REMEMBER WHO YOU USED TO BE

Peter Thornthwaite

HEDDON PUBLISHING

First published in Great Britain 2023 by Heddon Publishing

www.heddonpublishing.com

Copyright © Peter Thornthwaite 2023

A catalogue record for this book is available from the British Library

Paperback ISBN 978-1-913166-70-0
Ebook ISBN 978-1-913166-72-4

This is a biographical work based on true history with real historical characters. Includes appendices for data, maps and images.

Cover Image: Sue Challis
www.suechallis.co.uk

Cover Design: Catherine Clarke Design
www.catherineclarkedesign.co.uk

To Ted
From Pete.
Enjoy!
January 2023

For my sisters and my son,
and for refugees everywhere

Peter Thornthwaite lived in Oxford before moving to Brighton (Sussex University) in 1970. His further education included a year at Smith College, USA, postgraduate studies at McGill University, Canada, and back in England an unfinished PhD which, as he realised almost from the start, he had no intention of completing. There then followed years of changing addresses and equally itinerant employment; but slowly, sporadically a project was taking shape concerning his mother's family, the Lewinsohns of pre- Second World War Breslau: a story waiting to be written. In January 2021, after a respectable thirty years of Social Work, and having run out of excuses to postpone the project any longer, he retired and began the translating, researching and writing of *Remember Who You Used To Be*. This coincided with the second Covid-19 lockdown. The aim was to complete the project in a year, thus timing the ending with the fiftieth anniversary of his mother's death, 2 January 1972. Her German-Jewish background had fascinated him from childhood, but still more so after her suicide.

An early account of *Remember Who You Used To Be* under its original title, *Looking for Lewinsohn,* appears in *Second Generation Voices* (May 2022).

The author is married and lives in Shropshire.

REMEMBER WHO YOU USED TO BE

FOREWORD

Remember who you used to be, her father, writing from Germany, warned his *dear Gerdala* on 30th June 1939: four days after her eighteenth birthday; less than a month after her arrival in London; two months before the start of the Second World War. *It seems that you forget it very quickly.*

She was, and remained throughout the war, Gerda Resi Lewinsohn – from Breslau, though she kept that old address to herself – now living in England, fluent in English, with a German accent. Daughter of a once wealthy Jewish businessman, Elkan, who had established himself in Hats and Gentlemen's Outfitters. Sister of two estranged brothers, Kurt and Gunther, in Argentina and Ecuador. Niece of an aunt, Bertha, who was deported east in November 1941, and murdered.

My mother, Gerda, who is now (as I see her) twenty years younger than me – and the age gap between us is growing – seemed to spend most of her adult life forgetting who she used to be, but I realise she was really all the time remembering it. At the end of my investigations, I am still left wondering not only who she used to be but who she was. The answer, or answers, lay hidden (so I believed) inside more than thirty years of diaries and long forgotten family correspondence, and some answers did surface – though it took me another fifty years to see them. What I found myself going back to, time and again – the explanation had been there all

1

along, hiding in plain sight – was that terminal time in Germany. Her final months there, her frantic plans to leave, her *Auswanderung* – her emigration. I tried to see her there, in that vanished world of hers, at Scharnhorststrasse 31, Breslau, and penetrate the desperation that lay behind her early diary entries: *With every day that passes a bit more of my world is leaving. I had no idea there was so much of it until it started to leave. Now all I can think about is leaving too.* Is that what seventeen-year-old Gerda was thinking at the time? Maybe. I have to read between her lines.

Did she leave herself, as well as Breslau and the German Reich, when she finally got away? Then spend much of her adult life cutting the past, the childhood part, out of it? It is all speculation, though not without evidence. She was and remains interesting to me in the way that those acting out some profound inner unresolved conflict are *interesting*, if also very irritating at times. Her ending fifty years ago was, for me, when everything really began. Naturally, I couldn't let things rest there, as she had wished. No, I had to go back and find out what I could – investigate, interrogate the personal and private pasts of those who no longer had any say in the matter – though it took me half a century to get round to doing it. Doing it properly, that is; thoroughly, opening every last suitcase and trunk, going through all the records. It felt uncomfortable at first – ethically uncomfortable – an intrusion; a violation, even, and more than once I thought: *I really should not be doing this, I should not be here.* That was also its attraction.

Gerda wasn't a comfortable woman at the best of times, because she wasn't comfortable with herself. That she became my mother at all happened only though the most unlikely set of circumstances involving Holocaust and

World War. When she was seventeen and trying to escape, she could hardly have imagined meeting and marrying someone like my father; and as his effusive love letters to her reveal, she was so far beyond him as to seem a being from another world. Yet a wife and mother she was, or became, and I wonder when I first realised that she was really someone else entirely.

This is not her story alone. It is about her brothers, who also got away – what they made of their lives, and what their lives made of them. It is the story of the Lewinsohns of Breslau; an assimilated Jewish middle class family in Nazi Germany. This is their story as far as I can reconstruct it from the materials to hand, and if it is a sorely limited family history (which it is), it will have to do for now, because as far as I know nobody else has written about them, or is likely to. Anyway, this was never intended as a family history. It is mainly about a sister and a brother, Gerda and Gunther, forever estranged, forever connected. They were not unique in their differences and distances, hardly unusual – so unalike each other, yet so alike – but their relationship, as revealed to me on paper, seems extraordinary – more extraordinary than I ever supposed or could tell from Gerda's occasional but invariably negative and dismissive remarks. This is a story about two siblings, although there were three if I include the almost invisible third, the eldest brother, the first-born, Kurt. Gerda and Gunther are the ones I know most about from the records, the siblings that mainly concern me here. I was hoping to get to know them a bit better, through the diaries and letters, but somehow they seem further away than before – which is what happens, I suppose, when you only get to know people when they're dead. The third, Kurt, the most mysterious of the three since so little is known about him, made a comeback that took me by surprise.

What Gunther would think of this investigation, I can't be sure of course, but I imagine he would approve of it. He loved attention – it was a prime motive behind his letters to his little sister – so I think he'd appreciate my attention, and especially the many opportunities I give him to present himself in his own inimitable showman way and words. If nothing else, I have given Gunther a second life, and it comes as no surprise – indeed, it is often delightful to see – that he animates the page and makes the very most of it.

As for Gerda, I can easily imagine her reaction. She would not thank me one bit for my interest and attention. She feared attention. That was not always so. From her earliest diaries, it appears that she craved it. She came to fear it. When I knew her, she was the most private of people, often alone in her own secret annexe, her *Hinterhaus*. Only later, when I reflected on all the suitcases she had amassed (well over a hundred), packing them with papers from the past, and secondhand clothing for the future, did I begin to get their significance. They all contained her, and they were all packed in some kind of order known only to herself. It occurs to me now that this in itself – my mere mention of her hoarded suitcases – feels like a betrayal, for it discloses something about her she didn't want exposed. Perhaps she thought that in time they would all be gone like her, that we would find no use for her life's work, and discard it. She hadn't reckoned on me, or more accurately, on just how much of her hidden self she had left behind for me to find. No, she wouldn't thank me for what I have done. She'd hate me for it. But if she was able to think during those last moments – before all those pills she had saved for a special purpose took amnesic effect – she might have acknowledged to herself that, as she was finally about to forget everything, it was not after all what she really wanted. To forget. To be forgotten. By then it was too late. Someone else would have to do the remembering for her.

In a recently published book (2022), also by a son about a mother (*A Woman's Battles and Transformations* by Edouard Louis), he imagines his intimate homage as being a *home*, a *refuge*, for her. That is the exact opposite of what I could ever imagine for Gerda. And yet, perversely, I have written this book for her. She may have gone, but she left bits of herself behind for others to reassemble. Hers was an ordinary life. It was an extraordinary life, too. I think she must have realised, some part of her must have divined in a moment of astonishing clarity, the lasting and paradoxical consequences of her final act. So Gerda – like it or not – this book is for you, and for others also not at home in their lives.

PROLOGUE

Morgen – fruh – Ge - sta – po.
(Tomorrow morning - Gestapo.)

This staccato diary entry, dated 13th February 1939, records but does not state the purpose of the appointment, and there are no further entries concerning it or the outcome. It is there as a reminder – *Don't forget, Gerda, first thing tomorrow, Gestapo!* – although an imminent appointment with the German Secret Police, the Gestapo, in February 1939 in Breslau is not something she was likely to forget.

As this is her diary, she does not have to explain anything. She perhaps already knew the reason for the appointment at Gestapo Headquarters in Breslau the following morning, so there was no need to record it. If she didn't, then questions would have arisen – and they don't. Even so, I sense her fear – alarm – in the dashes separating the dread syllables. Those three words are stretched out almost to breaking point.

The appointment perhaps concerned emigration, getting the necessary papers (visa, permit) required. Though emigration was officially encouraged, it was (as her diary reveals) a difficult and drawn out business, especially for a seventeen-year-old Jewish girl with other things to think about, and possibly she had to inform the Gestapo of her progress. The appointment might have concerned accommodation. In February 1939, only Gerda and her father (her brothers having already left) occupied the over-furnished floors of Scharnhorststrasse 31; but as the year expanded, so their living space shrank, and the appointment with the Gestapo was maybe about reduced accommodation for them as Jews. But if so, why did she go alone without her **Tatta** – as appears to be the case? There is no mention of him, Tatta, also having to go **Morgen – fruh**. Again we are left guessing. Gerda doesn't have to explain anything. This is her diary.

Another possibility: the appointment is to do with a declaration of assets and really concerns her father alone, and perhaps she has decided to go with him for company and support. Elkan Lewinsohn, a prominent Breslau businessman, *Kaufmann von Herrengarderobe* (seller of gentlemen's clothing) was (or once was) prosperous enough to pay his part of the billion marks "atonement penalty" levied at that time on Jews.

As the outcome of that appointment with the Gestapo is nowhere recorded, I assume it went well, or if not well, that she survived it. She was not detained, and no one was arrested or deported, because by the next entry (15 February) she has been to the station to say goodbye to Gerd Nungen, who is off to Bolivia: **little Gerd**, whom she **didn't love**, though he gave her **a golden pendant** in parting, **a heart with a door in it**, which when opened revealed a miniature letter to her with the words: **Ich liebe dich**. As she later recorded: **What a good boy.**

Another Gerda – one with whom I have no connection – might have written a very different diary, if she had written one at all, but the actual Gerda whose diary this is – Gerda Resi Lewinsohn, to give her full name – *she* is the only one on offer. A different Gerda might have explained that visit to the Gestapo and recorded its outcome. And indeed some explanation, some

7

background detail, some external description, would have helped me better understand her situation. The only Gerda I know – the Gerda with whom I have some connection – is the one I've got in front of me and she, alas, is my sole guide.

My German language skills often default through long disuse to reliance on *Google Translate*, but I've translated her early diaries sufficiently to appreciate their limitations as well as my own. There is no description of where she lived, the house at Scharnhorststrasse 31, the streets of Breslau. When she goes out with her father, or on her own to visit friends, externally there is nothing to be seen. She felt no need to describe herself, other than by observing in passing that she is **rather beautiful**. Certainly it is good to know this, but some specific physical detail wouldn't have gone amiss. There is no description of other people – their appearance, clothes, surroundings – apart from describing someone as old or bald or boring. All were too familiar to her to require description. *She* knew what they looked like or wore, and hardly needed to describe it to herself. Maybe she was not the best observer of the world outside herself, but she was seventeen, and less concerned about what was happening outside than inside. As I recall, Gerda as a middle-aged woman had always more to do with interiors than exteriors, and I should expect no more of her as a girl at that time, in that place. Yet I can't also help thinking that, however sheltered, she *must* have noticed some big changes happening all around her. Given that her father owned several prominent shops in Breslau, and other properties, I would have expected at least some passing reference to *Kristallnacht* after 9th November in her diary for 1938-39. That historic month turned to December, and on to 1939, without any mention of shop windows broken, synagogues burnt and destroyed, or Jewish males rounded up and taken to Buchenwald. There are no swastika banners on the fronts of Breslau's main buildings in her diary, no street-wide political slogans. Yes, I know I am expecting too much. Gerda had other things on her mind. Mostly boys, from what I can gather, but again, am I being unfair? Is it likely, after the breaking glass of "The Night of Crystals", that Gerda would have wanted to hear windows break again in her diary? It may be that the inner, the private world of the diary, seemed a safe place, a refuge, where *she* still mattered. It made space for her.

Yet there is that reference to the Gestapo, and though it stands alone (I can find no reference to the Gestapo anywhere else in her German diaries) and lacks a before and after, there is a magnetism in the word, not just in the word itself but in the way she writes it: **Ge – sta – po**. I hear myself repeating those barbaric syllables. Why did Gerda separate them in that way if not to stretch out her anxiety – her fear? Or was it rather that, by uncoupling those syllables, pulling the dread word apart, she was exercising control in the only place (her diary) where she retained any?

In the untranslated tracts of her diaries there may well be references to the political and social changes of that decade. I don't wish to do her an injustice. Anne Frank she was not, and in her later life she was never political – not that I noticed. But there is no getting away from the fact that she was *there*, and how many others can still say that about their mother? Just being *there* – in the Germany of the late 1930s – that was enough in itself, without any direct commentary. It would be noteworthy even without the diaries. Did Gerda know how close to the edge she was? Something like fear, and desperation, surface in the diary for 1939. Her life till then might have seemed a world away from what was going to happen, though the ashes from the crematoria chimneys were not far off.

It's different for me. If I think about the Holocaust at all (and to be honest, I didn't give it that much thought till I re-read her diaries a year or so ago), I have the benefit of distance. There are memoirs and oral accounts I can dip into. There is Primo Levi. I can think of Gerda differently now, as one of the *saved*, though the last time I saw her she had more the appearance of one of the *drowned*. At any rate she got away with her life, she had a life of sorts, what more can you ask? Gerda got out. She was one of the *saved*. It took me a while to realise that the *saved* also drown. They just do it more slowly, invisibly.

What made me unearth the diaries again and resume, after a gap of nearly fifty years, scrutinising them, I'm not sure. A part of me regrets it. There were so many pleasanter things to occupy my time, and anyway I had been through them all before, to some extent, a long time ago, and knew what to expect. Why keep going back? There was surely nothing new, or very interesting, to discover. As my 70th year approached, I could have decided to leave the diaries until it really was too late to do anything about them and I had only dementia or cancer to look forward to. At the same time, I knew that the only discoveries still to be made lay many years behind me, and that was where I had to go.

I have heard that moths lay up to a hundred eggs in quiet, dark, undisturbed places. The eggs then change to white and yellow larvae that wriggle and nibble and gnaw away for as long as two years, feeding on wool and silk and the skin cells and hair in dust, and sucking up sweat stains and other spills. It is stretching a metaphor, but when, in January 2021, I reopened the dusty trunks and suitcases containing her old diaries, correspondence, miscellaneous papers, I could smell mothballs. It was one of the distinctive smells I associate with her, an almost aphrodisiacal odour. As I emptied one after another onto bed and floor, it seemed as if the moths she had feared and fought all her later life had got into these cases too, and in fact the mounds of diaries, letters and papers had in places the appearance of moth damage. Sifting through them for the best part of a year, I found pages missing, corners torn off, words eaten away. If there are such things as paper moths, then those little fat larvae had been making a meal of the Lewinsohns for many years and I had reached them just in time. It was an act of salvage.

It was inescapable. It was there, if anything more so in the later diaries and letters, implicit in everything she recorded and kept. There was really no way of getting away from it. The Holocaust and its lasting aftermath. Here, in these decades of diaries, was a Jewish woman's journey through pre-war Germany and post-war Britain. For me, right from the start, it was always the German diaries. They were the great attraction. It was there that most of the darkness had collected.

Gerda was born in June 1921. The following month, Hitler was appointed leader of the Nazi Party. Gerda grew up with the Third Reich. Before her 12th birthday, Hitler was made Chancellor and his birthday an annual holiday. The German diaries were the draw. The later ones, the diaries of the 1950s and 60s, I was at first inclined to dismiss as of no real interest. How wrong I was in doing so, it took me a further year to discover.

The diaries of her last two decades concerned a middle-aged woman of infinitely less allure (as I knew her so well) than her earlier incarnations – the Jewish girl in Breslau, the young woman in London. As I was to find, there was really only one Gerda from beginning to end. When she left the German Reich in 1939, she carried some of it with her. It is as much there in the later diaries with their tedious lists of mundane things and tirelessly repeated renunciations of the only sources of fun and joy to be found by someone in her situation. It took me a while to get what was really going on in the last diaries, with the blank spaces and gaps between her sporadic entries filling not just days and weeks but entire months. She was becoming more absent from her own life. Yet certain isolated dates are packed with words of an unimaginable intensity. For all her apparent preoccupation with superficial material things, she was a serious, a deep person, a *diving* person, and it wasn't until I finally acknowledged something similar in myself that I found it in her.

This house of ours is old, but the cellar is older, surviving the Great Fire of 1677 which destroyed the frontages of most of the half-timbered high street of this now declining market town. A local architectural archaeologist, who knows about these things, has identified Tudor bricks in the dank cellar. As you go down the uneven stone steps, you expect the door to slam shut behind you, and lock. And there you are, in the dark, because that cellar door stays locked. I mention this little anxiety of mine because I experienced something similar with the German diaries: I was going down steep stone steps into the dark, with the door behind me closing.

It was with the intention of translating the German diaries, and just needing something to get me going, that some years ago I visited the National Holocaust Centre near Sherwood Forest. This was something I had long intended to do, but in the end my partner, Sue, instigated it – as she has instigated so much else in my life. Really, I have her to thank for what happened next. While her life is lifted by energy and action and social engagement, mine has a tendency towards lassitude and withdrawal; so we complement each other nicely. It was Sue who got me to pack the German diaries into my black leather Calvin Klein shoulder bag. Going everywhere incognito is my natural inclination, but carrying the diaries seemed to commit me to further action. Yet I doubted they would be of any interest to anyone else.

What has the Holocaust to do with me? is something I still ask myself. Everything, of course. It has everything to do with me. Because of family, for a start. There were other reasons too, but for me family comes first and foremost. It is because of Gerda, and her brothers, Gunther and Kurt, and her father, Elkan, and Aunt Bertha, her father's younger sister. Family history is my specific special connection to the Holocaust. For me it is a question of what happened to the Lewinsohns of Breslau. What happened to Gerda I already knew, or thought I did; as for the others, I had an idea but lacked detail. They were one of the more fortunate families; they got out just in time, that much I knew; but even that was not entirely true. There were gaps. Elkan himself, the father, was one such gap. Did he get out and live, or did he stay and die? There were great gaps in Kurt's story, too. In fact, gaps appear everywhere in the recorded lives of Gunther and Gerda when you look more closely.

Before investigating Gerda's diaries and the Lewinsohn family correspondence dating back to the mid 1930s, that question concerning the Holocaust was not a particularly troubling one, and I seldom had occasion to consider it very deeply. In the 1970s, when I discovered Gunther's letters to her, I might not have noticed how often the word *gemutlich* comes up in them. Meaning *comfortable*. It is only more recently (over the last year), when I sifted through all the paper evidence with more scrupulous care and attention, that I pondered its special meaning for him. Gunther was forever describing things as *comfortable* – Gerda's letters to him, her family and life in England, their parallel but steadily prospering lives. It took me half a century to understand why everything had to be so *gemutlich* for him.

That word of Gunther's came back to me in the basement of the National Holocaust Centre as I looked at the people pictured on the brick walls: the families framed to last in formal studio portraits, or out picnicking in a green park; the excited girls aboard the *St. Louis* bound for Cuba from Hamburg in May 1939, waving goodbye to unseen family; a girl in Berlin being checked and charted by the white-coated racial hygienist; women and children queuing in long columns. Nothing *gemutlich* there, in retrospect. And all of them asking the same *ungemutlich* question: *What exactly have we to do with you?*

My mother's old diaries perhaps held the answer; but they too were uncomfortable. They were her private diaries. *Private*. Gerda had written them to herself – for herself – certainly not to exhibit them in public. And who knew better than her son how inverately private she was in all things, and how all this would have been utterly anathema to her? I mean – this place, my being here, my wanting to find out, and her old diaries in my bag.

In the Memorial Gardens I sat down by a sculpture – *Remembering The Six Million* – and remembered Gerda and Gunther. Before leaving for the museum, I had searched for them on my phone. Tapping in *Lewinsohn*, I had found it was a variant of Levinson, an Ashkenazi

Jewish surname, and that there are lots of them: Levinsons, Levinsohns, Lewinsohns. The search had netted a long list including *Lewinsohn, Gerda, Age 18, Estudiante*, and *Lewinsohn, Gunther, Age 16, Estudiante*. What a coincidence. To happen upon not just a long list of Lewinsohns and variants, but one coupling a Gerda with a Gunther, seemed more than coincidence and a good omen for the Holocaust visit. But a closer scrutiny of that fortuitous pairing had revealed that the Gerda listed was two years older than that Gunther, whereas the real Gerda was in fact nine years younger. Also, the real Gerda and Gunther were never Estudiantes (Students) living in Argentina. For all I knew, there might be countless other Gerdas and Gunthers linked together in internet lists, with other identities, other lives: all ghosts of the internet.

Relaxing in the Memorial Gardens, by a pond thick with yellow leaves, I tried to visualise her, Gerda, as she had last appeared. She had been gone too long and lacked a face. Before returning to those other anonymous faces on the brick basement walls, I examined the black sculpture in the gardens – *Abandoned* – and softly spoke the text out loud, *Out of the depths have I called Thee,* and waited. Nothing happened of course. She could not hear me.

Those German diaries were scribbled by a Jewish girl long before she meant anything to me. An almost stranger. And Gerda would have stayed that way if one or other of her wartime romances had worked out differently. Mostly they were written in Breslau, which is not to be found on any map of Germany after 1945. That fact alone – the strange provenance of the diaries – made them uniquely interesting, and this in turn made them less personal, more historical, more archival, and so it was that I went back inside the Centre with her potent history in my possession and handed it over to the senior researcher based there.

At the time it seemed one of the guiltiest acts of my life, as well as the most fraudulent. There was nothing Jewish about me, other than Gerda thinking of herself as Jewish – especially whenever things got difficult. She was so afraid of being found out. And there I was, with her Breslau years inside my leather bag like so much dirty underwear, claiming an inheritance I had no right to claim. A Jew is someone with a Jewish mother; that was my understanding. But was I really Jewish, or just trying it on to gain credence by identifying with this place, these people on the basement walls? It was not an inheritance Gerda ever wished on herself, or on us. She was ashamed of being a Jew, and afraid.

Meanwhile the senior researcher seemed genuinely interested in the diaries, though I noticed that she made eye contact with Sue. This was not unusual, and Sue had approached her in the first place, explained the situation, got her close attention. Not that I minded. It somehow exonerated me – as the mere bearer of the diaries, and otherwise an irrelevance. At least they were being taken seriously, treated with respect, and some of that rubbed off on me.

And watching them being handled and scanned was weird but thrilling. They were no longer my peculiar mother's diaries, but historical documents. She was in them, she *was* them, I could even hear her voice – for the first time in over fifty years. It drifted through the pages as if they were actual recordings, distant, crackling, foreign, but recognizably *her*. And as I listened the walls of words she had long ago constructed thinned to a membrane, a shifting sentient interface alive and quivering to the touch. It was then, when they were out of my hands, that I felt really for the first time the sensuous intimacy of her diaries. Always they had been mine to translate; it was never a question of *if* but *when*. The language wasn't a lasting barrier; I had an old A-Level in it and had once translated *Das Tagebuch der Anne Frank*. But I had no problem with this Holocaust Researcher arranging it on my behalf, and *at no cost* to me. Maybe she was thinking she had come upon another *Anne Frank's Diary*, a *Hinterhaus* hidden behind inaccessible handwriting for over seventy-five years. It was not inconceivable. *Well, Gerda*, I thought, *you kept that well hidden*. At that moment I regarded her with considerably more respect.

That Gerda was once not just a girl, but a girl in Germany, had always seemed most unlikely. It wasn't only that she kept her hinterland out of sight, apart from the odd tantalising glimpse. To my recollection, she had appeared fully formed as a 1950s mother, no different from others except in her unusual ability to swear in two languages (*Bloody Scheisse!*) and her accent, which got more foreign when excited or upset. Later – much later – something else emerged, something to do with Jewishness, but this seemed merely to add an extra layer of foreignness. As she was a bit foreign already, it made no real difference.

But that day at the Holocaust Centre it did make a difference. After handing in all the available evidence of her pre-war past, and leaving Sue with the researcher, I descended again to the basement – this time with a keener sense of connection. The question was not, what have *they* to do with me? – but, what have *you* to do with me? Everything, apparently. They reached out, they appealed – those photographs from a lost world on the walls: the ghettos; the deportations of dark-clothed columns past shadowed buildings; the girl tobogganing; the shop daubed with *Yid!* and *Kauft nur bei Deutschen!;* the twelve girls safely aboard a ship bound from Hamburg to Cuba on May 13th 1939 (just ten days before Gerda left the German port for England), not knowing that despite their visas they would be denied entry and have to return – some of them to their deaths.

In the few remaining suitcases – out of the multitudes she had amassed in her short life – there were, among other things, albums of photographs that would not have looked out of place on those Holocaust walls. Visitors like me could come and look at her family – at the dark-haired girl posing with an unlit cigarette and champagne bottle in a sumptuous room; the same girl astride her **Tatta**'s shoulders as he leans against a beached boat; that face of hers luminous in a classroom of unknown girls; little Gerda, placing the last wooden block on a pyramid pile on the floor. Visitors would take in, as I did then, the distances and differences, the foreignness of faces and places, and wonder what happened to her, what happened to that family, to their world?

And as I wandered from wall to wall that late afternoon, I remembered submerged things. She had not been utterly silent after all. She had told us things. About boys joining the Hitler Youth. About being excluded from school. If recorded or reflected in her diaries, such things made her a witness. All she had to do was *be there* and witness what was happening in the streets and shop windows. And she *was there* – after *Nuremberg,* after *Kristallnacht* – witnessing what was happening, things even she could not avoid seeing. It conferred on her a significance, a status, a stature previously unsuspected – and on me it conferred that strange sense of connection. At last I had a story to tell. It was *her* story – but I was part of it, and might legitimately frame my life differently, as somebody with an interesting history, or at the very least as somebody associated with somebody with an interesting history. Some of her magic was finally rubbing off on me. Through my mother, of all people, I had acquired a proxy sense of importance, of being *different*, which is a good feeling if the worst thing you can imagine is not being different.

As I browsed in the brick basement for what remained of the day, looking intently at walls, remembering other forgotten things, she came back to me in ghost glimpses. The woman I knew and loved. We were listening again to the Beatles song, *Hey Jude,* Gerda mistaking the name Jude for *Jude,* Jew, which at the time had made me laugh. Then, further back, with my bucket and spade in the warm Dorset sand – a happy memory – I remembered shouting out, *Heil Hitler!* Why I did so, raising my arm in stiff salute, I don't know, but that was the 1950s, when we were still winning the war in comics. *Heil Hitler!* It had such a happy sound, until I saw her face.

As Sue and I were leaving, still discussing the diaries, we saw that the wide dark fields beyond the centre extended under a huge hanging 'blood moon' – more burning yellow than copper or red. But as I add this memorable detail to my account of that seminal day, I wonder if in fact I'm confusing this first visit with my later one, in November 2021. Checking the internet, I confirm that the blood moon I remember so vividly actually appeared at the end of my second visit.

What we both recall (although writing this makes me doubt my memory) is that, at the end of that first visit in 2016, not long after the Brexit referendum, the researcher said she would be in touch about translations. My mother's pre-war German diaries were new and undiscovered, it appeared to me, and of interest to others. Among the many Holocaust memoirs (I had flicked through a few in the bookshop there) hers was different, if only because it was yet unknown. Who knew what might be hidden there? Gerda might not turn out to be another Anne Frank, but she had an equally interesting story to tell – one that did not end in a death camp. There was another reason for my excitement. This was not just another first-hand account of how that infamous time and place affected a Jewish girl who was there. This was personal. This was my mother. This was the woman I once loved, but for whom I once had little regard.

After two years or so, Sue emailed the senior researcher for an update.

Once I realised she had forgotten about the diaries, I started thinking differently about them. They had no special historical significance (as I had in fact suspected all along). Understandably, the researcher had more pressing commitments. It was a disappointment, but no surprise. In fact, it came as a relief, knowing that the diaries were safe again and there was no imperative to do anything about them. Gerda had nothing much to tell after all. A girl can be Jewish, live through the first six years of the Third Reich, leave for a country soon to be at war with her own, and still have not much to say about her situation.

Even Breslau, her vanished city (Wroclaw since 1945) was a disappointment, as I had discovered during a recent two-city budget break (Krakow and Wroclaw). No planes or trains go to Breslau in Germany, but it was easy and cheap enough to get to Wroclaw in Poland. Sue even got me a copy of an original German street map off the internet so I could find the streets where Gerda had once lived and walked. Thus equipped for my journey into her past, accompanied by my twin sister, we searched the entire city for Scharnhorststrasse 31 – and found half of it gone. The street was still there but ended abruptly before reaching No. 31, and though I retraced my steps – as if the missing part of the street might materialise with repeated attempts to find it – No. 31 failed to emerge from behind the concrete block of flats squatting in its place. The other address we had to go by, Victoriastrasse 65 – the two-roomed apartment to which Gerda had moved with her **Tatta** in April 1939 – was likewise missing. Victoriastrasse was still there, hidden behind its Polish name, but the section which once included No. 65 lay flattened under a concrete bus station. Returning to Scharnhorststrasse, looking up at an imagined ornate wrought iron balcony, I invoked that ghost of a girl – Gerda – looking down at me from a high window. By then, though, we were getting tired, our thoughts were turning to wine, and I had to make do with an inward conversation with our long absent mother: *So, Gerda, you never did go back to find out what happened to Scharnhorststrasse 31, but I did, and it's gone. Victoriastrasse 65 also, but I don't suppose you missed that measly apartment. They are both gone. Breslau, too. There is nothing for you there, or for me, or for any of us.*

As for the street name – *Scharnhorststrasse* – I later learned that it was named, like so many other streets in German cities, after a Prussian general from the time of the Napoleonic wars. A 1936 German battleship and the last (in 1945) of the Wehrmacht Infantry divisions were named after General Scharnhorst. No place for a Jewish family in 1939.

There are few public records proving that Gerda and other Lewinsohns ever existed before the war. There have been times, when searching the internet for them, that I have genuinely doubted their existence and decided that I must have imagined it. A similar sort of disappearing act was evidently what Gerda had in mind fifty years ago, when she expressed her last wish. *Burn all my diaries.* That was her alleged last injunction, though I found no evidence of it at the time, or in the half-century since. Had she left such a note, I'd have found it eventually, as I found every other paper record left behind. There was a note, certainly, but it communicated something quite different, less dramatic, less peremptory, and less likely to be remembered years later. Of course, it could have been a spoken, not a written, injunction. But if so, to whom might she have uttered it? No one ever mentioned it, and by the end she was virtually incommunicado. Speaking such transparently terminal words would have given the game away too; aroused suspicion. Anyway, the diaries were not burned, but dumped in the attic with her other junk. *Burn the diaries!* I don't think so. It's one thing to hear of books being burned by Nazi students in 1933; of extermination camp archives being burned to erase evidence of what they did; or of Kafka's dying instruction to his friend, Max Brod, to burn all his unpublished writings. Gerda was always going to be unknown. She counted on it. Why did she imagine anyone might even want to read her almost illegible diaries? As far as I know, I'm the only one to attempt it – and it has taken the best part of my life to do so, and I wouldn't recommend it to anyone.

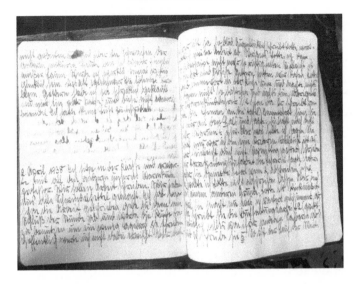

But assuming for a moment those were her actual words, then they suggest a wish to eradicate herself, erase herself from all surfaces retaining her personal imprint, destroy any written evidence that she was ever there. Well, that doesn't seem too far from the truth. It has become easier in time to think of her as an absence. My memory of her physical appearance has let in the light for years. There is also another way of looking at it. If those were really her words, they reveal just how much the diaries meant to her. Evidently a great deal, and rightly so. She is there in every word, exclamation mark, ellipsis. The diaries were mirrors to her. Even the most mundane, least interesting later ones, with their repeated lists, were cracked mirrors with fracture lines webbing the glass. It is no exaggeration to describe them as Gerda's testament, her opus, her imprint on the world – and its panzer imprint on her. And here's another possibility: she was afraid they might end up in the wrong hands. Somebody might read them, find out all about her, dig up the dirt. I am sure she believed there *was* dirt to be dug up. The only way to stop such an abomination was to instruct their instant immolation.

This is all speculation, which only gets you so far, and if it confirms anything it is merely a familiar sense of guilt. In the end (I decided) Gerda never wanted them burnt. Indeed, it is even possible that she wanted them found. Among the few books she read and left behind on a shelf, alongside titles such as *Never Love A Stranger* and *The Dream Merchants*, was *The Diary of Anne Frank*. Did Gerda once see herself as another Anne Frank? Maybe she did, before her diary entries and thought processes unravelled through the 1950s and 60s. Perhaps Anne Frank's diary, read and loved by millions, might have suffered a similar unravelling had Anne also outlived herself.

As it is, I was and remain the sole student of Gerda's diaries. Eventually I would be reminded of one of her phrases: *Genug ist genug.* Enough is enough. By the end, having read and re-read, translated and pored over everything she wrote for posterity, I had to agree with her. *Genug ist genug, Gerda, you were quite right.*

Another phrase keeps cropping up in her diaries: *Was Du nicht weiss, macht Dich nicht heiss.* What you don't know doesn't bother you. Or, more literally translated: What you don't know, doesn't make you hot. Some things made her hot, me too. So now I know. *Ich weiss, ich weiss, Gerda, and I have you to thank for it. If I hadn't studied every word you wrote, and all the paper evidence of your life, I would never have found you. Vielen Dank for mein inheritance.*

Was this a search for roots? Isn't that what people of a certain age do, legitimately? Family research. By January 2021, when the writing commenced, I had a working title: *Looking for Lewinsohn.* I liked the sound of it – at once personal and impersonal. Other Holocaust-related memoirs had similar titles and were also looking for lost connections, and there was something moving and melancholy about it too, because you know that some families just can't be found. The old family correspondence was for me as much an attraction as the diaries – often more so, as I could see them being written, having written such letters myself a few decades ago when there was nothing unusual about doing so, but I have never been a diarist. Letters are crying out to be read, whereas a diary occupies a private space. The correspondence I can read and re-read with almost a clear conscience. And they touch me, the Lewinsohn letters. They are not so much about their lives – they *are* their lives – all that remains of them. As far as I can tell, Gerda kept all her letters. From Gunther. From Kurt. From Elkan, or *Tatta* as she used to call him. From *Tante* Bertha, who did not write often, but whose few words are more affecting for that reason. There are letters from Jewish refugee committees, from people offering opportunities for domestic service. There are wartime love letters (quite a lot of these). Letters from London and New York, Quito and Pittsburgh, Buenos Aires and Cowley, Oxford. There is a mound of legal letters *auf deutsch* from Dusseldorf in the 1960s. There are intact letters, letters with pages missing, letters that don't begin, letters that don't end, letters with corners inexplicably torn off, undated drafts. And there is a jumble of other paper evidence, sometimes just as revealing: old shopping lists for items you'd no longer look for or find on supermarket shelves; receipts for goods once desired, long ago discarded; Christmas and birthday cards, such as this one I'm looking at now, which hoped (in 1943) that *never a cloud bedim your sky*. And then there are these little *weight cards* that I keep going back to (because they were such a large part of her life) recording (I regret to report) an increase of 5 lbs from 1942 to 1953. As for her *RATION BOOK (Ministry Of Food 1953 – 1954)*, I examine it again as if it was a page out of Kafka and not receipts for meat, eggs, cheese, sugar, tea. And there, upended on bed and floor: a trunk full of discoloured newspaper articles, mostly to do with the Eichmann trial in 1961.

Gerda was a hoarder. She kept everything – but so what? So my good fortune. So my future. When I consider her unusual circumstances – emigration – war – separation from family – only letters could cross such distances and diasporas. Thinking of Gerda as an emigrant, I am not surprised that she kept her letters. If she also had a tendency to hoard things of no apparent value, it had its roots in the fertile soil of separation .

Genug ist genug. Yet working laboriously through her papers was also a labour of love, and there were pleasures along the way – some entirely unexpected. As a surprise Christmas present, Sue arranged translation of passages from the diary for 1939. They covered the months following Gerda's arrival in London in June that year. Over Christmas 2020, which also coincided with my retirement, I had the unusual festive pleasure of reading about my mother's first unexpurgated sexual experience (not with my father, who came later) but with Joe – *the* Joe of wartime years, the one I would come to think of as *Berliner Joe*. The translation included a seduction scene in which Gerda evidently relished the role of seducer.

For the moment I will let that last sentence stand without further comment.

Fortunately, my last day at work (31st December 2020) coincided with the start of the second year of Covid-19 and rapid escalation of national infection. I could not have timed retirement better – to coincide with the pandemic at its peak. A new year. A second lockdown coming. An end-of-the-world-as-we-know-it lockdown. What luck.

From that January we were *all in it together*, as the government reminded us, invoking the Blitz. *Stay local*, we were told. At the start of the new year *local* shrank to a dying little market town in terminal decline, a high street full of empty shop windows, and an imposing but vacant and peeling old coaching inn at the crossroads. Under new pandemic conditions, the town looked marginally emptier and more abandoned than usual, the main difference being the absence of traffic and resultant eerie silence. There are positives in a pandemic, and it suited me having nowhere to go and nothing else to do. For me, Europe was opening up – the Europe of the Lewinsohns. Reading around the subject to begin with, I started with *Microcosm: Portrait of a Central European City*. In the beginning was Breslau. It circumscribed my initial research area. It was where Gerda had spent her girlhood from 1921 to 1939, and it was once home to the third-largest Jewish community in the Reich (over 23,000 at its peak). Every morning that winter, I climbed the worn oak stairs to the attic study (my own *Secret Annexe*) and I was back in the old world. As Theresa May observed in 2016, following the Brexit vote, if you think yourself a citizen of the world, you are *a citizen of nowhere*. Similarly, in 1933, Hitler spoke of certain people *who are at home both nowhere and everywhere*. Their words still resonate. So be it. *Nowhere* remains infinitely better than Brexit Britain. Actually I was more a citizen of *elsewhere*, which was where (if anywhere) I might find them, the lost Lewinsohns.

Remember Who You Used To Be is yet another pandemic memoir (a new genre) to come out of lockdown. There was nowhere to go but elsewhere. For me, though, there was a more potent stimulus. A nationwide pandemic was the right milieu – the right mix of national infection, fear, and social distance – for what I was writing. It leached into the words without my noticing at first. The state of the nation at that time suited the subject – so much so that I doubt I could have written it in a less toxic year.

AUSWANDERUNG
(EMIGRATION)

1

FROM GERDA'S DIARY

Breslau
Tuesday 27 December 1938

Soon another year will come. Soon we'll write 1939. What will the new year bring? The future looks quite black. We Jews are an unhappy people, violated, badly treated. As yet I can't complain too much. I still have enough to eat, to drink, and I can go out. But for how much longer?? Where will fate take me? To New York or England? Wherever, God is always with me. I am now exactly seventeen and a half years old and also in the most beautiful time of life. I had expected a different future for myself. My vocation was at one time to be Kinderfraulein or a cook. I would be happy to have such a respectable job. I had told myself, only marry out of love. I like a boy, 21 years old, called Horst Grotte. But this is also no great love. Then there is an acquaintance of Tatta's who visits us often. His name is Leo Lilienthal, a small fat 36 year old man who is always talking about marriage with me. If only to get the chance to get out of Germany, I would have considered it, but I came to the conclusion that God will show me how to be happy and satisfied. Which is why I'm not going to sell myself. But there is a decision to come.

Sometimes I read books by Guy de Maupassant, and see Marianne Licht and Ada Oschinsky. Most of the girls I meet make me sick. They are envious, jealous and cheap – all of them. Behind their nice words they are terribly stupid. To be honest, men are generally dumb too.

This afternoon I am going to town to get two dresses – no, a dress and a blouse – I have bought, two very beautiful pieces. In the morning I go to the dentist, an unpleasant man with a bald head.

Breslau
Thursday 29 December 1938

Today I am writing with a fountain pen for the first time. I bought it myself for 11.50 RM.

Yesterday nothing much was going on. In the afternoon I heard terrible, stupid music on the radio. I was also knitting a light blue angora scarf. There are already a few mistakes in it, but it still looks good. Then in the evening Leo Lilienthal came. I really quite like him, but I am not utterly in love with him. I always make myself look lovely for him when he comes, and to look glad when I see him, so it's not that I don't care about him at all. But to get close to him, to kiss him, or even worse to be kissed by him, that would be dreadful. Still, I came close to giving him a kiss, and getting one from him. And sometimes, when tempted to give him any encouragement, I am doubtful thinking about my future, and then I am tempted again to agree to marry him, if he is serious about it. But then I again say to myself, Gerda, Du liebst aus vollen Herzen. You could have someone else - someone you love with all your heart. Most people say I am beautiful, and that might be true. Why should I let false modesty rule me? Of course I'm not flawless, no, the opposite is true, but I am more beautiful than most of the girls. And I am young too. But I rely on

God. He will always show me the right way.

Yesterday we played cards until ten. I really like to play for money even if it's just some pfennigs.

This morning I went to the dentist again. Then I went home and sang some pop songs and accompanied myself with one finger on the piano. "Schon war die Zeit" and "Tango" - two very beautiful songs.

In the afternoon at four I met Gerd Nungen in town. That little boy makes me sick. He is 18 years old and madly in love with me. I always feel like a nanny dating him. There are no more boys or men left here. Am I ever going to find the Great Love? I am curious to find out.

Breslau
Monday 2 January 1939

Another year begins again. New Year's Eve was more boring than ever. At first I wanted to go out, though I didn't feel like it at all. Then Tatta said I should go to Siederers with him, but I also didn't feel like doing that, though staying at home on my own wasn't what I wanted either. I was not in a good mood. In the end I went to Siederers and argued with Tatta all the way there. At Siederers it was so boring with all the old people there that I left after half an hour. Actually I wanted to visit the Hoffmings, and I had already announced that I was going there, then cancelled, and went home afflicted, having had enough of life, not for the first time. If only I had my life again and could be completely satisfied. I stay much of the time at home, crying, actually for no reason. I think the reason for my bad mood is that I miss men and love. Because I can't call little Gerd a man.

Yesterday Leo Lilienthal came over. He too is going to

make me sick soon. I am never going to marry him. For now, I am still with Gerd, a cute boy but really nothing special.

My friends are Marianne Licht and Ada Oschinsky. I can't stand Marianne, but I do like Ada.

I take English lessons terribly often. Miss Lithauer and Mr. Gerson are my teachers. I can't stand Mr Gerson. I hope everything works out with England. I've got three possibles in mind. One in a village, and the other two in London. Where am I going to go? I am curious.

Am I ever going to find the real big love? I don't think so.

Breslau
Wednesday 4 January 1939

Little Wolfgang rang yesterday, he said Adieu, he travels on the 7th January auf Brasilien . . . Today I met Herr Gutfeld at the post office. A really nice man, 35 years old, but not at all my type. Really nice. Maybe he thinks I want him to be my husband? I will marry only out of love . . . I can't see myself getting out of Germany, I will suffocate here.

Yesterday I wrote to Steffi who is also in New York. And I am waiting for Gunter to write – dear Gunter. God help us. Show us the right way, and I shall go.

Peter Thornthwaite

LETTERS FROM GUNTER

New York
January 20th, 1939

Liebe Gerda

Please answer these questions promptly.

1. After having sold building in Scharnhorststrasse, will father move and where?

2. Is father of good health?

3. Is father very busy with the matter of emigration?

4. What happens with both my parrots?

5. Would it be possible to send me over a photo-apparat?

6. When will you definitely start to England?

7. Is Aunt Bertha frequently your guest?

8. When will you get your passport and clearance certificate?

9. What can Kurt do with regard to the helpless situation of father?

10. Have you the chance to take with you some garments and outfit in case of emigration?

11. What do undertake all your friends in Germany to increase their chance of emigration?

12. Where will you go, to London or in a rural part?

When you want any information please ask me, I may give informations at any time.

Today I am with my best regards

Guenter

New York
den 3 Februar 1939

Liebe Gerda

I acknowledge with thanks your letter of 26 January and am hurrying to fill out the questionnaire and return it to you. Such a questionnaire always has its problems and therefore I cannot guarantee that I have answered it sufficiently. It is dated 3 November 38. You should have been interested in getting this done a little earlier to get a declaration of "no objection". Should there be any further questions I'll be happy to answer them for you.

Do you finally have a chance to get out? Why does the Tatta write so little? How is he actually? I only get telegrams from you, nothing more. Don't do anything wrong now. Instead submit immediately to the Berlin Consulate. Should you go to England any time soon, definitely don't forget to take with you the Affidavit. I think you're pretty careless with these formalities. You could also write to Steffi Posner. Definitely write to the London addresses I provided. Make sure that father can emigrate as soon as possible. I have done everything possible to help you, I can't do anything more for the moment. I suppose that when Father submits the Affidavit, a way will be found.

Meanwhile any message from Kurt?

If you were here in the U.S you would soon get a job. They go like hot cakes to the girls who come here. In the college here I have been taught with many girls my own age – all very nice girls from Southern Germany. I have been in much doubt whether I should stay in New York. I don't know what will happen to me as a visitor. I would very much like to be in Baltimore where I could work in a hat factory.

By the way, to get you an Affidavit I had to use the picture you gave me from Foto-Fix. As you can see, it was a complete success.

New York is preparing for the World Fair. There is life and bustle here that you can hardly imagine. Unheard of! During term I go to the cinema and often see, for two hours mid-day, splendid cinema programs with stage show and Swing Orchestra as the ticket is only 15 cents. In my opinion one learns better English or better American than if you hear it only in School English.

Here you can buy cheaply the finest dishes out of cans to warm yourself up. Tomorrow I'll make 3 cups of cocoa, Toast, 1 Philadelphia Cream Cheese, Kosher sausages etc, and tune in to all the best music on WABC Radio Station. The American slang you hear causes me great difficulties. At times people here just can't be understood. I am determined to take the next opportunity to get to know everything.

Is Klara still with you?

Next time I'll write in English. I am curious to know how your England-Project is getting on.

Warm greetings from your brother Gunter

Greetings and kisses to Tatta

POSTCARD

615 W 143 street, ap. 44 NewYork City
February 8, 1939

Dear Gerda,

Acknowledge receipt of your post-cart and I hope that in the meantime you have got the papers, which I filled out. I am very enjoyed about your news that now you have a real chance in getting out of Germany. In every case dont forget to take with you the Affidavits sent to you the other day. It would be easier for you to stay in England when the English organizations know that you have immigration papers for U.S.

Why does not write the Father?

My best greeting, Gunter

FROM GERDA'S DIARY

Breslau
Friday 10 February 1939

No post yet. I have so many obstacles because of the Declaration of No Objection. Everything is going to work out. You should never worry too much.

In the afternoon Ada Oschinsky visited us. She is a very nice girl. I really like her. In the afternoon I really annoyed Tatta. Bento Zadeck told me to come over and Tatta didn't want me to. But then I pretended to cry and so we finally went.

Gerd will go to Bolivia next week. I might give him a present.

Time to sleep now.

Gerd tomorrow at 10.30.

Breslau
Saturday 11 February 1939

It's nearly 10.30. Gerd is probably going to arrive downstairs. Soon.

Another day is passing. Gerd didn't come this morning. He's ill. Seems like Gerd is really upset about needing to go that far away. I think he loves me very much, but I don't love him at all.

Breslau
13 February 1939

Today I got a letter from England, from Abraham Reform

Synagogue in London, about a position. Tomorrow I have to go to the Gestapo.

Gerd didn't come again this afternoon. He is still a bit ill.

Another day gone. Where has the time gone.

Morgen – fruh – Ge-sta-po -

Breslau
15 February 1939

I've been to the station. Gerd left forever, to Bolivia. I did like him lately, he is still a little boy, and now he will be on his way, nach Bolivien. Anyhow, when I saw him, for the last time, I didn't love him. He has given me a golden pendant, a heart with a door in it. If you open the door there's a little letter which says, "Ich liebe dich". What a good boy. I wish him all happiness for the future. I have never kissed him all the time we were friends, and luckily I didn't have to when he left. I only kiss who I really love.

Later today I went to see Ada. We've had a nice talk. I still like her very much. I spoke about Gerd a lot with Ada. I still didn't find anyone better than him yet. I am in a pretty bad mood now.

In the evening I stayed with the Hoffmings until 9.30. But I do not intend to go there again. It's been horrible there. Tatta plays cards the whole night, drinks and smokes. He's very unsympathetic then. Lilienthal was there too. Such an ape. He makes moves on me all the time.

Hopefully the postman is going to bring me something tomorrow.

Breslau
21 February 1939

I'm already in bed and will turn off the lights to sleep, but only after writing a few lines.

I got a postcard from Hamburg from Gerd today. A real love card. He is missing me very much, and at the end he sent greetings and kisses – which is oldfashioned actually. He didn't get one little kiss from me either. Well, for all I care he can have as many kisses on paper as he wants. But I was happy about the card. I really want to have a boyfriend again, but a really nice one.

Mr. Gerson gave me an English lesson. I can't stand him. He is stupid.

Breslau
23 February 1939

The postman gave me another letter from Gerd today. An even more exuberant one. He calls me his cute lady and greets again. Outrageous!

I still didn't find a new boyfriend yet. Sad enough. Well, maybe it's going to happen.

Breslau
26 February 1939

Today was a very boring day. Terribly tedious. Leo Lilienthal wants to speak to Tatta all the time. I can't stand that old man. But I want to make him addicted to me.

Today I wrote letters to Gunter and Lotte. Hopefully I get post myself soon.

Ada wanted to visit me today. But I'm not really in the mood for visits. And I won't go to Hoffmings.

I still don't have a boyfriend. I really miss having one - a real one. Not someone like little Gerd again. No, I want someone I really do love and with whom I can learn to kiss.

Today I am unhappy with myself. I always go back to the same faults, the laziness and the carelessness. It's horrible, and I really want to change myself, but most of the time I can't find enough energy.

Well, I have now handed in the papers. I hope I filled them out properly.

That was a great sigh – again! How is it all going to turn out?

Seventeen-year-old Gerda's interest in older men such as the **small fat** Leo Lilienthal (aged 36, late December 1938) and **the really nice Herr Gutfield at the post office** (aged 35, early January 1939) probably says more about what was happening towards the end of that decade in the Third Reich as it approached its Nazi zenith – specifically what was happening for its Jews – than it does about her taste in men. After 1933 when Hitler became Chancellor; after the Nuremberg Laws of 1935; after the climactic "Night of Crystals" of November 1938, emigration became *the* "topic of conversation" in "Jewish circles". Breslau was being emptied of boys and young men – leaving for Palestine or whichever of the world's doors remained open to them. By 1939, almost half of the Jews in Breslau were over fifty years old. With that going on, Herren Lilienthal and Gutfield probably appeared relatively youthful, and I can see why - **dreadful** though it might be to be kissed by him – she came close to kissing Leo. As for those nearer her own age, little Wolfgang was leaving for Brazil, Gerd Nungen was off to Bolivia – leaving behind that gold pendant heart **with a door in it** – and **there are no more boys or men left here**.

Twenty-one-year-old Horst Grotte had also left, and there is no further mention of him after 27th December, perhaps because he was "no great love" and was anyway just another absence. Of all the boys and men mentioned, only Horst Grotte has some kind of internet afterlife (as far as I can find , having searched for every one of them). Most of the information available concerns his father, Prof. Dr. Alfred Grotte, an architect in Breslau, and the four "Hannukah drawings" that have survived him, three of them depicting a boy lighting Hannukah candles in 1937, 1939 and 1940. Alfred Grotte was killed in Theresienstadt on 17th June 1943. Horst's mother, Klara, was murdered in

Auschwitz. It is recorded that Horst fled Germany in 1939 and settled in Bolivia and later Colombia.

Gerda's brothers had left, too (Kurt to Buenos Aires and Gunther to New York), leaving her with Tatta – who at the time seemed to be getting on her nerves as she was arguing with him all the way to "Siederers", leaving after half an hour since it was **so boring with all the old people there**. Her snapshot of him, playing cards all night, drinking and smoking at "Hoffmings", suggests more than annoyance: estrangement. She was missing **men and love** just when she was looking for both.

It is obvious to me now, but when I first started translating these diaries I didn't notice how her words reflected so clearly what was going on around her. She did not have to explain anything.

Something else I missed at first reading – or rather I did not discern the connections – is also obvious with closer scrutiny. That notable entry of 13th February – **Morgen – fruh – Ge – sta – po** - is surely connected to that of the 26th, which includes the statement: **Well, I have now handed in the papers. I hope I filled them out properly.** This in turn takes me back to Gunther's letter of 20th January and the question (No. 8 of his 12 important questions): *When will you get your passport and clearance certificate?"* That must have been the reason for her appointment with the Gestapo: it *was* to do with obtaining the necessary emigration papers. My initial surmise had been correct, but I was less certain then, more prone to speculate. Aside from how the syllables are separated on the page, she reveals no anxiety or fear, though she surely shared a communal Jewish dread of an authority which viewed Jews as vermin and pressured them to leave while also making it more difficult for them to do so. Its powers of arrest and deportation, its 7am appointments for applicants (or more accurately, supplicants), its boundless state control, and then the prospect of its official scrutiny of a **beautiful** seventeen-year-old girl denuded to *eine Jude* – all this might have made her speculate as to the real purpose and outcome of the appointment. I am almost certain, too, that she went alone. **Morgen – fruh – Ge – sta – po** sounds such a lonely statement. One last observation – regarding the **terrible, stupid music** she heard on the radio in the afternoon of 27th December. She doesn't identify it, so I am again left to speculate. Might it have been music to goose-step to? Military marches had occupied the German airwaves since 1933, and with Breslau one of the most potent radio stations in Europe, there was no escaping it.

2

TO GERMAN JEWISH REFUGEE COMMITTEE
DRAFT LETTER (UNDATED, 1939)

Dear Sir

I beg to ask you if you could give me a chance of being trained in diet – cooking. Having in view to go to USA later on where my brothers are trying to get me an affidavit, you would give me an excellent opportunity to prepare myself for my emigration.

I daresay that I am well experienced in cooking and baking.

TO GERMAN - JEWISH COMMITTEE COORDINATING
COMMITTEE FOR NURSES, WOBURN HOUSE, LONDON.
DRAFT LETTER (UNDATED AS ABOVE)

Dear Sir

Having learnt that you are going to train Jewish girls from Germany as nurses I beg to ask you if you have a vacancy for me.

I am seventeen and a half years old and healthy, not afraid of any work and should very much like to attend and to nurse sick people.

My 2 brothers being in America trying to get me an affidavit I shall go over after some time. By this training you would give me an excellent chance of earning my living there later on. My father is going to emigrate very soon and my mother has died some years ago. That is the reason why I am anxious to go out instantly and to prepare myself for a profession abroad.

I beg you to consider the special circumstances of this case and that the danger of being left alone is approaching.

I thank you in advance and beg you to give this application your kind consideration.

Yours f . . .
enclosed please find my short biography and 2 photos.

TO THE INTERNATIONAL AU PAIR INSTITUTE, VICTORIA, LONDON SW1.
DRAFT LETTER (UNDATED AS ABOVE)

Dear Sir

I beg to apply to your kind assistance in seeking an au pair post with an English family. I am seventeen and a half years old, the daughter of a highly respected merchant here, attended a secondary school till my 14th year. After leaving this school I attended a school for household and domestic science in Breslau for one year where I learnt cooking, baking, sewing, ironing, and gardening. From September 1937 – June 1938 I attended Victoria College in Prague in order to improve my knowledge. I took the English examination with distinction at the German University there.

Returning home I entirely dedicated myself to the

household economy. My mother having died early I am accustomed to work independently. In addition I am fond of children and interested in music. I am looking forward to an early answer and thank you in advance for your assistance.

UNDATED DRAFT LETTER (AS ABOVE)

"Household"

Dear Sir

I beg to apply to your kind assistance asking you if you could procure me a place in a household (town or country, by preference in London). For this reason I submit you the following particulars.

My 2 elder brothers are in America and try to get me an affidavit. My father is going to emigrate now and my mother died early. Having no chance to get out of here at the moment and being much afraid to be left here alone I entreat you to get me a chance for I am quite desperate about my future.

I beg to consider that I don't intend to emigrate to England but only want to go there for a temporary stay in order to wait there till I shall get a visa to America.

I am of good appearance, enjoy good health, and able to adapt myself to any conditions. If you see your way clear to helping me in my difficulties about my emigration I should be deeply grateful to you.

This was to be no "Kindertransport" emigration – she was just too old for that – although in the 1960s, in a letter to the lawyer in Dusseldorf handling the case for compensation from the German government for the family's financial losses suffered during the Third Reich, Gerda was to describe leaving Germany by Kindertransport. Towards the end of February 1939, at the age of 17 years and 8 months, her childhood was not a distant memory, but she was having to arrange her future fast, seeking offers of employment from private English sponsors primarily for some kind of domestic service.

That Gerda was looking for such work in England reflected the reality of her situation. It was the best she could do in the circumstances – it was what certain English families wanted, and all that could be offered. That she was from an established bourgeois Breslau family, had attended Victoria College in Prague, where she had distinguished herself in English, and by her own account made a good impression – these might secure for her a position as a domestic. Although her own family once had servants, it is doubtful anyway that she would have aspired to anything more. In the 27th December entry her vocation is to be "Kinderfraulein" (nanny) or cook, and she went on (in these February drafts) to make the most of her training in domestic science and her cooking, baking and sewing abilities. As for Gerda's desperation about her future, I am certain that also came across in the letters she actually sent. They were desperate times, but forgetting for a moment her situation as a young Jewish woman in unusual times – aside from marriage, what else could she realistically expect?

She had no mother to advise her. That was doubtless something to be thankful for, since it also meant that Gerda had no mother to leave behind, no mother to join the queues of those selected for a disposal as yet unimaginable in February 1939. Fortunately her mother had died. There is no reference to her either in the "German" diaries or the later ones, and it seems that she would be remembered only for dying early. Whereas "Tatta" expands in the space she vacates – fat Tatta, who amounted to Vater und Mutter rolled into one, with flesh to spare. With his massive head and torso, the father fills the German photograph albums, while his Frau (also large) is allocated just two photographs. In one of these, a formal family composition, there is no Gerda. The boys, Kurt and Gunther, are there, dwarfed by their parents (the mother seated, the father stern, straight-backed and patriarchal in jacket and breeches), but judging by the height of the boys, their little sister was still unborn. I recall only one photograph – of that large, unsmiling woman bending over her baby – where Gerda (if it *is* Gerda) is with her mother. That nameless person may have once filled gaps in those old albums (who knows?), but her daughter evidently found no need to mention the absent mother again. Neither (as far as I know) did her brothers. Gunther once referred to her, in a letter from Ecuador written at or near the end of the war, but then it was only to ask his sister if she remembered the date of their mother's death in Breslau. Whether or not Gerda was able to supply this information remains unknown.

Her father was a different matter. He seems to expand inside each photographic frame, as if even the expansive seascape they escaped to each year, with its beaches and boats, barely allowed sufficient living space for such a man. *I am Elkan, big Tatta, merchant of Breslau*, the image seems to say in its high-waisted, genitals-defining woollen trunks, *and this little girl sheltering beneath me is meine kleine Tochter, Gerda*. In one such photograph, undated but well before 1933, when such holidays came to an end, he stands at the water's edge, shoulders back, legs wide apart to make a pyramid space for his crouching daughter, as he arches over her.

3

LETTERS TO GERDA

Hampton-in-Arden
January 25th 1939

Dear Miss Lewrnsohn

I am wanting someone who can do housework, plain cooking, and who is fond of children. I can offer you a good home, with comfortable bedroom and kitchen-sitting room. I understand that you can speak English and are accomplished in needlework, I am sure that you would suit me, it is someone refined that I require, someone who can help me with the housework and whom I can leave my little boy with happily, it is not very often that I have to go out in the afternoons, but if I do I must know that I have someone responsible.
You would have a bicycle at your disposal, wireless in the kitchen, your outings would be Thursdays from lunch-time and Sundays. The wage I am offering you is 17/- a week.
If this position interests you I should like to hear from you immediately. Do you think we shall be able to get a permit?

Yours Sincerely

Mrs. M. Catlin

Hampton-in-Arden
January 31st 1939

Dear Gerda

Thank you for your very nice letter. I shall apply for the permit immediately, but I am afraid that we shall be two or three weeks obtaining it. Now Gerda in the meantime I should like you to realise and know all the possible drawbacks to this position, as well as the advantages, because I should not like you to take this big step only to find that you are disappointed. I want you to be quite sure that we can make you happy here.

Firstly, please realise that this is quite a small village, it has not even a cinema, which means that you will, for your amusements, either to have to go into Birmingham which is a 20 minute ride by train with 1/10d to pay for your return fare, or you will have to cycle about 2 miles to a large village named Solihull. Secondly, I don't think that there are any other German girls here, but this is compensated by the fact that there are clubs in Birmingham where you would doubtless find friends. There are, of course, plenty of girls in Hampton, but I don't think that they would suit you, as the ordinary English maid is very uneducated and unintelligent. There is one exception, and she is employed by my neighbour, and is a very nice woman who I know would always be glad to see you and return your visits.

I do so hope that all this has not put you off the idea, but I think that you should know everything for and against when you are coming so far from home.

Yours Sincerely

Mrs. M. Catlin

Hampton-in-Arden
February 22ⁿᵈ 1939

My dear Gerda

I have had such a disappointment, and I am sure that you will also be upset. I had a letter from the Ministry of Labour yesterday, informing me that no permits were issued to foreigners under 18 years of age. I had no idea that there was an age limit, it is all very difficult.
Now Gerda will you write to me as soon as you become 18, and if you would still like to come I will again apply for the permit, it will only be three months, and you would then come when the nicest part of the year is beginning.

Yours Sincerely

Mrs. M. Catlin

Peter Thornthwaite

LETTER FROM GUNTER
(NO ADDRESS - NEW YORK?)

Feb.28, 1939

Dear Gerda

To day is a very bad weather – better: the weather is very bad today – it pours from the sky. It is quite impossible for me to leave my home; the streets are always very dirty and full of mud. It is a very good exercise for me to write English letters and for you it means likewise a very smart training to read my writing, to pick out the mistakes of the content and so to check them in your mind. I will not fail to repeat again, what I mentioned in my letter to father, that your clever letter is a testimony for your good English knowledge. I am obliged to be jealous, for I have much trouble in writing and understanding English. It was a pity that the last year in Germany I spent in learning Spanish. I aspire to learn the American pronunciation so fluently that nobody more is supposing that I am of German origin. You know English and American is very different, especially the American slang is very particular.

I am convinced that if you would succeed in getting to London you would enjoy it very much. You remember I had always been so afraid to go abroad and now I feel so well. I am very fond of the American mentality and let us hope that as soon as possible you will be able to state it with subject to the English life.

The girls in this country have mostly a very good income, though it is not necessary for them to work so industrious like men. For young female persons like you it is very easy to find a good job. The girls in this country know that they have the best chance to make money and therefore they are very proud and selfish. They have in all situations of life here the preference. I have no good opinion about the American girls, for they have all vices and frivolity, Their conduct is very silly. Girls in the age to 30 years are roll-skating on streets. Roll-skates is the great fashion with nearly all girls. They ride along the side-walk. They like to wear coloured sport-hats with feathers of an altitude of about one foot. Their faces are lavished with powder, their cheeks are specially marked with a pure red colouration. This shall produce a very healthfully look out and emphasize it. Naturally almost all youngster must smoke on streets and the white paper of cigarettes becomes completely red by their poignant lips always treatened with lip-sticks. In their mouth they have a mint-bonbon, their skirts are very short, they like to wear shoes with very flat rubbersoles and heels and by the open tip they show their big toe. And the whole purpose of their life is to dance swing. I dont like that type of girls, it is too superficial for me. Dont imitate these dreadful qualities!! Just this minute my neighbour communicates me that he is going to forward his oversea-mail to the harbors post-office and therefore I will shut up.

Your brother Gunter

LETTER TO GERDA

North-Western Reform Synagogue Refugee Aid Committee 1st March 1939

Dear Fraulein Lewisohn,

I was so sorry to hear from you, in your letter of the 25th. February, that you will not be able to go to Mrs. Catlin until you are eighteen – I knew that you could only come to England as a guaranteed child before you reached this age.

I am now doing everything possible to find you a temporary home, as a guaranteed child, until you can go to Mrs. Catlin in

June, and if I am successful, I will write to you at once; you will have to join a transport and come to England on what is called a "Collective Permit", but this is only possible if I can find some-one to take you under these conditions. In any case, I am doing everything I can, and I will write to you again as soon as I have any news for you.

LETTER TO GERDA
FROM LONDON S.E.15

March 4 1939

Dear Gerda

I have just received your letter and am hurrying to catch the post.
I filled up the form on Thursday and possibly there may be no objection to your youth. If there is, they will be sure to tell me and I will then guarantee you as you say.
I think you may feel quite sure of leaving Germany before your Father.
My daughter knows a lady who is working on the Committee and I will see if she can help us at all.

Cheer up!

Sincerely Yours

Mrs. M. Stainton

LETTER FROM GUNTER

New York
March 4, 1939

My dear Gerda

This morning still lying in my bed, I received your handsome letter written again in English. Your very good manner in writing English causes me to tremendous admiration. Where received you such enormous knowledges? I suppose the last time you must have been only sitting down in the Elkan-Stool very closely the radio always studying English-lectures. The average education and knowledges of American and may be of English people is not of high rank. People prefers for conversation a most easy and simply way to express their thoughts. However instead of this, people like it to use a lot of accostemed slant-words, pronounced in a very peculiarly sound so that a stranger like me is incapable to understand. The expressions: Go ahead, come on, what is the matter with you, hello, hello, sure how are you, shut up, are to hear dayly 100 times. It is nearly disgusting! Listen, in your writings you must pay attention that your written "w" not looks like a "r", that can easily give misunderstandings. I am very excited and curious to get from you the first news of London and to know how you feel standing on your own feet, earning the first money. No Reichsmark but engl. Pounds and Shillings! Probably you will be very fond of the event to start in a new life in freedom! Yesterday some one let me know that Suse from Breslau, now living in London, lost her position and reputation because she offended very severely her employee, Her insolence is not only a harm for her, but it means a loss for many refugees at all. Indeed, I wrote Lotte and till to-day her answer is still outstanding. By this I am broken heart. But what a good chance since I have your spent address of Steffi. I am going to write her a detailed letter. I will thank her because she was so auxiliary to you.

Father wrote, you are so busy in the kitchen and you would have great capacity in doing house-work. People here is not so fond of "Mensche" like you, they prefer to play Bridge and Domino; however I play in old freshness Cello and Trumpete. Just yesterday I played the first time in the Young Men Hebrew-Association-amateur-orchestra. I am happy to be introduced in a real, good situated American society. For your stay in London I give you the advice to take up immediately the social intercourse with only English citizens, for only by this you can learn English fastely and correctly, whole looked away from other advantages which would following from this. Oh, how lovely, my neighbour in the drawing-room is just listening to the latest hits. All people are singing it on the streets. A waltz, - Umbrella!

I am very proud to have for many presentations in WABC-Broadcasting & movies free-tickets, so that I don't get out of amusement and in consequence of this I become lazy, silly and gluttonous.

Finally I present you my sincerely regards. Your brother Gunter – Israel – Heinz (beloved from all delightful girls of this town)

(*Mensche* = people).

LETTERS TO GERDA

London S.E.15
9 March 1939

Dear Gerda

I sent your letter to my daughter who took it to the lady who works for the Refugee Committee, she is an Austrian Jewess. On Monday she searched for your card and found it, she has stopped the form which I filled up, which would have gone to the Home Office and made difficulties, and is doing her best to hurry on the guarantee which I am giving for you. Ordinarily it would take two months but she hopes to get it through in four weeks. I do hope it will be in time for you.

I have never enquired as to your religion, whether you are an orthodox Jew. I do not mind what religion you profess but I think it is better to have some religion, as it helps one to have a good life.

I wonder if you quite understand what your position will be in this family! You and I will work together during the day but you will not have your meals with us, not because of any idea of inferiority, but because we are usually only together at meal times, and we want to talk about matters which concern only ourselves. I am sure you will understand.

The work of the house is not heavy, as we have all labour saving devices. I am sure you will not find the work hard. My woman, Mrs. Hands, has been very ill with "flu" and is still away. She has worked for me for nearly 20 years which proves that I am not an unkind mistress.

I hope that you will remain here. I have heard of English ladies who have taken trouble to get a German girl to England and the girl has left them after a little while with some insufficient reason. I do not like changes and I hope that you will be happy enough to want to remain with us.

The house is on a hill and we look right over London with all its lights. We have a nice garden with a big old oak tree in it.

The two dogs are mother and son! Whimsie and Winkle, they will love you.

We think that if you come to us you will find here a happy home.

PS I have kept, for the present, the certificates and your photo. Your English is excellent. I had to pay fourpence on your letter.

Sincerely Yours
Mrs. M. Stainton

London S.E.15
31ˢᵗ March / 39

Dear Gerda

I am afraid I have no very good news for you. Although I received on February 28ᵗʰ a notice that the Continental organisation had given you a very good report, yet, because a different Committee is now dealing with your case, you have to fill up the enclosed form and forward it to the proper authorities.

I have been assured by my daughter's friend that your case is to be dealt with specially and that the delay will not be so great as it would be ordinarily.

I am very sorry about it and I think it all seems very stupid, but I am assured that I can do nothing to hasten matters, there is so much what we call "red tape" about it all.

Today is a lovely sunny day and everything seems hopeful. You will be glad to get to this peaceful country, and this pleasant home.
Sincerely Yours
Mrs. M. Stainton

North-Western Reform Synagogue Refugee Aid Committee
4ᵗʰ. April 1939

Fraulein Gerda Lewisohn,
BRESLAU,
Victoriastr. 65,
Germany.

Dear Fraulein Lewinsohn,

I received your letter and health and birth certificates safely. On Thursday I shall take them myself to Bloomsbury House, where I have some influence and hope to get the matter arranged very shortly.
I note that you have written to me from a different address – I have Scharnhorststrasse 31 in my records as your address; please be sure to let me know which address is correct, as we cannot risk any letters miscarrying.

FROM GERDA'S DIARY:

Breslau
Mittwoch, den 26 April 1939

Still I have not got the Permit. Therefore I pray every day. Perhaps God hears my prayer.

I think I am a little in love with Katz.

But then there is Peter who "ist doch auch so niedlich" (cute). When I came over he said, so that I could hear it, "Fraulein Lewinsohn . . ."

(ist doch auch so niedlich = is so cute too)

By late April 1939, Gerda and her father had moved to Victoriastrasse 65 – which address no longer exists, but then neither does Scharnhorststrasse 31, or Breslau for that matter. Back then, though, it was mainly those identified as *Juden* who were losing their addresses. "Lebensraum" (living space) was what Germany and German citizens wanted and would get, but for the Jews of Breslau the allocated "Lebensraum" was an estimated seven square metres of space per person and restricted to rooms shared with other Jews in *Judenhäuser* (houses for Jews). It was fortunate that the Lewinsohn household had dwindled by 1939, with no mother or brothers taking up space, because by then Jews were not allowed out in groups of more than two, and if they did go out, they had to keep walking, as public benches in Breslau were for Gentiles, *fur Juden verboten* (for Jews forbidden) as were the parks, as were the cinemas (of which there were 27), the theatres, libraries, sports and other public facilities. But they were still allowed out in April 1939, and in May also; they were not prohibited from leaving their apartments until September, and that was only for night time from 8pm until 6am. Her father, a diminishing figure as I see him then, may have joined other Jews at the Financial Office in Breslau-South with queries about the 20% (soon to increase to 25%) of the assets to be paid, while she went out on her own. Or he might have stayed at home most days, in their shrunken apartment, with other things on his mind arising from the *Aryanization* or *dejudaization* of businesses and properties and life. It was a time for letting go of things. But among these various losses they did gain something: an additional middle name, *Sara* for her, *Israel* for him, to distinguish them from citizens. They were not yet distinguished by a Yellow Star with *Jude* inscribed inside it. That was to come, on 1st September 1941, just in time for Elkan; too late for Gerda.

I see from her diary entry of 26th April that Gerda was still going out and meeting "cute" boys like Peter, who identifies her by name, audibly enough for her to hear him and for her to feel just a little excitement. Things couldn't have been too bad, because by 1st May, Gunther is commenting on her "delightful German written letter", while in New York he has "a grippe".

4

LETTER FROM GUNTER

New-York
May 1, 1939

My dear Gerda:

I took in receipt of your delightful German written letter and found out of the content that there is reason enough to appreciate your skilful proceed in your emigation-matter.

All your writing I got unto now from you were always obviously logical. With respect to this fact I hope and trust, that you will succeed in putting aside the last tremendous hindrance impeding you.

When I get post from you the first thing what I do is staring on the envelop's stamp, for I am expecting that the picture of Hindenburg soon will turn over in the bust of the old king of England – Georg V.

You must be current endeavoured to get the outstanding papers from that family in England. Take it easy and let us hope and trust that in a couple of weeks you will be able to find a new home in England.

Since about 6 days I have to suffer from a grippe. By rising in my head, the grippe caused so tremendous pains, that I was incapable to open my eyes. I was forced down to bed; before the door of my room I put a notice "Mr. Lewinsohn is out of order".

In the meantime my disease deceased a bit. I was able to ride to the Mount Sinai-Hospital for consultation, free of any charge, and now I feel that I would be on the right way to recovery.

My influenza upset me so terrible that I lost concentration to procure all the essential papers for my intended settlement in "Equador S.A". Meanwhile I could advance in my preparations and I am going to get the permanent visa for Equador. Probably I don't fail in my opinion that father will not be particularly enjoyed about my Equador-divice, but in spite of all what would be opposed to my arranged shift, I made up my mind in this matter.

On 5/3/39 I ride with railroad to Havana/Cuba, from there with autocoach to Miami/Florida. The remainder of the trip takes place by steamer 2. class "Orbita" (The Pacific-Steam Navigation Company) down to the harbor of Equador. Guayaquil. Please look at the map!![1]

I am very sorry that father and you have some trouble in settling the question of your apartment. It is well imaginable for me, that especially father is missing a lot of comfort in your poor 2-rooms-flat. Nevertheless in consideration of the fact that Dallmann are nice and clean neighbours, I suggest you still to remain in this flat, even under the threats of Klara. Father who, by remembering Scharnhorststr.31, including service of Bruning and Klara, became very awkward with going, must now give proof of self-disciplin, undependent of any comfort and services once given.

Now will father exist abroad when he is not trained to shine his shoes or to, for example, wash dishes? When father will stay

---

[1] It was not until December 2022 - during proofreading - that I noticed Gunther's error. He informed his sister, in his letter dated May 1st 1939, that he would be leaving New York for Ecuador (which is spelled here as *Equador*) on 5/3/39. Checking dates, I think he must have meant 5/6/39. The itinerary of his onward emigration also appears confused here.

abroad he has whole alone to take care of his gentleman-duties. Then there is only one room, no Klara nor anybody else. Then is all up to him! Therefore father would do very good practicing a little to live, or at least to try such a life, under modest conditions, after the principle "serve yourself"!

I am enjoyed that Aunt Bertha is finally residing in Brandenburg, one of my aims has been reached by this! My best regards and kisses dein Bruder Guenter

LETTERS TO GERDA

London S.E.15
8th May 1939

Dear Gerda

I received a letter on Saturday which looks hopeful. I have sent the fee and am to tell you to apply for a visa to the local British Passport Control Officer, to whom communication has already been sent.

The Committee with notify me of the approximate date of your arrival.

Steffi rang the other day (that means she phoned) to ask if you had yet arrived. I will tell her when I hear that you are coming. She seems very happy.

PS They have given me a new address for you so I am sending this there. I hope it is all right.

Sincerely Yours
Mrs. M. Stainton

Peter Thornthwaite

North-Western Reform Synagogue Refugee Aid Committee
8th May 1939

Dear Fraulein Lewinsohn

I am very much pleased to be able to inform you that the Home Office have granted your Permit.

You must immediately apply to the British Consul in Breslau for the Permit and Visa, and they will give you all the necessary information.

I hope that you will have no further trouble and that you will come here as soon as possible.

LETTER FROM KURT

Buenos Aires
May 21, 1939

My dear Gerda!
Thank you for your lovely letter. What understanding and subtle taste! You've become a wonderful person – what a shame we can't have a face-to-face chat! The verse that you recalled, I know is very vital, every teenage girl overflowing with illusions should read it. Your letter shows that you have become a practical and sober-minded girl, although free from the despicable absence of the ideal of an average person.

You wonder about my relationship to my father. And to me it, on the contrary, seems quite logical. I love my father very much, not because I owe him a lot, but because he is my father. Otherwise there would be degeneration, inhuman confusion. If

69

I was and am a bad son, if I was constantly frightened by gloomy memories from childhood, then the main fault for this lies with the father, his lack of complexes, his thirst for power and his selfishness. A poor teacher, the father should understand that children develop their own personality, which should not be led, not raped. Therefore, my father was my disappointment.

Dear Gerda, when you fall in love one day or when you decide to go your own free path, you will feel your father's selfishness!! I don't doubt it for a moment! Now I again insist that the distancing was due to the fault of my father. This is not about ingratitude or lack of love, it is about something completely different.

I am very sorry that my father is in a bad position. If I could help him I would have done it today. But in terms of invitation, Argentina is the worst country. I turned everywhere to call my father, but this is impossible. I must provide proof that I own property and have an income that allows me to fully support the person who is being called. Doesn't the father know that countless emigrants want to take their relatives overseas, but cannot do it?

As already mentioned, my affairs are very bad. Working with meat (for a number of economic reasons, it seems to me inappropriate to tell you about this in detail) sometimes brings me 80 dollars. I'll probably leave this occupation and go to paper.

My father's unworthy suggestion that marriage could improve my position I reject.

Say hello to dear dad
I love and kiss you heartily, Your brother Kurt.

Kurt's letter might not have reached her in time. It probably arrived as she was leaving – or after she left – though it found her eventually, since it is there in the cache of letters from that period. What she made of it is unknown, but Gerda, too, was distancing herself from her Tatta – if more for practical than psychological reasons. What Kurt has to say about his father appears uncaring in the circumstances, but also anguished. By 21st May 1939 it appears that *the father* is the main source of his embitterment, more than Nazi Germany. Even the father's desperate situation provokes more irritation than compassion. Does the father not understand that *countless emigrants want to take their relatives overseas, but cannot do it?* It is yet another burden for the eldest son to bear. Then another possibility arises – censorship? Did Kurt deliberately expunge from his letter any criticism of the German authorities in case it ended up in the wrong hands? Such censorship did develop during the Third Reich, and Jewish letter writers might have feared that their letters were being read by others. Still, there is no disguising the fact that Kurt's darkest thoughts were as much to do with "the father" as the fatherland. There is no mention of his mother – no mention of her at all anywhere by Kurt or any of the family – probably because by this time she was already long dead. No reference to his brother either. But he is fond of his little sister, with her *understanding and subtle taste*. What he means by her freedom *from the despicable absence of the ideal*, I'm not sure. Its opacity may have more to do with the translation. Perhaps Kurt meant that, though practical and grounded, she is also idealistic, and it is the *absence* of idealism in others that is despicable. That must be it. There is no reference, I see, to her imminent departure from Germany, which is strange given her desperation (as evident from her diary). Possibly she had not written to him about it, concocting instead a *lovely letter* to allay any anxieties; yet his reply is a little egotistical. Is he not touched by the plight of the family left behind in Germany?

As for him, he had left years before, as is clear from a much earlier letter (only recently translated) dated 17th November 1935 – the earliest (to my knowledge) of the surviving Lewinsohn letters.

Peter Thornthwaite

LETTER FROM KURT

My dear Gerda!

Thank you very much for your lovely letter from the mountains! Finally, a few lines from you again. I have not seen you, or talked to you, my dear sister, since I left. I have lost sight of you, so to speak, that is, I always see you in front of me as the little girl who played with toy trains with Gunter or amused herself with her dolls. And in the meantime, you were becoming a young lady, and your last letter gives the delightful impression of a sensible person. Time flies!

I hope that you will soon describe to me in detail what you are doing. Do you have a couple of cute girlfriends? Do you still belong to the Zionist youth group you wrote to me about? Are the Friedlander girls from the corner of Charlottestrasse and Goethestrasse still in the Augusta-School? What is Gunter doing with his music? Does your father often visit Litauer now? Does Gunter sometimes take you to the hatter? Have you happened to meet some of my old acquaintances – Bergheim, Hans Jevitz, Fritz Rosenstiel, Hans Bauchmann, Heinz Frenkel, Kurt Markus, etc? Do you get on well with Aunt Johanna? I hope: yes. (As for me, my family attachment increases the further I am away from home). Are Ilsa Holz from Scharnhorststrasse and Ruth Schein from Lammsstrasse still in Breslau? Please write to me soon.

Personally I'm doing well in the circumstances. That is, my health is all right except for a runny nose, which affected me unpleasantly when tonight I could not distinguish gasolene from kerosene and filled the Kerosene Lamp with gasoline, which almost exploded when ignited.

In farming, by which I have been earning my daily bread, I find great satisfaction. At supper I feel that I earned this meal honestly and in good faith. Who'd have thought that the "impractical", the "idealistic" Kurt one day would earn his living by feeding pigs?

My current activity? I wake up at 4:30. At 5 o'clock I clean and fill the cauldrons in which fodder and sugar beets for cattle are boiled. At 6:00 I feed the pigs. 6:30 coffee. 6:45 I milk 9 cows. 8:00 I break for cheese, meat, etc, and 1 bottle of wine or rum. 8:30 – 12:00 a lot of outdoor work (currently: harvesting sugar beets, ploughing the vineyard, felling and sawing spruce and stacking them in cubic meters. 12:15 lunch. 13:00 – 17:00 more outdoor work. 17 – 18:30 milk the cows, feed the pigs, lock up the sheep. 18:30 dinner. 19:00 end of the working day.

Tomorrow we have a feast as it is the chief farmhand's birthday. Menu: noodle soup, oysters, sausage and buttered bread, Russian-style beer, goose liver pate, veal in carrot sauce, beefsteak, cheese, stewed fruit, cake, coffee and brandy.

But you must not think I am happy now. Quite the opposite! Completely isolated, living among people who are utter strangers to me, with the frightening uncertainty of tomorrow. No help at all from Jewish authorities. No intellectual life. I cannot properly dress and maintain myself. I lack all the little things, of which I recently wrote to father – that are almost more important than food and indispensable if one does not want to fall into the darkest misery.

The natural and healthy life here in the scenically wonderful Perigord strengthens my energy, but I worry about my future and fear destitution.

For the next three months I am carefree enough! Did I mention that I had a decent suit and coat made?

Now, dear little Gerda, I'll end this letter.

Your loving brother, Kurtel.

Many greetings to dear father and Gunter and Aunt Bertha.

PS. I strongly advise you to visit the Paula Ollendorff School in Breslau.

By 17th November 1935 Kurt, then in his mid-twenties, was part of the post-1933 exodus of Jews from Germany. He did not go to Palestine, or to North or South America, but to rural France where even an *impractical idealist* might earn his *daily bread* by feeding pigs. In 1935 there was none of his later bitterness about his father. His tone is light, when thinking of his little sister as a girl with her train and dolls, and darkens only when thinking of his future. There is affection for the family left behind. Something has happened in the four years between the two letters to embitter him and turn against "the father".

By 1935 it was evidently still possible for a German Jewish girl to enjoy herself, as her *lovely letter from the mountains* suggests. By 17th November, Hitler had been Chancellor for nearly three years, books had been publicly burned in Berlin and Breslau, Jewish shops boycotted, and the Nuremberg laws distinguished Jews from German citizens. By September of that year Gerda lost political and civic rights, including the right to sexual contact with Aryans (although at age 14 she may not have minded the prohibition). By 1935 she would have noticed restrictions on education. It is not known if Gerda ever visited or attended the school recommended by Kurt. Paula Ollendorff, then prominent in the Jewish community, established houses for Jewish infants and girls in Breslau, and a school to prepare girls for domestic service. There may be some reference to it in the yet untranslated tracts of Gerda's early diaries. [2] All I know is that some time in 1935 she wrote from the mountains

---

[2] In writing this, I overlooked evidence included in Gerda's letter, drafted early 1939, to the International Au Pair Institute in London (pg 47) in which, though not naming the Paul Ollendorf School recommended by Kurt, she appears to refer to it when stating: I attended a school for household and domestic science in Breslau for one year...

to her distant brother. She was on holiday. In mountains. There are photographs to prove it – and she is joyful (as I can see from one of them), at this high point in her life, in Kitzbuhel, in an ankle-length coat with wide leopard-skin lapels. Could she have been only 14? She looks older. She wrote to Kurt from a ski resort in Austria – the very place where, in February 1939, Eva Braun was to spend a week skiing, before going back to the Berghof to await the return (in early May) of spring sunshine and her Fuhrer and tea on the sunny terrace.

Did Kurt's letter of November 1935 trouble his little sister with its words of *darkest misery* and *destitution*? There is no extant diary of that period, no surviving letters from her, to reveal her thoughts. By 21st May 1939, when he wrote to her again (there are no known letters from Kurt to Gerda during the intervening years) her troubles were almost over.

5

FROM GERDA'S DIARY

Breslau
20 May 1939

Immer noch Breslau. But not for much longer! It should start tomorrow. First nach Berlin. Dann nach Hamburg. Am 24 Mai – mit President Harding nach London. I will celebrate there and determine the position with the Staintons.

To my surprise I have got the Permit! I have also got the Visa. I have many nice clothes to cram in.

Hopefully arrive 12. Juni 1939.

JOURNEY NOTE
(NOTEPAPER HEADED UNITED STATES LINES):

Reiseaufgang (start of journey)
23 Mai 1939

It is a quarter to 12 Nachts.

I have experienced so much that I can hardly grasp it. The fabulous food. Wine as if it was bleeding. The next course always better than the one before. And the music too. It was like a fairy tale. I thought I was dreaming, but for once this dream should succeed . . . Girls play. Yes, play. The whole of life feels like a play to me in which I have the main role. Sometimes I play with childlike naivety, only in this play I have no partner . . . Cinema, too – a cute film with Claudette Colbert. Unfortunately I couldn't understand most of it as they spoke in American slang. After the film the ship departed. I am going away all alone. What will the next day bring? I am very curious. I am a little in love with one of the ship's employees . . .

Peter Thornthwaite

LETTER FROM TATTA

Breslau
30 May 1939

My dear Gerdala!

I received your card and both your letters and was pleased that you fortunately landed in London and were well greeted by your people. Tell me, my dear child, how did you get to Paris? I don't really understand and you don't write in detail, only cursorily. Perhaps you don't have the time for it now.

I was in a terrible mood in Hamburg when you left, and I immediately left for Berlin, where I stayed for two days. I am very anxious about you and feel very lonely.

I am extremely pleased that you have made it and am convinced that you will settle in well. You write to me that in London that man you met is nothing to you, and I ask you to remember who you used to be here. It seems that you forget it very quickly.

Here everything is the same, for the time being nothing has changed, but now I have to come to grips with and pursue my emigration as quickly as possible. I must and I want to get out as quickly as possible. In the meantime, you do your part, my child.

I received a card from Gunter, he is on his way to Ecuador and has visited friends in Panama who were very happy to see him.

I have not yet seen Klara, and I don't want to see her any more either. Coffee I make for myself, and soon Aunt Bertha will do this for me. I eat mainly at the railway station.

You haven't told me yet whether you have received your things. The forwarding agent charges 129 RM. Quite a lot! Please write in detail how it was on the ship and how was the food. Did you get seasick?

There are a lot of girls of dubious reputation going to London.

Please don't get involved with them! Move only in good company.

I don't hear anything from Kurt. Write him a letter: Kurt Lewinsohn, Parana 358 111 E, Buenos Aires, Argentina.

It is enough for today, my dear child. Be greeted and kissed by me, my little Tatzelwurm.

Dein Vater

(This letter was initially dated 30th June, but 'June' was then crossed out and 'May' inserted.)

LETTER FROM AUNT BERTHA

Breslau
June 8, 1939

Dear Gerda!

I have read all your letters from faraway London and am pleased you like it there and seem to have it pretty good. Looks like you're in the right spot. I was delighted that you took the first place among those to be greeted; it is proof of your good upbringing.

There is nothing special to report here. I come back each morning to clean up and make coffee for your Tatta, and I surprised him quite a bit because apparently he did not think I could make a bed. Miss Klara comes in two to three times a week to do the main housework. So you see, dear Gerda, your father is sufficiently cared for. Of course he is very anxious about you, and every day he asks for mail from you, so do please write as often as you can. It is the only thing he can enjoy now. Please write me a nice letter directly for a change. Your Aunt Bertha.

LETTER FROM TATTA

Breslau
12 June, 1939

My beloved Gerdala
I received your dear letter dated June 8th and was very happy to hear that you are fine. I thought right away that you'd have to work a lot. The English do not employ people for pleasure or out of human kindness. Besides, work is good for you and gives you an appetite, and you will become strong and healthy. Dear little Gerda, you wrote that you will get the luggage soon; does that mean you don't have it yet?
Now, my beloved child, you must take pains to make sure that I get out of here as soon as possible. As long as you, my child, were with me, life was still bearable, but now I feel abandoned and my longing for you is greater than before. So you must get me a permit from someone. The Gestapo is urging me to emigrate!

Your loving father.

FROM GERDA'S DIARY

Monday 12 June 1939

London!!!
   A new chapter begins.
   I have really landed in London and will be the whole time here.
   Die Schiffsreise was lovely. On the ship I got to know a 19 year old boy. He is perfect. Really. A Berliner.
   In Paris I was with Joe ganz allein. But nothing happened on the way . . .

? June 1939

Yesterday I was in Hyde Park with Joe and his friend, also a good looking boy, Karl. But I prefer Joe. It was so cold there that I held onto both of them, and Joe kept pushing our arms away, but he sometimes also stroked mine. I believe that is what he wanted to do, but I am not entirely sure. I like him very much, but I also have a terrible snaky feeling. . .

Peter Thornthwaite

LETTER FROM TATTA

Victoriastrasse 65
Breslau
30 June, 1939

My beloved little Gerda!

I have finally received your clear lines and am pleased about your well-being, but I am all the more annoyed that you have nothing positive to tell me about the whereabouts of the typewriter! I have conducted research here and found that the machine was placed in the box under the supervision of customs officials. The box was then wrapped and locked with two locks, and you received the keys!

How did the typewriter get lost? It can only have been left in London during customs clearance and got lost there. It cannot have been stolen on the way! It means a big loss! Consider, the typewriter is worth 186 RM, and the gold duty is just as much, so that's 372 RM all in all! That is a small fortune when you take into account my Dalles. You must get possession of the machine again. You have to blame customs clearance. Don't be so lax and act immediately!

That you can do so little in the way of my departure is more than regrettable. You've shot for the moon and now you are helpless and powerless to help me. You lack the necessary time because you have to keep up constant correspondence with your friends. I forbid you to waste so much time uselessly. Of course you then lack the time to write to me punctually. You write to me that your friends can't achieve anything for their families either. That's just not decisive at all! The purpose of getting you there was not that you can work as a maid in London, but that you manage to find people who can vouch for me for the short time I would stay in London. Since I have an affidavit for America,

Gunter would then request me to go to South America. Somehow it has to work! Staying here is impossible! Yesterday two Gestapo officials visited me again and inquired when I'm leaving. So you see, I'm not interested in whether there are pretty women in London, but I have Zores

You have forgotten everything, my child, because you are relatively well off over there. My dear little Gerda, I don't need to assure you that I am also very worried about you, but now Tachlis.

Meanwhile warm greetings and a thousand kisses from your loving father

(*Dalles*: Yiddish for financial hardships. *Zores*: Yiddish for trouble. *Tachlis*: Yiddish for focus on the task ahead.)

That she left Breslau, first for Berlin, and then Hamburg; that her father had accompanied her to Hamburg; that she then left Hamburg, eventually arriving in London on June 12 1939 – these are the recorded facts. But how did the journey from Hamburg to London involve stopping off at Paris where she was, in her words, **ganz allein with Joe**? The outward bound journey on the President Harding bound for New York on 24th May 1939 is evidenced by the ticket she retained:

UNITED STATES LINES
EINSCHIFFUNGS- VORSCHIFTEN (EMBARKATION REGULATIONS) PRESIDENT HARDING FUR 24. MAI 19390.15 UHR

I'm with her father in asking: how did she *get to Paris*? The internet gets me only so far: the President Harding did leave Hamburg on 24th May 1939 bound for New York, stopping off at Cherbourg and Southampton. Did she disembark at Cherbourg, take the train to Paris, stop over in Paris with Joe, whom she had met on board, and then on to England, arriving in London 12th June? But it is clear from the letters (30th May, 8th and 12th June) from her father and Aunt Bertha that she had arrived in England well before 12th June. To confuse matters more, a short note (dated 4th March 1940) from her new employer in London S.E.15, states: "Gerda Lewinsohn came to me from Breslau in May 1939. She is clean, honest, and willing." It is not stated for whom the note was intended, and while it is complimentary (in a typically English way), it doesn't clarify how Gerda arrived in S.E.15 in May and also in London on 12th June. The 12th June arrival date is even announced in her diary with CAPITALS and three exclamation marks !!! It was a date to be remembered.

It appears that something happened that she did not share with her father, and I am equally in the dark. There are facts here, but I may never get to them.

Another question: What was she planning to take with her aboard the President Harding? (I see that Gunther was also wondering about this on 20th January 1939: Question 10 concerning *some garments and outfit in case of emigration.*

Clothes: of course she had to take some of her good clothes, including perhaps that ankle-length coat, with the wide leopard-skin lapels, from her skiing holiday in Kitzbuhel, and those baggy Turkish trousers she wore when ice-skating. There were restrictions on what could be taken, so she had to limit such baggage, which might not have been easy for her. Apparently, allowable luggage was not so limited, given her diary entry of 20th May 1939: **I have many nice clothes to cram in.** How many is *many*, I wonder? Obviously not the hundreds of dresses an Eva Braun could amass, but still, the Jewish girl's extensive wardrobe was subject to difficult selections before departure, in view of the numerous restrictions.

What else might she have taken? Money (no mention anywhere how much, or how little, she took). Diaries? Certainly her 1939 diary, but how far back did she go? Diamonds? Possible – but risky. Somehow the family fortune, reduced to diamonds, either went with her on 24th May or was later sent to her in London. It is clear, from irritable references in her father's letters to the forwarding charges, that much was sent on to her – including a typewriter which she lost. As for the gold duty he also had to pay – it adds to the cost (to him) of her leaving.

You haven't told me yet whether you received your things (letter of 30th May). Such things were clearly of great importance to Elkan Lewinsohn. His beloved daughter has just abandoned him, and already she is not telling him things (the trip to Paris with Joe), not even bothering to acknowledge receipt of the things forwarded to her at his considerable expense. Such things mattered. It is easy to see in his concern over the loss of the typewriter a greater concern – the loss of his daughter – but he was still a businessman, and things measured in RM, *Reichsmark*, also mattered, and he was still teaching his daughter the value of things. Things like a typewriter worth 186 RM, which you could not afford to lose.

What assets Herr Elkan Lewinsohn still had by the time his daughter left him is unknown. She never said (and probably never knew) and it is nowhere recorded, unless in archives in Krakow or Wroclaw. The Lewinsohns were once an established, well to do middle class family, and in fact (from what I have read) being Jewish did not mean they were not well integrated, even in a city where Hitler's party took 43.5% of the Breslau vote in 1932. Herr

Lewinsohn was a prominent and respected *Kaufmann* in this more "liberal" of German cities. I have no evidence that any men stood outside his shops in 1933 with a sign warning *DEUTSCHE kauft nicht bei Juden*, or scrawled great swastikas across them, or if his windows of hats and other attire had contributed to *the Night of Broken Glass*. The family had money, but by May 1939 Elkan's assets had been stripped. And when she left him in Hamburg, it was just another loss to accept, not only of her – the daughter who was still his beloved child – but of himself as the overarching father, the *Tatta*, between whose legs Gerda once sheltered on the beach. Elkan was relieved to see her leave, I imagine, but possibly guilty too because she was going away and he could not go with her as her protector, and I wonder, too, if he envied, even resented, his daughter, because she was getting away and he was staying? By the time Elkan boarded the train for Berlin, she was aboard the President Harding. At this juncture in her diary and life are there no words of sadness or regret, no tears for Tatta? Not that I can find hidden inside her cryptic German script. She was not yet 18. She was getting away – at last! A delay of another month or two would have made all the difference. Whatever saying goodbye to her father, home, childhood, German Reich, and half her wardrobe, meant to her (and she never wrote it down or said), her mood as the ship was preparing to leave was indeed euphoric. She was excited, it was all wonderful.

By the end of June 1939, there is something new – reproach, bitterness – in his letter to her. There is also fear.

6

LETTER FROM GUNTER

Guayaquil/Ecuador S.A.
July 2, 1939

Dear Gerda

After a silence of about two and a half months I just come from getting a letter of father. Really I am glad to learn that you succeeded in getting to London. When I got your letter during my stay in New-York, I must confess it very frankly, I feared that you are not skilful enough to realize your intended emigration. You will understand that I am most curious to learn how do you like to stay abroad, in a country of other customs and of strange mentality. I suppose that you will be fond to have regained your liberty absolutely. Is it not smart to have freedom in every respect? Under these conditions of freedom even the hardest work will be taken easy. I live nearly one year abroad and it is completely out of any imagination that there would give a time that I could live again in Germany. I hope that in the meantime you have had enjoyable days together with Steffi, movies, theatre, dance etc. But at this occasion I will not fail to warn you before a lot of emigrants. Most of them, specially those who are not able to find any job, like it to abuse the fate of the other emigrants who have forgotten the persecution of Jews in Germany, and abroad they pursue continuously their vicious play, cheating one emigrant the other one. I give you one advice, the best way in order to succeed abroad is to join original English circles. You will have by this the best entertainment, you will learn very quickly the language and you have the greatest chance to advance. I wrote you the other day that in spite of good English knowledges it will be very difficult to understand English people. They dont only like to speak distinctly slant but also very soft, they dont open their mouth at speaking. It is impossible to understand them when they have a pipe in the mouth. Please write me very comfortably about your first impressions.

Now you can write to me without any limitation what was going on in Breslau with Tatta. From time to time it is possible to speak some passengers proceeding from Breslau, but it is not clear what they report. They only particularly point out that it is very urgent to deliver Tatta of daily persecutions from the part of the Gestapo. I studied the new emigration-law for Ecuador and found out that momentary there is no chance to enter this country. Besides of this for emigration to this country father had to bring up 500 dollars. It is very questionable whether father will be able to get out 500 dollars by his liquidation of fortune. Father wrote in his last writing that he is desperated and of broken heart. He told me that he accompanied you to Hamburg. Please communicate to me whether father's health has suffered under the Nazi-events? Drank he much brandy? What is the matter with Aunt Bertha? What is up with Klara - Gisa – Frl. Walker? One emigrant just told me that Miss Walker has been very kind to father, she has confessed herself to assist father as long as it had been possible. Kurt, the filthy fellow, had already kept in silence. Father is very excited why he is not writing. We both together must now do anything to ease the fate of father, we cannot wait as long as Kurt is redeemed from his insanity. Let us hope that soon you will do a bit for the favour of father, coordinating with me. It is always a shame for me to write father that instantly I cant be helpful. Consider, we all belonging to one family have brought us in security. Now we must make all efforts to get out father of the country of barbarism.

My best regards and kisses Dein Bruder, Gunter

LETTER FROM TATTA

Breslau
5 July 1939

My beloved Gerdale

I received your dear letter of July 3 and note with satisfaction your efforts to get back into possession of the typewriter. The machine really can't have disappeared off the face of the earth.
 I would like to meet your desire, namely to come there to give you a few resounding slaps (converting into a few big kisses). Without you, my child, there is no sun! You shall not be weak and faint and shall achieve something for me.
As far as I know, it is difficult for people between 42 and 60 to get to London, but for people over 60, and that applies to me, it is easy to be requested, especially by their children.
Why should I mind if you write to Kurt and Gunter? I don't quite understand!
I can't tell you much else that might interest you. My health is quite good.
Your letters are nice and charming, just write to me often. Innumerable kisses

Your loving father.

ADDITIONAL NOTE FROM AUNT BERTHA INCLUDED IN ABOVE LETTER

Dear Gerda

I also want to "participate" with a few lines, thanking you for all your greetings. Write often, every available minute. The Father is always very happy about your nice and humorous letters (not to be confused with "whimsical"!)

You should not forget your mother tongue completely. There is nothing new here, all going on as usual. I'm also learning English now. I have my first lesson tomorrow and I'm looking forward to it, so that I don't speak English in such a way that it sounds like Chinese. Then I will send you a sample of my new dress, it will be very nice.

Now what's new with you? Do you already have some nice admirers or even suitors? Do you still think you're pretty or have you already neglected it? Don't!

Do you know, dear Gerda, don't you know a way I could get to England? I'm very good at housekeeping now, and the dear father can even confirm it for you! But I won't come unless there is a position, since I'm no longer of the proper age to come as a housekeeper, but only if a position requests me. So, I would be very grateful to you, dear Gerda, if by chance you would know something like that.

Warm greetings, dear Gerda,
From your Aunt Bertha

Peter Thornthwaite

LETTER FROM AUNT BERTHA

Breslau
den 17. Juli 1939

Liebe Gerda

Your "Tatzelwurm" was grumpy from the start today as he is long missing a message from you. Hopefully one will arrive tomorrow. Meanwhile I will write to you today.

I gave you the address of a cousin whom you will find at 70 Finsbury Pavement, London Also, dear Gerda, I have some requests to make.

Firstly we got an invoice from Tinny's for 2 dresses costing 100.50 RM (deposit 50 RM, cash 39.50, 11 RM remaining). One dress was 35 RM, 4.50 RM for alteration, and the other, the blue dress 56 RM, alteration 5 RM. The Father wants to know if that is right. Hopefully you will remember.

The cousin is 22 years old and has been living several months in London where he is an official. A girlfriend of yours, who knows him, lost his address and then by chance found it again and contacted him, and then she wrote to us to find out how we are. I have answered and received a nice letter from her and his address in London. You must write to him a card. He can perhaps be useful to you. Definitely write to him that you would like to meet him. The Tatta thinks that's right too. Perhaps he can also do something for the Tatta to help him get out soon.

You have to try everything.

Now, dear Gerda, I hope all goes well with you. We hear very little from you now. Write again soon, a long letter.

Warm greetings
from Aunt Bertha

LETTER FROM ELKAN LEWINSOHN

Breslau
18/12. 39

Dear Frau Salomon

I thank you most cordially that you were so thoughtful letting me know about my daughter Gerda. I had great concern about her going and I am happy to hear that she is fine. Now I have a big request to make, that you let her know I am in good health, and that I would like her to write to my son in Quito to ask him to get a Visa for me as quickly as possible for my own emigration. It is utterly impossible to procure a Visa here. I am very worried that I have received no message from him and that he does nothing at all for my emigration. I know that Gerda would wish to write to him about this immediately and impress on him the urgency.
Please send her my warm greetings. I would be very pleased to hear from her again. My anxiety about my child is limitless, and I've cried many tears.
Aunt Bertha sends her greetings and hopes you are well.
Thank you so much for your kindness. I remain with best regards

Elkan Lewinsohn

My new address is Gartenstrasse 34Gartenhaus 1.

UNDATED POSTCARD FROM GERDA

London S.E 15

Lieber Tatta,

Just a quick few lines as I am fully occupied. Why don't you write? I hope everything is ok. Send me a message soon. From Gunter and Kurt I have had nothing for a while. I have stayed healthy. Greetings to Aunt Bertha.

Warm greetings and kisses von Gerda

Remember Who You Used to Be

Her old photograph albums: they must have been among the things her father forwarded to her at a cost of 129RM. They tell me more about her childhood, her life in Germany, than she ever did. Whether she looked through them in her room in S.E. 15, or if she was too busy enjoying what Gunther refers to as *movies, theatre, dance etc* and with regaining her liberty *absolutely*, I have no way of knowing. Those albums are falling apart, and many of the photographs once framed inside them have also left their home, never to return. The surviving ones speak to me. In one – a portrait of her as a young girl, maybe five or six years old – she sits cross-legged on a chair, with her dark teddy bear, one paw raised, on the covered table beside her. She is looking but not looking at the camera, evidently in a world of her own... but also not of her own, as she is wearing ear phones connected to some hidden device. Her hair is dark, with a straight fringe, her distracted face plump, and she wears a pale dress with wavy embroidery. As I leaf backwards and forwards through time, I find other Gerdas – all recognisably her, but at different ages and in different settings. Here she is on a patterned day-bed, leaning on a cushion with a star design. And here, an unlit cigarette angling from her lips, one hand clasping the neck of a champagne bottle (another bottle in an ice-bucket), a Pierrot with outstretched arms at her side, a dark figure of some beast at the back – all reflected in a gilt-framed mirror behind and to the right. Looking more closely, I see wide baggy trousers down to the knees, presumably the photographer's legs. Here she sits (in an adjacent photograph), putting the last wooden block on a pile of blocks on the floor, the same Pierrot, his shiny black hair slicked back, lolling against her left arm, a large expressionless blonde doll in the foreground, while Gerda with a straight black fringe is smiling. Still aged six (the date underneath is 1927), sitting sideways on a high-backed wooden chair and holding open a picture book as big as herself, the little German girl is wearing earphones and appears distracted by what she is hearing, and you notice the garters holding up her thigh-length stockings.

In this other album the photographs are all of beach scenes, and in one (a group photo of 1933 with other swimmers in the sea) she looks her age in a dark swimsuit, while younger children in the foreground make faces at the camera, and underneath the photograph a word next to the year gives a clue as to the place, but I can't make it out. All the other photographs in this holiday album include Tatta, and I wonder if he is anywhere to be found in any taken after 1933‡.

More than photos of people much closer to me in time and place, her German albums speak mutely of distance and disappearance. In the one I am studying now she straddles her father's white-shirted shoulders as he perches on the edge of a beached boat, his hands holding her steady; while in the boat an unknown girl wearing a hat turns to face the photographer, and (passing the boat at that moment) an unknown boy looks down at something only he can see.

In the one next to it Tatta, corporeally sculpted by his trunks, leans – not nonchalantly, for his posture is assertively upright and stiff even when leaning - against the striped awning of a shelter with a wicker seat. There is some further concession to the beach in the long-handled spade he holds over his left shoulder and the rubber ring in his right hand. Meanwhile a diminutive Gerda, grinning and holding her rubber ring against a sunburned leg, relaxes on top of the shelter above him.

---

‡ In fact, "Tatta" does not entirely vanish from the surviving family photographs post 1933, though he is absent from most of them. He reappears occasionally, as in the snow scene pictured at the bottom of P. 76 where, unusually, he seems to be laughing heartily. Judging by Gerda's appearance, this undated photograph can be no earlier than 1935 or even 1937, during family holidays in the mountains.

Before I close the album of beaches, I allow myself one final study of her father – serious-faced as always, bare-chested and wearing loose waist-high white linen trousers – half kneeling behind her, while she looks down, preoccupied, at something she is making with sand.

Herr Elkan Lewinsohn, alone in his room in Breslau (though it appears that his sister, *Tante* Bertha, visited daily and made him his coffee), might have revisited the photograph albums before forwarding them to his daughter in London. In Elkan's *limitless* anxiety about his missing child, those memories of the prelapsarian pre-1933 past may have given him comfort and distress. I try to picture him there, as he sat drinking coffee, or *much brandy* (as Gunther feared), his stern, set Germanic face (as I imagine it) collapsing with tears. The bereft father: *desperated and of broken heart.* He might not have been thinking (as I do over eighty years later) that the camera *fixes* such appearances as these albums hold, and so *saves* them from the flow of further appearances. But if he did open those albums before forwarding them to her, he may have felt something like it, though he was not to know then that he would never see her again. There is a telling phrase in his letter of 5th July 1939 to his lost daughter: *The machine*, he wrote (referring to Gerda's missing typewriter) *really can't have disappeared off the face of the earth.*

From the little his daughter disclosed about him, it seemed that Elkan was one of those assimilated patriotic German Jews who believed that Hitler wouldn't last, that things would return to normal. She may also have mentioned that he had fought in the First World War, although an internet search actually suggested a Russian origin, which was news to me. Anyway, whether he was born in Breslau, or moved there from some other part of Germany, or even from Russia, he was an established businessman in that most liberal of German cities by 1933. From Gerda's typically piecemeal account, her father did not share the post-1933 despair widespread among Jews, instead believing Nazism a passing phase. He belonged to das Vaterland, as das Vaterland belonged to him. Urbanised, bourgeois, if not quite secularised (Elkan, his son Kurt, as well as other Lewinsohns unknown to me, were listed in a Breslau synagogue in 1930), he was otherwise a model of integration. If he had also fought in the First World War, such proof of patriotism was surely protection enough. This was not a *country of barbarism,* after all.

In one of the books by the side of my desk, about Breslau Jews, there's a photograph of people gathered at an assembly point for deportation, autumn 1941. It captures them, in their shapeless, thick winter clothes, their woollen hats and scarves, waiting outside a hut, while officials in dark caps and long dark coats (possibly belted, but it is hard to make it out) attend to them. The woman to the left in the foreground is slightly stooped and holds something to her face. It could be a handkerchief. To the right of her, a chair is tilting, and further to the right, in the corner, is the handle of what looks like a pram.

Elkan Lewinsohn was still in Breslau in late summer

1941, though probably unaware of the memorandum dated 26th July 1941 by the chief of police explaining that Jews would be removed from their homes and deported. From 1941, deportations, administered by the Gestapo, were well underway throughout Germany. A lot was happening, and about to happen, but it is unlikely that Elkan was aware of most of it. He was not privy to memoranda concerning the "various possible solutions" of the "Jewish Problem", including the "Final Solution"; or to plans for the extension of Auschwitz and the construction of Birkenau; or to reports on another possible use of Zyclon B. In November 1941, a thousand Jews in Breslau were arrested and sent to Kovno, where they dug their own graves and undressed, before being shot , but by then Elkan was elsewhere. As far as I know, he was still in Breslau in September 1941, by which time he would have been required to wear the six-cornered yellow star. By then he was not allowed out at night. Then there were the *daily persecutions* from the Gestapo, mentioned in Gunther's letter, but not detailed, and it is unclear what Gunther had in mind exactly. Possibly he was alluding to the changes of accommodation, the *Aryanization* of assets, appointments with the Financial Office in Breslau-Sud, or with the Gestapo. If Gunther, the most assiduous of the siblings in finding things out, is vague on detail, and if Kurt, *the filthy fellow*, was keeping *in silence*, and if Gerda was otherwise occupied in London (*movies, theatre, dance etc*) – then I don't see how, eighty years on, a distant relation like me could be expected to know exactly what Elkan – Aunt Bertha, too, for that matter – were going though at the time.

As can be seen from their correspondence of that period – the few letters still available and barely translatable – Elkan and Bertha revealed some aspects of their situation. There is that telling phrase about the missing typewriter. There is Bertha's hopeful/hopeless question: *Don't you know a way I could get to England?* There is the evident anxiety over paying the *invoice from Tinny's* for two dresses. There is Elkan's *limitless anxiety* in the letter of December 1939 to Frau Salomon – the friend or acquaintance who appears just once in the correspondence. Although I have no written evidence for it, fat Tatta was losing weight. What food was available to him in his reducing circumstances, I don't know; but I think it was more to do with his anxiety, and certainly there were stomach issues. It was as if he had ingested the toxins of Germany. He still loved his country, perhaps more so than ever, and to see (in external events) the cancerous cells growing, reproducing, invading, destroying the social tissue... Elkan Lewinsohn might have felt it spreading through him.

Although relieved to have fled the country to which he would never return, Gunther worried about those left behind. There is evidence of this in his letter of July 1939, in his concern about his father's health and dependence on brandy under Nazism, and the loss of the family fortune. Gunther was unsure what was going on over there. Having spoken to people leaving Breslau, he remained uncertain and unclear. Gunther worried about family, but as a recent emigrant himself he had other things on his mind, as well as advice to give to his sister concerning the unscrupulous emigrants cheating on others and the importance of her finding *English circles* – where, presumably, people could be trusted, even if they could not be easily understood because of their *slant and soft way of speaking*. As for Gerda, she certainly had other things on her mind, with time only for a few fleeting words to **Lieber Tatta,** as she was **fully occupied.**

LONDON, QUITO, BUENOS
AIRES, PITTSBURGH,
OXFORD

7

FROM GERDA'S DIARY

(Red Tagebuch)
London
Tuesday, 24 June 1939

Ich liebe Joe ich liebe Joe ich liebe Joe, ich liebe ihn so sehr that soon I cannot endure it any longer. Liebst Du ihn really? A funny state of affairs! He is still just a boy, I believe he has not yet kissed very much.

I love him very much.

When we are together I am stupid and offhand.

I am always singing to myself that song: nothing comes easy . . .

Joe, Joe, Joe

POSTCARD

London W14
June 27, 1939
9.30 pm
(Just received your card)

Gerdale, Liebes Du,

How happy I was to get your card.

And only yesterday on your birthday I was feeling so agitated and missing you so terribly . . . Today is nearly at an end, and I am so happy that I must answer your card.

Today I have written a card to Ada, as follows: I should like to know what for you are looking into my pocket-book!? May I tell you that 1. It is impolite of you. 2. You are curious (that means being curious of course!) and the next time you would better mind your own business. Yours, etc.

. . . You silly little thing, how could I be angry with you when you write that you love me? I am very happy about it and want to jump up and send you this card now. I wish I could see you earlier than Friday.

I love you and kiss you
Your
Joe

FROM GERDA'S DIARY

London
July 3rd 1939

I don't entirely trust Joe. It would be pretty much the same to me if he had done it . . . In the evening the Doctor and I prepared supper and the Doctor met Joe at the door. He was awfully nice. I would really like to know whether the Doctor likes me at all. I don't like him at all in that way. Joe said he was flirting heavily with me. Whether he is jealous at all, I don't know, but it almost seems to be so. Oh Joe, if only you really loved me or at least a little! I can't figure you out. And then Joe and I made coffee together, the Doctor also helped us with it. He seemed to get on quite well with Joe. Then Joe said he had to go into my room to fetch his coat.

I was planning to stay downstairs and wait until he'd come back but he called, Why aren't you coming?

Me: I'm waiting for you.

Him: I'd prefer you to come here.

So I went up to him (a little bit nervous) and upstairs I asked him where his coat is and then he says, It's downstairs.

Me: So why did you come upstairs then?

And I tried to go out quickly and he blocked my way and said, Now don't run away straight away. And then we hugged and kissed.

But I must say I've read so often that the kiss makes you lose your senses and takes your breath away, whereas I knew exactly what was happening and I was internally quite cool. Will it always be like that for me or do I just not love Joe enough? He said, My little girl, I love you so much, you have to get rid of this petit-bourgeois behaviour and you must become a free person. And then I said, I'm already free.

In any case he professes to love me. Maybe it's true, maybe not! I'll see how it goes. On Wednesday I've arranged to meet up with Joe at 4.45 pm at Marble Arch. Hopefully it will be nice.

London
Undated

Today I got some post from Tatta and also from Lotte. I hate Tatta. There isn't even a trace of sympathy let alone love. I wouldn't like to ever have him in England. Lotte writes very nicely but soppily and illegibly. I can't really be bothered with post any more apart from that with Joe.

The photos of us are still not here. If they'd already arrived on Friday, that's when I was together with Joe for nine hours non-stop. First of all we were at Lyons Corner House for something to eat and then we went to the cinema to watch "Confessions of a Nazi Spy". It was a bit soppy. But Joe was into it. Then we went to Hyde Park. On the way Joe started a dangerous conversation because it could have easily led to an argument. Then in Hyde Park we lay down on the grass and I had to say, in spite of all my efforts, I love you. But it didn't come out very convincingly. Well perhaps it will come.

London
Undated

Then we went to visit Ann and we picked up an advocaat. We didn't stay there for long. Then at home and on the stairway I said to Joe, Do you know what I fancy? And I meant by that that I could drink an egg cognac.

Him: Do you know what I would like?

Then I laughed that he wanted to drink me and I told Joe.

Then he said, May I? And suddenly he gave me a kiss that actually came quite unexpectedly. Then I drank and he drank too. Then I said that tasted good which then sparked exciting conversations.

Then he said, That's a good way to end.

I said, On that note? Does it actually have to end?

Him: That ended well.

Me: How come we ended it all then?

Him: Shall I repeat it again then?

Me: Yes (although I hesitate a little). I wanted to go quickly down the stairs.

Then he said, Don't run away from me. And we kissed each other again like mad.

Then we went for a little walk and did some shopping.

Then he said, They could think that we are a husband and wife going shopping in the evening.

So I said that we looked too young.

Him: Age doesn't really matter, but we are both free to do what we like . . . so first of all we'll go to America together.

I said, No! And that was the end of it. I will always say No to that. Joe can't bear it.

London
Undated but same day in the evening – 9 o'clock

I believe I love Joe, I think about him constantly and have a little yearning for him, and yet I still have a feeling of doubt and mistrust of him. Just what should I think about that? Is that just in my imagination?

Hopefully.

Well, we're meeting each other again the day after tomorrow. Otherwise there's nothing new. Mrs S – and her daughter are back again.

London
Monday 10th July 1939, 4 o'clock

I'm sitting in my bedroom and I'm having a little quiet period – bit of peace and quiet. However I will go and make a cup of tea soon. Yes, well, I haven't written for days and I've got a whole lot to tell. So "Chapter Joe" hasn't ended yet. What happened on Wednesday?

I met up with Joe at Marble Arch. He arrived late. I wasn't angry about it because that sort of thing can happen and especially in London. I wanted to go to the cinema to see

Fred Astaire and Ginger Rogers but Joe suggested that we should go to the Waggon Orchestra.

There we queued up for a long time. In the end it was too expensive for Joe, two and six for standing room, and he wanted to leave. But I'd been looking forward to it and wanted to go anyway, but since I didn't want to go alone I paid for Joe. That is to say, he paid me one and six and I paid the rest. At first he refused a little bit but then he took it. And that's how it should be. Instead of always letting someone pay for me, I was the one who got it.

I had a bit of a strange feeling towards Joe afterwards. The performance was amazing. I really enjoyed myself and I bought sweets for one shilling and Joe and I had a good time and scoffed ourselves and we were standing pretty close together and we were holding hands. I felt really happy there. It was so sweet of Joe the way he secretly dried his hand first before he reached out for mine. Finally he found it – my hand. It was directly under my bust. But that was really lovely.

Aren't I a terrible girl? Yes, well, then we went to Hyde Park afterwards and Joe was really sweet. We laughed a lot and we were being stupid (always making sh-boom at each other). No kiss the whole afternoon. That was quite pleasant for me. After all what is a kiss?

POSTCARD

London
July 17. 39
7.10 am

Liebes Gerdale
You have slept in my bed! How immoral!!I hope that hasn't

confused you. You lovely girl, don't think too badly of me. I had better quickly give you my new address in case you want to write something else to me . . . My dear little girl, I have to go in a few minutes. Don't forget about me entirely until we can be together again.

In love
Your
Joe

FROM GERDA'S DIARY

London
Undated (July?)

I don't get repulsed by it any more but I don't feel anything when I'm doing it. Perhaps I don't love Joe enough or I'll always be like that, so lacking in feeling. I feel much more when Joe holds my hand and when we're walking arm in arm or he inadvertently brushes against me. Only once – that was yesterday – when I was at his house and he kissed and hugged me and I felt a tiny little bit.

Yes, well, yesterday: Sunday. We met at Joe's. I was supposed to meet him at 4 o'clock, but I didn't get to Joe's until 4.45 pm - no, it was even as late as 5 o'clock.

He was awfully angry that I came late. Very, very angry. He put tea and cakes in front of me and the tea tasted of washing up water and the cake looked so sweet that I didn't want it.

Then he showed me photos. His father looks hideous. Joe doesn't like him very much either. Then naturally the hanky panky started. I was being nice to Joe, but remained quite cool on the inside and knew exactly what I was doing.

Suddenly Joe said, What are you thinking about?

I couldn't exactly say to him, I'm thinking about the fact that kissing is a revolting thing. It is extolled in all songs and it is supposed to be so wonderful when the boy sticks his tongue in the girl's mouth.

No, I couldn't say that, so I said, I'm thinking that you are unshaven today.

I'm not very poetic, am I? Whether Joe feels anything when kissing I don't know.

He said, I love you so much I'll never let you go.

Rubbish, nonsense. I like Joe but I don't love him. I know that for sure. Sometimes I imagine that I love him, but it isn't true. If another good looking boy came along who was interested in me, I would be exactly the same with him as I am with Joe. I have to feign love towards Joe. It has to be like that as without him I would have no pleasure in going out.

Otto Lob, Joe's friend, is a good looking nice boy, but I couldn't ever fall in love with him. He's just too childish. But I can make use of boys like that. At least I can show them a thing or two.

Right well, Ann wasn't there. We waited ages but she didn't come. I was quite happy about this as I didn't want to endure any girl like that and she has annoyed me.

She phoned me this morning and was very angry. She said she was there at 5.30pm. It doesn't matter anyway.

POSTCARD

London
Sunday – (no date, probably July)

My dear little girl,
You can hardly imagine how happy you've made me again . . .

We both have made terrible mistakes. But that should and must change now . . . I am quickly writing to you before I go to sleep. Excuse the writing, but I am writing this on the bed.
Silly, lovely, sweet girl, you are and remain meine geliebte Gerda. I know that I love you and nothing can change that.
Your
Joe

FROM GERDA'S DIARY

London
Undated (July?)

Well, then on the train I had a real antipathy towards Joe. He talked about breasts endlessly. He didn't look anything special yesterday. He'd had a haircut that didn't particularly suit him. Green trousers, brown jacket and a blue hat.

Yes, well, on the train I was increasingly cool. He asked me if I didn't love this kind of conversation. I said that it made me think he was quite a different person to the one on the boat. He said he couldn't understand why people always avoid this topic and how the world would be a better place if etc. etc. etc.

POSTCARDS FROM JOE

London
July –

My dearest Sweetie-pie!
Your letter has reached me and makes me curious . . . I was pleased to get signs of life from you . . . You know that I love

*clarity above all (the schoolmaster again) so write clearly what
you mean. I am open to you. But write to me in London where
I'll be tomorrow. I am sure that I will be going to Herne Bay,
but I don't believe before the 25th. In any case I'm looking
forward to seeing you.*
From Your
Joe

London
August 15, 1939

Dear Gerda
*Please do not forget to bring tomorrow my picture as I need it
for my registration at the police station.*
Longing for you.
Joe
See you 5 pm Marble Arch!

London
Sept 12, 1939

My dear Gerdale,

*Many, many thanks for your lovely letter. How happy I feel
sometimes, and how terrible I feel sometimes. You can imagine.
I am definitely at home from 5 pm and hope that perhaps you
can come and see me . . .*

Hugs and kisses
Your
Joe

Peter Thornthwaite

FROM GERDA'S DIARY

London
Monday 25th September 1939, 11.30am

I just have a little bit of time. Soon I have to clean the drains. So – it is getting more exciting and more interesting. Joe asked yesterday if I would marry him and I have said yes. In plain German, we are engaged, but . . . there remains a "but". I have not won by a long shot. Because I suspect that Joe doesn't take getting married very seriously.

Why? Well, first Joe should buy an engagement ring and take with him one of my diamonds. He pretended to – but I discovered last night that he didn't take a diamond, therefore he doesn't have any intention to buy rings, or is there another reason behind that?

Secondly, Joe thinks I'm not completely frank with him when I tell him that I don't feel anything – absolutely nothing - during sexual intercourse (geschlechlichen Verkehr), and he believes perhaps I would tell him the truth if he promises to marry me.

But he's got the wrong end of the stick, poor little thing. I will not walk into his trap. Regardless of how strongly I feel I won't tell him. At this point I don't feel anything at all, so I don't have to lie.

So after all I don't look upon myself as being engaged, even if it looks like that, and I won't tell any of it to another soul. Joe hasn't told anyone either, and he's asked me not to say anything. Another reason why I don't believe he really wants to get married.

The best I can do now is to wait and see what happens. I won't discuss the engagement with anyone. Joe is only 19 and needs permission to marry. Perhaps he won't get it, and perhaps he wouldn't tell me if he did: he might say that he couldn't get it and that would be a very good "excuse". In any case, I don't trust him at all. The only thing I know for sure is that he does love me very much: otherwise I wouldn't have such love bites on my shoulders, and yesterday he didn't want to let me leave at all.

But Joe will never show me how much he loves me.

Now we'll draw a line under all of this.

I will always try to take the right path, the path that God will show me, even if it is extremely difficult and I often stray. But in general I have already improved a lot, and I was never as beautiful as I am now.

If Joe doesn't marry me then it just wasn't meant to be. Whatever God does is the right thing. I will make my own way without Joe, with God's help, and I hope I can be strong and brave enough to take up the fight with destiny. With or without you Joe !!!

It will have to be somebody else. Because I will want to marry at all costs, but only someone who I love. But deep inside me I still hope that everything will work out with Joe.

London
Thursday 28th September 1939, 2.30pm

Isn't life strange! But at the moment, wonderfully exciting and interesting. So, the story with Joe continues to run and it's getting more gripping, it's like a film, and at the moment we have arrived at the most exciting point. When will this film finally finish?

Hopefully a "happy" ending. I like to watch films with happy endings, especially the film of Joe and me, and which must have a happy ending. Whatever God wills.

Well, the situation which happened with falling in love developed exactly as I expected. Joe sent the letter and he asked me to marry him that evening. I was very happy, but I wasn't totally sure. I know my struggle is not over yet and Joe must marry me. There is no other man that I would even consider.

And so, the following took place yesterday: I went to Joe in the afternoon. Joe said he had something important to tell me. I already knew beforehand that this concerned the engagement and that it would be that he took it back.

He went on and on without coming to the point. He said that he had been a great idiot on Sunday (very complimentary to me!). I have to admit that although I had never trusted the whole thing, it was a terrible disappointment for me. I saw my beautiful castle in the air break down and it would have been truly wonderful to wear an engagement ring and to be able to tell everyone that I am a bride.

But I said to myself what God does is well done. God sees that if in the future life isn't so good for me, that I do believe in him and that I am and will always be grateful to him.

So I hope that after a few months I will get over this disappointment and be OK again.

Why did Joe do this? I am not at all clear about that. But I know this a little bit:

1.   Joe doesn't trust me, he believes I will immediately use him badly when we are married.

2.   Because I told him he can flirt with as many girls as he wishes when I can't see it; in front of me he is not allowed to flirt at all. What I don't know doesn't hurt me.

That does upset him. He thinks I would do exactly the same. Ach! If Joe knew how terribly jealous I am, and how every time it pierces me in the stomach when he behaves nicely with other girls. Ach! The stupid man doesn't have a clue how much I love him and for now will not know – or perhaps never.

Then we went to the Variety. Harry Roy played. He was fabulous. I was much livelier and in a good mood. I thought to myself: Joe I will still get you, and I know exactly how much you love me.

Then we went home. Home to Joe's and it was as if I was tipsy with happiness, excellent. Joe became increasingly strange and I believe firmly that he was angry with himself and that's what he should have been, that was the punishment for the disappointment. Ach!

And then I seduced him. This time it was the other way round. I knew that he desired me but that he was angry about my excitement and didn't know what to do. Perhaps for once he didn't know what to do. Therefore he said, You want to today, but I don't want to.

That was an immense sacrifice by him and I can understand from that how much he loves me. I said, Joe, I knew this beforehand. Ach! You can't really tell all this, I only knew that I had won.

But afterwards, he was doubly ashamed of this. He told me actually, afterwards in bed, that he was engaged to Gertie and that they were going to get married, that she didn't really suit him because she is not an energetic person, that he is a swine, that he is blessed with having such a lovely girlfriend (meaning me) – and I, the idiot, believed him. But thank God, not for long, and I didn't show him any weakness.

But already, on the bus, a light went on, and I felt that all of this was strange and I wouldn't be surprised if I had got it wrong. Joe believes I spend my days now crying with chattering teeth: if only he knew that I have seen through it all – but Sunday evening he will find out.

Peter Thornthwaite

POSTCARDS FROM JOE

London
Sept. 29, 1939

Liebes Gerdale,

Many warm thanks for your lovely letter. I am going to be quite brief in this card. I officially invite you to a party here on Saturday. Evening wear is required - also bring a suitcase. Please come as early as possible, but alone. Extra holiday after 11.30 is highly desirable.

Until tomorrow

Cheerio

Joe

London
October 12, 1939

Dear Gerda

It is very unequal to love two people at the same time, one more than the other. That you don't believe it doesn't change the facts. How am I to answer your questions? Please write immediately (no phone). If the danger has passed, I believe we can go on – on the basis of going on together.
Your Joe

FROM GERDA'S DIARY

Weds 11th December 1939

I am still with Mrs. Stainton. The old woman checks everything I do with my hands and every mouthful I take, she looks at every bite and everything I put into my mouth. I have a good attitude though, I "smile through clenched teeth".

I have been tempted on numerous occasions to hand in my notice, but I don't do it, I want to stay the course until I am perfect in everything I do. My present responsibility is not to show pain and to work fast, whilst always being friendly, polite and very nice. In everything I go with God, and God will help me so that I succeed.

It is very difficult, I could hardly finish this sentence when the old woman called me again: Gerda, please clean the window ledges. It is now three thirty, I was just about finished at 3.15 and then it starts all over again from the beginning.

They are using me very much here – these two-faced English people. When I'm not here any more then they will have to have two people instead of one. They won't find another Gerda. It means sticking it out. God wants this and what God wants is well done.

I have horrendous pain in one of my feet, but I don't want to show it in my face because nobody is allowed to see anything. These are the tests God sends. It is easy to believe in God and to thank him when one is well, and it should be the same when you're not well. In any case, I am beautiful as a picture and have lots of luck in love.

Everybody turns around in the street, even the policemen cast loving glances at me. Although – I haven't found the right one yet.

Joe was not the right one. He was until recently still very much the big love, he was extremely in love with me and I also liked him very much, but the asshole stank lately so much that I felt nauseous and all of a sudden I didn't love him any more, because I wanted to throw up.

After that I received a proposal of marriage from a very nice but very dull man, although he could really kiss and he had a fantastic car. But he's not for me.

Then there was a doctor from Vienna; after that an Englishman, very stupid. I haven't loved anyone, and except for the nice Englishman with the car, not let it go as far as a kiss.

I have a date on Friday with a Communist, but perhaps I'll meet someone else before then, and then I'll leave him standing.

God will always show me the right way to take and I will make every effort to take that path without weakening. Strange, deep within me I'm waiting for a call from Joe. Would I nevertheless love him? I don't know - "waiting and drinking tea".

Emigrants like Gerda were "avid for news about Germany" (or so I have read somewhere). There is no evidence that she was. In all the diaries, German and English, her country of origin is rarely mentioned, if at all. This doesn't mean that she wasn't thinking about it, that it didn't come back to her at times, but if so she kept it to herself. Yet as far as the evidence goes, she didn't even do that, for it is nowhere to be found in the one place where she did keep things to herself. And with Germany wiped off her map – just as it was doing the same to other countries – she was also erasing Tatta, or so it appears. I don't know what he could have said in the letter she refers to in her undated (probably July 1939) diary entry – **today I got some post from Tatta** – but it roused her to write: **I hate Tatta**. I have not seen the letter to which she refers, or any other letter from him around that time likely to excite such a reaction. I have translated his 1939 correspondence with her and can find nothing untoward. On 5th July he was complimenting her on her nice and charming letters; there is only the slightest of reproaches in his *just write to me more often*. The same cautious reproach is in Aunt Bertha's letter (17th July) when she writes that Gerda's *Tatzelwurm* is *long missing a message from you*. That her *Tatzelwurm* longed to hear from her is hardly cause for hatred. But – wait a moment – I think I have it. Going back to his letter of 30th June, I see that he refers to Joe – the Joe she met on the boat – as *nothing to you*. This is not her father's verdict but her own, yet it might have rankled. If it did, it was nothing compared to her likely reaction to what followed: *I ask you to remember who you used to be here. It seems that you forget it very quickly.* As if unaware of the pit he was digging for himself, the tactless Tatta warned her about the many *girls of dubious reputation going to London*. His daughter might have interpreted this not merely as fatherly advice that she should not get *involved with them,* but as a warning not to become such a girl herself. Whatever the truth of the matter, there is no space in the diary, from July 1939 to year end, for Germany, or for Tatta and his situation there, or for Aunt Bertha, or for anyone she once knew in Breslau. And that makes all the more room for Joe, who from 24th June occupies all the available diary space. She has found her inner *Lebensraum,* and it is love. It is also short-lived. By 3rd July she does not **entirely trust Joe**. By 10th July **Chapter Joe** hasn't ended yet. But – as she implies – chapters must end sometime. The month has not ended before she has a real (and understandable) **antipathy towards Joe** with his green trousers, brown jacket, blue hat, and endless talk of breasts. By 25th September she feels **absolutely nothing** during sexual intercourse with him. Despite the imprint of his love (**love bites on my shoulders**), Joe does not want to marry her, as was revealed when he did not take up the offer of one of her diamonds for an engagement ring. And he is perhaps a little stupid in not realising that she has **seen through it all**. His punishment, it appears, is to be seduced. Without noticing (till now) I keep switching from past to present tense – unavoidable when their diary entries and postcards, their brief love affair as the world is turning to war, are so present-tense. *It is happening now.* That is how I read them, briefly forgetting that they were written over eighty years ago, although such *forgetting* can't be quite true since I am having to translate them. But for them it is *happening now,* all the more intensely given the time and place: June-December 1939, London. Halfway through this first love of Gerda's, Chamberlain was to announce in a broadcast at 11:15 am on Sunday 3rd September that "this country is at war with

Germany". With *Germany* – Gerda's ex-country, Joe's ex-country. This must have contributed to the intensity of their moment, although I notice that neither Gerda nor Joe mentions it. Within minutes of the momentous broadcast, air raid sirens were sounding in London. You don't hear them in her diary and his postcards. There is no mention (none that I can find as their translator) of what might have been, for Gerda, a still more momentous announcement on the radio: that places of entertainment were to close with immediate effect. Now that really would have been bad news. Now that I think about it, the closest they came to thinking about what was happening in Germany and the world is that film they watch near Marble Arch, *Confessions of a Nazi Spy*, and even a film of such apparent relevance to her aroused little interest (**a bit soppy** although **Joe was into it**). Gerda preferred to hear at the *Variety* (28th September) Harry Roy and his Band, who were probably playing hits from 1931 and 1939 like *My Girl's Pussy* and *She Had to Go and Lose it at the Astor*. **Fabulous** was Gerda's verdict, though I wonder how they were there given the closure of places of entertainment after the announcement of war. Maybe they had reopened late September. After all, there were still no air raids in London, no *Blitz* yet, despite the mass issue of gas masks that month. No mention of air raids, Blitz, gas masks, sirens, blackouts, and very little about London itself in her London diaries. I presume, in one of their meetings at Marble Arch, that the restaurant she refers to (its name is illegible in her undated diary entry) was Lyons Corner House. There was a Lyons Corner House then at Marble Arch – one of its *Maison Lyons* – a *vast place* (I have read) with four or five levels, each with its own orchestra, but you would not know this from her diary. Joe's little postcards supply more of a sense of place. In the one dated 12th September there is, hand-drawn in green ink, a street map to help Gerda find Oval Road from Camden Town Station. In his picture postcard to her from Plymouth Lido (18th July), you can see six women in bathing costumes and wrapped in towels leaning over an iron railing above the pool with its lanes, swimmers, and central fountain. What he was doing in Plymouth in July 1939 is undisclosed, and the writing (also in green ink) is illegible apart from a reference to *Herne Bay*, the words *mein liebes kleines,* (my dear little one) and *GEFUHL* (FEELING) in capitals. Other than the dates (when given) of the diary entries and postcards, and the references to Marble Arch, Hyde Park and venues like the *Variety*, there is little externally to locate the two lovers. Most conspicuous by its absence is the war. It seems that something more cataclysmic was happening in her life at that time – something to do with first love and first sex. I am assuming this was her *first* time; while not actually stated, it is the subtext. If it is not her first time, then it is surely her first experience of love's divisions – not only between her and Joe, but (as she is only too aware) between the two Gerdas. It is *there* – all her difficulty then and later – in the painful pleasure of anguished, self-indulgent introspection; in her unspoken response to Joe's **What are you thinking about? I'm thinking . . . that kissing is a revolting thing.** For all my wry reporting of the great events in her life, I can imagine the seismic event that the collapse of her first **big love** was for her. Other things were going on of greater moment in the world outside. In September 1939 it took just weeks for Poland to collapse before the world's first experience of the blitzkrieg. How much attention she was able to give to such matters can never be known. Her diary is no guide. My guess is that her own internal strife occupied her far more. There is something else to be noted. Gerda and Joe are both in London, but this is still a *German* love. Her diary and his postcards are in German. He is **Berliner Joe**. They are just off the boat. He must register at the police station. Though Britain took them in, they are still enemy aliens – or soon will be, with Chamberlain's announcement of war. Theirs is a *refugee* love. The time and place and circumstances are everything. *5pm Marble Arch*, Joe writes on 15th August, just over two weeks before that historic broadcast – though still over a year before incendiary bombs were to drop from the London sky. Countries are about to collide and collapse, but *they* – Gerda and Joe – are meeting for love, and it is necessary for them to agree exactly where and when they are meeting. Funnily enough, it is his few words, not hers, that resonate the most: *5pm Marble Arch*.

8

BORIS BAR
PASAJE ROYAL TEL. 2296

HOY 9 DE OCTUBRE

POR MOTIVO DE FIESTAS PATRIAS

GRAN CENA BAILABLE

amenizada por el

famoso acordeonista señor Gunther Heinz

Con su Repertorio enteramente nuevo

MENU ESPECIAL   CUBIERTO $ 4.00

ROXY NIGHT CLUB

PRESENTA

Y LA FAMOSA
COSTA RICA SWING BOYS

GUNTER HEINZ

EN UN FORMIDABLE REPERTORIO

MODERNO

DEDICA SU

MATINEE DOMINICAL

A LA JUVENTUD GUAYAQUILEÑA

con su acordeón

ROXI NIGHT CLUB
ESTA NOCHE NUEVAMENTE EL MARAVILLOSO
ACORDEONISTA
GUNTHER HEINZ

Deleitará al Público asistente con selecto Repertorio de Música Nueva, acompañando a la Orquesta COSTA RICA SWING BOYS
DOMINGO COCKTAIL BAILABLE
de 1 a 4 p. m.
Nuestra Cocina es Especial — Nuestro Servicio diario esmerado en Banquetes y Agasajos.

LETTERS FROM GUNTER

NO DATE OR PLACE STATED
ECUADOR, AUTUMN 1939?

Now I stay here in Ecuador two months and I am glad to have found the possibility to live here in a town still with a lot of civilization. Not only to live but to earn too! Since I come here I have become member of the greatest Ecuadorian Jazz Orchestra, "Blacio", playing in the smartest night-club restaurant. I am engaged for a salary of 250 sucres monthly. Besides of this it is possible to collect money by plenty of tips. Every week I play in the radio "Telegrafo" accordion-music. All members of the orchestra are 100% South Americans. Nobody is speaking German, but I have good Spanish knowledges.

Meantime I took an unfurnished room in the finest and newest cement-house of this city. I bought a new steel-bed with all supplies for about 60 sucres. In spite of my enjoyable beginning there are still some oppressing clouds on the horizon, for in this country I have only permission to have an occupation in agriculture and industry. In the meantime I am registered at the Consulate of the United States, for the only purpose why I determined to go to Ecuador was to find a way to go back legal to the U.S.A. Here there are plenty of emigrants, most of them come to Quito, Rio-Bamba, Cuenca, or other mountain towns because the climate of Guayaquil is not supportable for them. Indeed the climate can be terrible, and I can't say with certainty whether I shall be capable to blow every day 8 hours only trumpet. And plenty of diseases here too! Palodismo! Malaria! About 75% of all children die in consequence of this diseases. Nobody is preserved of palodismus. I must keep me prepared for this disease. The consequence of malaria is 5 days highgraded fever.

The life here is typically tropic, like in the story of 1001 Nights. Donkeys (excluded of me) are the most used instrument in traffic. Bare foot Indians, full of louses and bed bugs, live scarcely before their wracked cottages, picking up louses from their heads and eating them like epicures. On the other side, modern American life with smart Buicks, sky-scrapers, modern coffees etc. The manner to work here is most slowly. It is all manana, manana, with the meaning: do not work today, when you can delay for tomorrow.

My trip to Ecuador was very adventurous. I rode with the bus from New York to Miami, then with steamer "Cuba" to Cuba, and then with steamer "Orbita" to Panama. From Salinas, harbour of Ecuador to Guayaquil derailed the train under tremendous noise, however I kept nearly unhurted.

In spite of all torments I believe to have done better to go here than to marry in New York a girl only with the aim to become legal.

All my dishes I take here at Mister Woolff, who is known to you by his restaurant in Breslau. His daughter "Baby" is fond of me, but I don't like her. Here around Guayaquil grow the finest and sweetest oranges and bananas. All the day I eat these fruits . . .

**Quito, Ecuador
May 6, '40**

Liebes Gerda

Some time ago I received a letter written by you in September of past year sent to the post office Guayaquil. As in the meantime I moved to Quito, this letter remained about 8 months unread in G'quil. Always again I'm glad to read that you feel well at family Stainton – and that they are nice to you. In the meantime also I received a comfortable letter from Tatta. He is very complaining that yet nobody redeemed him from his unsupportable stay in Germany. He want to know exactly when he get his visa in order to come to me. I'm very busy and endeavoured to settle the immigration for him but still I went to such a lot of hindrances that not yet I can say definitely when the asked immigration papers will get in his possession. Another question is his passage. Until now he had only the one chance to use an Italian ship. But who knows whether in future also it will be possible. To settle this matter is very expensive, I need for this purpose a lawyer. It is said that to procure father an immigration visa will take nearly half a year and by this circumstance it will become questionable whether father can get out of Europe. Nevertheless I'm continuously trying my best to increase fathers get out of Germany. The third important point is that the chance of immigration to U.S.A. will no longer last too long. Father has like you a good affidavit and our giver of affidavit is trying to increase our soon immigration.

Father asks to you that from now on your writings to him shall be remitted to me and I shall forward them from here directly to him. Father asks in his letter why I don't try to bring you out of England to this country. I will answer this question. The difficultys to attain a visa would not be less than with Tatta. Besides of this I believe that in this still savage country whose principal population are poor-class Indians would not satisfy to you. I know very well that there you enjoy the protection of the family Stainton – and you are not afraid to stay as long in England as comes the moment to get over to U.S.A. I can emphasize always again that I can make here a good living as musician but in spite of this I shall prefer the U.S. A woman cannot earn much money here in Ecuador but in U.S they find very easy a good job.

Before I step to U.S I will undertake a round-trip into some border-country of Ecuador. - It is possible that in next time I go to Dr. Hans Schein in La Paz/Bolivien to participate in a smart swing-orchestra. Every night I hear the station B.B.C in London excellently and so by radio I caught the nice hits: My

Prayer, A Little Street in Singapore, South of the Border, At the Balalaika. etc. That will be enough today.

Now it is up to you to write to me. Also the writing for Tatta please send to me. Best regards from your brother Gunter

Quito/Ecuador
den 26 Mai 40

My dear Gerda

Many thanks for your comfortable letter. Really I'm glad that you in London can make a very good living. My birthday I spent without any celebration because I'm always severe working like you. I have my occupation in the smartest Bar of this country, leading there the Band and presenting me as accordion-soloist.

Here I found quickly the way to glory, and the crowd in the Bar is always delighted to have a touch with the "Gringo" - how he plays and sings. Yes, sing too. People have discovered that Gunter – Heinz has a good voice. So, I sing always the latest hits in Spanish and also in English.

I got an offer to play in an other Bar here in the city where I shall work less and earn more. To-day still I cant say how to build up the future but you see I'm on the best way! With regard to this matter I advice you for an aspiration to earn more than you earn instantly. I took notice that you have in mind to immigrate to the U. States and this intention of you will be backed well when you have built up a reserve of money. Besides of this I have to say that I regard it as our duty to have safed money for the purpose to be helpful in fathers endeavourments to get out of Germany.

In the meantime I tried my best to bring father outside of Germany. I was ready here at the government to make a deposit of 500 US dollars but unfortunately the law changed and it seems to be nearly impossible to get entrance to Ecuador. But in spite of this I will not tire in my endeavourment to bring father out of Germany. Should I be successful in getting him abroad, would you be ready or, better said, able to support him cooperating with me?? Any support from Kurt we have not to expect!! Please answer me this question in your letter promptly! One week before I received from father a cable asking urgently for help! The matter with time has become very severely, and I hope that you also will be endeavoured to help father abroad.

How do you enjoy my English? I speak better than I write.

Now for some other news! I have instantly correspondence with Dr. Schein, whose wife is living former in Breslau. He lives in La Paz and he is always asking in his writing whether I can come to him. He has an orchestra there. You must consider that here in South-America is a great need of musicians.

The reason why it doesn't give musician here is that most people cant live in a height of average 8000 meters. This height is for weak people hurting the lungs and heart, however I exist very well and have a big program for the near future. Past month I bought a magnificent radio-set with 5 tubes with short-wave and I spend much time listening to the B.B.C station in London, which I hear loud and clear.

My best regards and kisses

Gunter – Heinz
Boris-Bar

Quito/Ecuador
October 30, 1940

Dear Mrs. Stainton:
I am the brother of Miss Gerda L who came from Breslau/Germany as refugee to you finding occupation in your esteemed house. Unfortunately my father and me, we are without news about the fate of my sister since a couple of months. I would be very much obliged to you if you would give me an information with regard to the situation of Gerda. Has she come in a concentration-camp or has she had an accident. My father and me, we are very sorry that she is absolutely silent while some time ago she wrote frequently. Please be so kind to give me asked information as soon as possible. I will try to get her here to Ecuador if it would be necessary. I thank you in advance for your answer and I am with best regards Gunter-Heinz Lewinsohn

LETTER FROM GERDA TO GUNTER

London S.E. 15
Dec. 1st 1940

Dear Gunter,
That is now already the third letter I write to you without getting a reply. I understand that these are results of the war and I am quite sure that you are perfectly alright. It is impossible for me to get any news about Tatta. I worry a lot how he is getting on and would be awfully happy to hear something about him. - I hope you are still getting on nicely. - I don't see any Germans at all. I've lost every connection with them. Even from Ada or Steffi I hear absolutely nothing. I wonder how they are getting on. As

for me I am very well indeed. Mrs. S – passed away recently. So I am maid to her 28 year old daughter and her 34 year old son (who is in love with me and I the same and whom I am going to marry), Please don't laugh, finally I am 19 years old. He is very much like you in his character but that doesn't disturb me. Well perhaps that doesn't interest you very much. - We are all sleeping together on mattresses on the floor, I haven't been in a real bed for now nearly a year because of air raids. I find the war terribly thrilling and exciting, if it wouldn't be for Tatta. I would be ever so much happier if he would be with you or another safe spot. Now dear Gunter not too many reproaches in your letter. I hope very much that this letter will reach you. I haven't heard from Kurt since I am here in London and I really don't expect to hear from him anymore. I think he doesn't want to have anything to do with his family. But perhaps I hear from him one day. Finally he is my brother isn't he? Well so long With love I am
Yours Gerda

LETTER FROM JEWISH REFUGEES COMMITTEE

Cables: Refugees, Westcent, London
18th March 1941

Dear Sir/Madam,
We have received an enquiry from Quito Committee, Ecuador on behalf of your Brother, Guenther H. Lewinsohn of Quito – Ecuador Casila 837 who is anxious to have news from you.
Will you kindly let us know whether you are still at the same address and what we can say in reply, and will you also communicate with the above-named at the address mentioned.

Peter Thornthwaite

LETTER FROM WAR ORGANISATION OF THE BRITISH RED CROSS SOCIETY AND ORDER OF ST JOHN OF JERUSALEM

Foreign Relations Department
13th May, 1941

Dear Madam
We will certainly make an enquiry for news of your father and this will be speeded up if you will let us have the following further particulars about him:- his age, nationality, and the date and place of his birth. It is certain to take some two or three months before we can receive a reply to this enquiry but it will be forwarded to you immediately it reaches us.

LETTERS FROM GUNTER

Quito/Ecuador SA
Boris-Bar
Apartado 807
Undated

Dear Gerda:
I am glad to have your letter of March 23rd 1941, and took notice that all with you is o.k. Why do you not write oftener? Father and me, we were so afraid that something has happened to you. Therefore we must advice you again to write always as soon as possible. Miss Laskowitz who meanwhile arrived here coming from Tatta told me that father is enjoying of good health and of rather good mood. However unfortunately he appreciates the cognac now more than in former times. I deposited here in the immigration-office 500 dollars for fathers come-here. I hope that father had been successful in his

135

endeavourments to get visa for Ecuador. Referring to this concern I am expecting a favourable answer from father. Should it result quite impossible for him to come here I would be compelled to withdraw the 500 dollars which I met at his disposal here as landing-money. Or I would like to make arrangements that you would find a chance to come to me. I feel very lonesome and I wished you would be here. It would not be too difficult to find a job for you, though the business-conditions in Ecuador instantly are not good. But it is up to you whether you will come here. Also it is depending on the possibility to make a cruise to this country. Last not least it is a question of money too! Make up your mind and let me know your opinion with regard to my suggestion to come here.

In Ecuador I stay already about one years. Most time I spend in the capital Quito. I am quite well in making a living here. I am musician and advertising painter too. I feel well here in every respect, but nevertheless I am trying to find a real chance to get to the U.S. Perhaps you remember, I brought from U.S coming an affidavit with me. The result of preliminary examination of my documents by the U.S Consulate is that I would get visa; in that case I would obtain an additional affidavit. I make all efforts to find such substantial affidavit, I write to many persons but not now I have been successful in finding an additional affidavit. When nobody will deliver it I run the risk to lose my chance to get visa. For the next time in spite of all intentions I have, I will remain here.

Yesterday I sent my birthday congratulations to father. His birthday take place on June 16 and he will become 63 years of age. To-day I will take opportunity to present to you my best wishes for your birthday on June 21. Have a nice time on this day and I am wishing you luck and good health for future times. Let us hope that Father, you and me will find together very soon. With Kurt my relations are broken and I would not like to have a touch with him. Besides of this, he is quite unable to make a living.

Now I will close. Please let me hear from you. Write not only to me but also to father. Elkan Lewinsohn, c/o Gunter H. Lewinsohn, Quito/Ecuador, Boris-Bar, as indicated on the head of this letter!

Once more "Happy birthday to you!" My best regard and kisses from your brotherGunter-Heinz profesor de musica!!

Quito/Ecuador S.A.
Boris-Bar
Apartado 807
June 28, 1941

Dear Gerda:
Father and me we are very pleased to have taken notice that all with you is o.k.

Yesterday I got a cable from father, as following: "I got visa for Ecuador! Trip to Ecuador only possible passing through the Argentine. Kurt shows himself without any interest regarding to my endeavourments to get transitvisa for the Argentine. Therefore you must try to procure me transitvisa at government of the Argentine by having a touch with the Consul of the Argentine in Ecuador!"

Meanwhile I had an appointment with the Argentine Minister who pointed out that he is not entitled to give visa, but only direct the government of B'Aires. I am on the best way to obtain a transitvisa for father, however have to sacrify about 65 U.S dollars in order to be successful to deliver him. The passage to Ecuador is very expensive and still it is a problem how to make arrangements to embark. The lowest price for the voyage-ticket would be 450 dollars. I dont possess such a lot of money, because more than 500 U.S dollars I deposed here in the government-office as landing-money.

As soon as father arrives here you would have a chance to come here. Then it would be depending on you to come here or not. My chance to come to the U.S had become very small. For the next time I will not move from here. Here I will meet me at the disposal of father and help you as good as I can. Please make up your mind to let me know what is your desire. I remember that on June 21 you had birthday. With some delay take my best congratulation.

With Kurt I am no more corresponding since about 5 years so that I have no idea what is the matter with him. Also I am not curious to know something about his fate. Aunt Bertha is still assisting father as used.

Are you still enjoying yourself by the three doggs from whom you told me? I advice you to come here, then the time would not be so lonesome for you nor for me! Please let hear from you!

Please write some brief lines for father directed to me! My best regards and kisses. Your brother Gunter

LETTER FROM GERDA TO GUNTER

London S.E.15
29th Aug 1941
First page (rest missing):

Dear Gunter,
Now as you know I am alright, I am writing ordinary posted letters again. I am still keeping fine, couldn't be better, am very happy etc etc. I hope the same from Tatta and yourself. The doggies are fine too. They had liver for dinner and are completely satisfied. But they want me to go out for a walk on One-tree-hill with them. Which is a little mountain nearby. It's lovely today. I am sitting here in my brown velvet slacks and am having quite a nice time although it is

not my day off. But I'm not so very busy today as the woman comes today who does the house once a week . . .

LETTERS FROM GUNTER

Quito, Ecuador
Boris-Bar
Apartado 807
October 10, 1941
(First page of letter, rest missing)

My dear sister Gerdale!
While writing this lines to you I'm sitting very lonesome in the nice Russian Boris-Bar. Today is Friday, and this day is very silent in contrary to Saturday and Sunday where all seats are taken and a multitude is listening to the clever music of "Gunter-Heinz".

Now in this solitude I am remembering of you. Naturally my remembrances and impressions of you are always the best and, frankly said, I am proud to have a really cute and nice sister. To everybody I am telling that in London I have an intelligent sister. Many people are interested to read your magnificent letters, but when my friends here want to see a picture from you so I must confess that I possess only one old Photomaton-photo proceeding probably from the year 38. Meanwhile you have become a real lady. When will come the hour that we meet again? I will say it again, that here you will be able very easy to make a living as female work. I advice you to study the art of to cook and to bake, and doubtless you would have good chances. Nevertheless I can't but to emphasise that between London and Quito exists a great difference. Particularly you as young lady would feel this very strong. London, a modern city with all comforts, while Quito like a lonesome and boring village. It is up to you to decide.

Just as I pointed out that Quito is like a village, by this fact I am not in possession to deliver you the silk stockings you asked from me. Silk stockings are here imported goods, and it will be most difficult for me to obtain the right of re-exportation. So I have to reveal to you that this time I can't comply your demands . . .

Quito, Ecuador.
Undated
First page(s) missing

Father is very enjoyed to have received your lines. I hope that soon he will answer you. I have much trouble with father and already I spent much money for him. Father has visa for Ecuador!!! Now I am trying to find out a way to bring him here. I spend a lot of money to get transitvisa for Argentina but all in vain for the government in B'Aires is not ready to give transitvisa before is deposited 365 U.S. Dollars, expenses for the air-trip B'Aires – Quito. As already 500 dollars I met here in the immigration office at disposal of father now I am unable to spend further 365 dollars for his trip. Momentary I am going to make my efforts to realize his trip via Cuba. Father is now brought on the list of those people who will come to Ecuador via Cuba. Let us hope that all my endeavourments to help father immediately will have full success. Though my income is rather small, I am proud I can announce to you that I will take care of him, then he will have to eat and to drink. Naturally I would be obliged to you if you would contribute something to make comfortable his stay in Ecuador.

To day there will be 2 years and two months that I stay in Boris-Bar and I am pleased that you also make a long time without interruption are employed at Staintons. The other day you mentioned that perhaps you will be obliged to give up this job, however I hope that still all is o.k. Have you much work? Do you take care of the dogs? You wrote that it is very hard to find social-intercourse and you cant find somebody to get married! All this is unnecessary! Wait until the war is over! Let us hope that the democratic nations soon will shout Victory and then all problems you have and I have will be solved quickly.

Please write as soon as possible and also for Tatta. My best regards and kisses your brother Gunter

LETTER FROM TATTA

Quito/Ecuador S.A.
Post Restante
January 20, 1942

My dear daughter Gerda:
Today I only will announce that I have arrived here in Quito. Unfortunately I suffered extremely on my sea trip and my state of health is awful. Gunter is assisting me as good as he can. Two medical doctors are taking care of me. Let us hope that soon my disease will better a little. Please let me hear from you! Many thanks for the nice pictures you sent to Gunter. Please don't write to the direction of Boris Bar because Gunter left his job there.
What is the matter about the goods I gave you the other day? Did you sell or are you still in possession?

My best regards and kisses your father

It was only after several readings of the above documents – all correspondence, mostly from Gunther – that it hit me what was missing. Gerda's diaries. There are none for this period from late 1939 and the end of the affair with Joe, through to 1942 and her father's arrival in Ecuador. When Gunther refers to her letter of March 1941, he took *notice that all with you is o.k.,* and this is repeated in his letter of 28th June. September 1940 to May 1941 was the period of the Blitz, and there is no mention of it in the extant correspondence. Gerda may have recorded some of her observations of it, as other ordinary people did – the sandbagged buildings, blackouts, falling masonry, litter of glass, splinters of wood, black dust and debris of bricks, bomb craters, second Great Fire of London, Anderson shelters in the gardens, outside walls of houses blown off to expose strangely intact interiors with marble clocks on mantels and uncracked mirrors. If she noticed such things in S.E 15 or elsewhere in London, there are no diary entries to evidence it because there are no diaries. In a life marked by gaps, this remains one of the most noticeable. Maybe the lost wartime diaries of Gerda Lewinsohn will one day turn up. Meanwhile, her London during the Blitz remains as bare and blank as the moon for all that it is described or evoked, and indeed that is how I visualise it, empty street after street, half lit in the *subdued moonlight* of specially screened lamps.

Absence is what Gunther notices too, though in his case it is not the absence of the war in London or the falling bombs or the Blitz, but the absence of his sister. Re-reading the above correspondence, several things stand out, but none more so than Gunter's anxious letter of 30th October 1940, to Mrs. Stainton of S.E. 15 , asking for news about *the fate of my sister: Has she come in a concentration-camp?* He obviously can't mean a *German* concentration camp, as she is not in Germany, yet that is what I instantly thought when I first read this letter, because naturally I associate "concentration camp" with Germany: they go together. It is understandable that Gunther would have concentration camps in mind, but he probably meant an "internment camp". Following the declaration of war in 1939, about 70,000 German and Austrian UK residents were classed as "enemy aliens" – who then had to register at local police stations. Of the three categories into which they were divided, Gerda was surely categorized as "C" and so exempt from internment and restrictions. Most (not all) of the Jewish refugees were in this benign category, and I think I would know if she had been interned. There is somewhere, in all her papers, official documentation confirming this.

That Gunther made this inquiry reveals how anxious he was. There was his father's worsening situation, and then there was the *fate* of his little sister, who had not corresponded for months and had been *absolutely silent*. Their correspondence during this period is notable for its gaps. It is her turn (on 1st December 1940) to complain of *his* silence: **That is now already the third letter I write to you without getting a reply**. Forward to 18th May 1941, and Gunther has written to the Jewish Refugees Committee for news of Gerda. Their anxiety was spreading in all directions. The metastases of not knowing can be seen in the letter of 13th May 1941 from the War Organization of the British Red Cross Society, promising Miss Lewinsohn that they will inquire for *news of your father*. It is easy for me, having scrutinised these wartime letters, to close such gaps, categorise this correspondence, file it away in blue folders, reassure all concerned that, for all their anxiety, their letters eventually received replies. They remained in contact (Kurt excepted). But I also get some idea of the reality behind words like diaspora and dispersal.

Fortunately – from the *still savage country* of Ecuador, full of *poor-class* Indians *picking up louses from their heads and eating them like epicures* – Gunther was able to pick up *loud and clear* on his magnificent radio-set *with 5 tubes* the BBC in London, although it would take over a year for him to hear (from 6th July 1941) *London Calling*; by which time he had informed his sister of their father's visa for Ecuador. Gerda – far from the internment her brother had once feared – is relaxing (29th August 1941) in her **brown velvet slacks** and about to go for a walk up **One-tree hill with the doggies who are completely satisfied, having had liver for dinner**. It is a shame that Gunther can never seem to remember accurately his sister's birthday, which (as I could have told him) was not 21st June, but the 26th. Probably he remembered it as the 21st because she was born in 1921. It is a minor point. There were more major issues, and Elkan's late *Auswanderung* was to bring one of the more prominent of these to the fore.

"The father", as he is sometimes referred to, left just in time – in late October 1941 – when mass deportations were common. From October 1941 to February 1942, about 58,000 Jews were deported from the Reich and sent East. Elkan Lewinsohn's letter to his *dear daughter*, announcing his arrival in Quito, is dated 20th January 1942 – the date of the Wannsee Conference, convened by Reinhard Heydrich at a villa in a Berlin suburb. Among the Nazi elite attending this conference was Adolf Eichmann, who took the minutes, recording the "various possible solutions" to the "Jewish Question" under consideration. Well before Elkan fled, Zyclon B was being trialled at Auschwitz, anticipating Germany's much lauded *Vorsprung Durch Technik* (advantage through technology).

While Gunther was still struggling *to bring father outside of Germany*, and anxious that his little sister might be in a *concentration-camp*, it would be reasonable to suppose that her thoughts (once she had got over Joe) were occupied with the Blitz and the Battle of Britain; and in fact – in one of her rare surviving letters, dated 1st December 1940 – she described the household at S.E. 15 all sleeping together on the floor because of the air raids. The Blitz (originally from the term "Blitzkrieg" or "Lightning War") was approaching its height when Gerda slept on the floor with the others, the Luftwaffe night bombing campaign having begun that autumn. She was nineteen years old, in another country, nightly bombed by Germans, which might have still seemed a little strange to her, and what she expressed to Gunther was the excitement of it all: **I find the war terribly thrilling and exciting, if it wouldn't be for Tatta.** It would be unjust and unkind of me to think that she mentioned her father as an afterthought.

What she perhaps could not have anticipated was the question in his letter of 20th January 1942 – the question half hidden in its allusion to the diamonds in *the goods I gave you the other day*. It was hardly "the other day", since his daughter had left him almost three years earlier, and it sounds like he had become so habituated to secrecy and disguise that the habit had followed him to Ecuador. It also appears that he had deliberately avoided, in previous correspondence with her, any mention of "the goods" – perhaps out of fear that letters from Germany would be scrutinised by the authorities. Safe now, he was alluding to something of some importance to the surviving family.

It seems to me remarkable that they had been able to smuggle such "goods" out of Nazi Germany in 1939.

Brave, too, considering the likely penalties if found out. It is less remarkable that some (most? all?) of her father's fortune had been turned into diamonds – that the tailors and hat shops of Schonfeld & Co, not to mention other properties in Breslau and elsewhere, had been turned into such stones from South Africa. Whatever their value at the time – doubtless a fraction of the former value of his "assets" – they were portable property and could be concealed in a suitcase or trunk. That is what I imagine happened in May 1939: the assets, such as they were, emigrated with Gerda.

What she took with her out of Germany, and what was subsequently forwarded to her at some cost, has never been (until recently) a matter of particular speculation. Fifty years or so after she left home and country, I found in an attic, at the bottom of a tea chest and wrapped in old newspaper, a bone china tea set marked *Dresden* and decorated with dark pink roses. It was just my cup of tea, and as no one else wanted or claimed it (being in the attic it had to be "junk"), I appropriated it. It is still unclear what happened to it some years later; all I know is that it is gone. It was the identical porcelain tea set she had brought over from Germany, or so I supposed. It was when her *Auswanderung* first took shape for me, and for years I associated it with the fine bone china tea set: both had to be handled with delicacy and care.

As for the diamonds, the story about them seemed less likely. The *Dresden* tea set, though fine, had little actual value and, as such, it was the kind of inheritance I expected, worth maybe £15 or £20 at most. I might even have sold it for about that. Whatever became of it, the tea set had one great advantage over the diamonds: it was there, it existed, I had it in my hands. I could imagine her father forwarding it to her (carefully wrapped against breakage by Aunt Bertha) with the other things of more sentimental than monetary value, such as the photograph albums. Diamonds were a different matter. Not that I ever doubted their existence – more the apocryphal story about them.

During the war, the diamonds were hidden inside the lining of her gas mask until the day an official came round, while Gerda was out, to collect the gas masks. The story gets vaguer still at this point. Why she was out, where she went, she never mentioned. It was never made clear why the gas masks were being collected in the first place. Were they no longer required? Unlikely – given that the Blitz was at its worst while she was still in London. Did they need servicing or replacing? As I lack detailed knowledge of gas mask administration in the Second World War, I can't say. As for the *lining* of the gas mask, was there such a thing, and if so, could diamonds be hidden inside it? How many stones were there, and how big were they? It seems an unusual storage place for diamonds – although it meant that, wherever she went, she had her gas mask and therefore her diamonds with her. Except on this occasion when an official was coming to collect them.

By July 1939, nearly everyone, including children and babies, received a gas mask – one of the millions manufactured in a Blackburn factory. Even the fashionable dummies in department store windows wore gas masks, and children looked at their mothers from behind Mickey Mouse masks. Issued with cardboard boxes, they were to be carried at all times as *Hitler will send no warning* and *Don't Ask! Carry Your Mask!* Air Raid Wardens, armed with football rattles to warn people of suspected gas attacks, carried out monthly inspections. So – the "official" in the story of the missing, presumed lost, diamonds was an Air Raid Warden, and during one of their monthly inspections some fault was found with Gerda's gas mask, requiring it to be taken away and replaced. It may be that by *lining* she meant *filter*, which was perhaps clogged up – making its heat resistant insulate (asbestos) less pleasant to have clamped against her mouth.

It still appears unlikely. If she had to go out at the time of the monthly inspection, did she simply forget about the diamonds? Surely she'd have temporarily concealed them elsewhere in her room, possibly inside her clothing. As she probably kept the mask in her room, did the warden go in there to get it, or had she left it out in the hallway? Maybe she was leaving in a hurry to meet Joe. I know that she still had the diamonds towards the end of their time because, on 25th September 1939, the diamond she had suggested he take away with him to buy her an engagement ring was evidence he had no intention of marrying her – for he had *not* taken the diamond. Looking again at that diary entry I see that she wrote **one of my diamonds** (my italics), which suggests that she was already thinking of them as *hers*. This is perhaps why, in later correspondence with her brother, she gets so tetchy with him for repeatedly asking after the diamonds. After all (I imagine her justifying herself), *she* had smuggled them out of Germany, *she* had taken all the risks, and anyway she never expected to see her family again.

My mother almost never mentioned the war to us, still less her time in Germany before the war, but she did refer occasionally to the lost diamonds – which was extraordinary in itself. For her to refer more than once to something from her remote past was more than unusual. At some point I understood that she had them in mind because they were the money she should have had – her lost inheritance. That money would have made all the difference. No more scraping and saving. But a year or so ago, in January 2021, when I really began investigating these matters, I suspected there was more to discover. It was certainly true that Gerda missed her lost inheritance, I remained sure of that, but there was something else in the story of the diamonds, eluding me. With that in mind, I searched the internet for any information I might have missed. Though the Blitz did not begin until a year after the war commenced, there was (I learned) from the start a fear of poison gas bombs, with a quarter of a million deaths expected in the first week alone. The Ministry of Home safety issued advice on how to wear a gas mask: *Hold your breath – Hold mask in front of face with thumbs inside straps – Thrust chin well forward into mask – Pull straps overhead as far as they will go – Run finger round face piece taking care head straps are not twisted – If out of doors turn jacket collar up to stop gas drifting down neck, and put on gloves or put hands in pockets – Put up umbrella if you have one* . . . Apart from helping me picture a gas-masked Gerda putting up a black umbrella against poison gas pouring from the sky, this useful information did not get me very far, and the story of the family diamonds remains apocryphal. What happened to the diamonds – the Lewinsohn family fortune – is as unlikely as the stones themselves to come to light.

One last thought on the subject. Watching *Casablanca* for the hundredth time the other day, I was struck by an early background scene in Rick's Cafe between minor characters who have no further place in the story. The woman is saying: "Can't you make it just a little more – please". After examining the stone or stones, the man replies: "Sorry Madam, but diamonds are a drag on the market. Everybody sells diamonds. We have diamonds everywhere." It is December 1941 in Casablanca in French Morocco, and it was during this same December (but colder) that Gerda was working as a domestic servant in London S.E. 15. Whether she still had *her* diamonds by then, I have no way of knowing; but if so, they might have been as much "a drag on the market" as in "Rick's Cafe".

9

LETTERS FROM GUNTER

Quito
April 30, 1942

My dear sister Gerda

To-day I have the painful duty to communicate to you that father is dead! Father who had arrived here in the first days of January had been very sick. The doctors examination has resulted that father was suffering of many diseases. He had caught a malaria, then dysentery, however his principal illness would be found some time later. A medical doctor finally discovered cancer of the intestines. The tumour already had been of horrendous evolution. Father was treated by a famous clinical physician, later he transpassed to a great public hospital where three operations had been made by a surgeon who is specialist in such concern. All operation had been in vain because the cancer-tumour couldn't be removed.

Father embarked on the end of October 1941. He arrived in Barcelona with the feeling that something goes wrong with his health. The food on board of the steamer, Isla de Teneriffa, was awful and soon by becoming ill of dysentery he lost much weight. Completely exhausted he landed in hospital of Cuba, Nevertheless his trip to Ecuador was going on by means of air-

plane via Colombia. At fathers arrival here I was more frightened than agreeable surprised for he was incredibly slender like Kurt, he was pale and sleepy. When I offered him brandy he rejected. In spite of all the first time he resisted very well. He has given proof that he was a man of tremendous vitality. As ill as he was he liked to walk around with me through the streets of this small town. Soon he felt that here he found that what in Germany he could not find, the liberty and the manner to live quiet and not to be persecuted. Is it not a mad misfortune to die amidst the idea to spend some happy years on the side of his son?

Father spoke so often from you and wanted to know why you dont write. I am convinced that you as well as me are appreciating father as a man who always treated well his children. Nobody in the world can be better than he was. He not only was a capacity in business life but specially in his private life and with regard to his family he was a man who cant be surpassed by nobody. All what he has done for us never will be forgotten. If you would have an idea how much he was suffering and persecuted before he shut his eyes you would be shedding many tears.

My heart indeed is completely broken. I saw him suffer about 4 months. Nobody supported him. I was the only. I brought him excellent food to the hospital. Each day I was taking care of him, I was his nurse. I was talking with him about various matters and he always shouted: "Why does Hitler not die before I die." He always was very talkative until the last few days when he lost nearly completely his consciousness by the great loss of blood and pus.

I trust that when next Sunday will take place his burial and I will do my last honour to him you will do it too after you are in receipt of these bad news by dedicating him the prayer of Kaddish.

The last few months have been terrible for me. I lost my nerves and finally I lost my small fortune I had. Now I am *without a shirt. I hope that later you will be able to give me back a great deal of the money I spent for medical doctors liquidations and for prescriptions, but don't sell the jewels which father gave you the other day.*

Expecting from you very soon a comfortable answer I remain with best regards and kisses your brother Gunter

Quito/Ecuador S.A
July 2, 1942

Dear Sister:

This will acknowledge receipt of your letter of April 13, 42 directed to father, wishing him a soon recovering.

Unhappily father arrived here in January with a deadly disease and he died on 30th of April. Already on beginning of May I announced you by means of an air-mail letter the death of father. I gave you a very detailed description of all and though not yet I got confirmation of you I hope that meanwhile you took notice of this bad news.

Father spent about 4 months in the hospital and I took care of him. He suffered awfully, all operations by the surgeon had been in vain. Father had been buried here and I am sorry that you had no chance to see him before he shut his eyes.

Your letters always are very interesting but why do you not write oftener? I cant advice you to give up your employment. It would be absolutely wrong to look for a job as a waiter. Keep out at Stainton's – and be endeavoured to become a good cook. As cook for instance you would here make lots of money.

Instantly I am living in a pretty apartment occupying two nice rooms with my own furnitures, but now as father has dead this dwelling has become to big and comfortably for me alone. Besides of this I spent so much money for fathers disease that I will not be able to live any longer here at expensive rent. Now it has become extremely hard to make a living as musician. From time to time I get a job as advertising painter or I give lessons in accordion or some other instrument.

Please write again as soon as possible. Are you still keeping both the nice dogs? What is Ada O. now doing? Let hear from you! Best regards and . . . . kisses (hoo, hoo . . .)Your brother

Gunter

By the time Elkan Lewinsohn died in hospital in Quito at the end of April 1942, people were being gassed at Auschwitz – with one report witnessing how an SS man in a gas mask opened a roof hatch and dropped the powder in. As Nazi efficiency increased with more regular usage, it was found that a politer and pleasanter manner, when inviting people to take a *shower*, proved more effective than brute force, putting them more at ease before killing them; and having them strip first meant that the clothes would not have to be removed afterwards from bodies. Such improvements at Auschwitz were already well underway when Elkan was dying from an intestinal *cancer-tumour of horrendous evolution*, with Rudolph Hoess among others deciding that the crematorium planned for Auschwitz would be located in the new camp at Birkenau where the screams would not be heard by other prisoners. Selections were in progress by the end of April 1942, though it would take a few more months for the process to become *systematic*, and it would take more than a year to build the new crematorium.

I have found the above information about Auschwitz in a book of that title by Laurence Rees. I was also struck by the photographs included in Chapter 2 and by one in particular from July 1942, which shows a smiling Heinrich Himmler (whom Rees describes as not at all unusual in appearance, bespectacled, with a "tummy") with Auschwitz Commandant Rudolf Hoess who is standing stiffly to attention in belted uniform and boots. As detailed in this history of Auschwitz, by July 1942 thousands of Jews from Slovakia and France had been transported there, including children separated from their parents (it was subsequently found that such separations impaired the efficiency of the killing process). By the summer, Jews were also arriving there from Belgium and the Netherlands, even from Guernsey, which in April that year had added a further three to the total. The "killing capacity" of Auschwitz was much improved during 1942, albeit limited to the "cottage" gas chambers of "The Little Red House" and "The Little White House". Facilities were developing elsewhere, with building work beginning on Treblinka in May 1942. The industrialisation of murder by the state was clearly advancing. 1943 was the "year of transformation" for Auschwitz, with the first of four crematoria opening at Birkenau in March – and it was in March 1943 that Dr Josef Mengele arrived at the camp.

By then Gerda, for whom 1943 was also a year of transformation, had joined the ATS.

As the women's branch of the British Army, the ATS (Auxiliary Territorial Service) started in September 1938 and by September 1941 had 65,000 uniformed cooks, clerks, storekeepers (and others in appropriate positions). By the end of December 1941, the National Service Act had called up unmarried women aged twenty to thirty to join one of the auxiliary services, including the ATS.

Yet another internet trawl netted the above information, which has at least the appearance of hard fact. No such reliable information is to be found in Gerda's diaries during this period. In fact to refer to her "diaries" is misleading, since they amount to loose, torn-out pages. One such page – or rather, half a page with the final sentence unfinished – has this: **March 1943: Another long, boring day again. I am not happy. I am so unhappy in love. I eat much too much and get fatter every day. God give me the strength to slim. Please, please, please! I never know if I love Martin, or if it is madness as he believes. I wait for it. I wish to God I wasn't so bad, but also not especially good – as I wouldn't wish this on myself either. I am very bad to myself and . . .**

A further loose note, dated **Samstag, den 26 Marz 1943,** carries on in the same vein: **I am not happy, but also not terribly unhappy. I find life very boring. Every day I get uglier and fatter. If I were beautiful, I'd find a man who loves me. I want to marry soon, have children, and if I'm lucky this will take me to the end of my life. Perhaps that's too much to ask for. But why? Why? Why? Why must I always be so alone? With Martin is it enough? I don't believe I love him. Or is it enough?**

Her note ends there, like so many of her jottings, on an unanswered (unanswerable?) question.

Meanwhile my question, as I rummage through this jumble of loose diary notes and other papers, merely concerns chronology: did she join the ATS in March 1943? If not, when? For some reason, getting the chronology right, the actual sequence of events, matters more than I expected, so I spend half my time searching the paperwork for factual evidence; and one thing I *have* discovered is that it is not simply a matter of looking, but of knowing *how* to look – how to put things together.

For example: this torn-out page before me now, undated of course, records a moment of arrival. A sizeable corner of it is missing; the first truncated line now has only its ending . . .**station in time,** and the next line down begins: . . . **ely girl from Breslau with the name of Lewinsohn.** The line below this is: **Journey tiring. Quite nice girls.** And finally: **Arrive in . . . castle.** *Newcastle* – as confirmed by the address at the journey's end, in large letters underneath her last thoughts on the train (**feeling rather miserable** and **I'll have to stick it out**):

**Recruit Gerda L Platform 3A No 1 Company 19
A.T.S./ T Centre Newcastle-on-Tyne.**

Nearly all the remaining fragments from her time in the ATS are undated, but assuming they date from 1943, and trawling for evidence, it is not long before I net it. In a typical entry, she complains: **The girls here are a very rough crowd and poke their noses into other people's business. They don't like the Jews and unfortunately I am one. Not that they treat me very badly but now and then I have to suffer. I work very hard and try to be as efficient as I can. Dear God help me to become a useful person of society and not just a useless being. Make me dainty and gepflegt and tidy . .**

"Gepflegt" translates as neat, well looked after, well groomed, and also refined, elegant, sophisticated. I am sure Gerda desired to come across as all the above. Which she probably did, if the love letters she received during the ATS years are anything to go by. As, for example, this from George of "India Command", dated 12th July (no year stated):

My darling Gerda, Just a few lines to let you know that I still love you and am constantly thinking of you and wishing myself back with you, darling. Not much has happened since I last wrote, but I will make this letter as interesting as possible if I can. A few days ago I went to the pictures and saw a very weird film called "The Cat People". Hope you see it. If not, it was about a girl who changed into a panther whenever she was kissed and then killed her lover. Silly I know but entertaining! Last night I saw a film about spies and diamond smuggling and what have you, all rolled into one, with murders included. I am still working in the cookhouse and thinking of you every day. Well Darling I am still waiting to hear from you as so far I have received only one letter! I don't know where your other letters have got to. They must have got lost in the post. It seems that everything is getting lost in the post nowadays. Mother sent me 200 Players cigs in March and I haven't received them yet. I am now without a Blighty fag – terrible isn't it. My birthday was on the 1st of July so mother will send me some more cigarettes. I do hope I get them this time. Well cheerio for now until I hear from you. Please write soon. With all my love darling from your loving George.

There are then about a hundred crosses for kisses (I haven't counted them all) around the words I Love You.

Did George write to her on 12th July 1943? I can find no reference to him in any of the scattered entries from that period, including the only note I *can* definitely date – even though it is undated – in that she refers to her birthday (26th June) as "yesterday":

Yesterday it was my birthday. I am 22 years old. Schrecklich alt. If only the right man would come.

Since Joe I haven't fallen in love with anyone. Warum?

Lieber Gott, I would so much like to find a nice man who loves me and whom I love terribly. I feel so alone and unhappy – very often. There are not many girls I like here. They are all boring and catty. We have lots to eat, but I would so much like to be slim and beautiful. I find it terribly hard to resist. But I have to keep on fighting.

This evening I am gong to play Ping-Pong in der Stadt.

Sometimes I am lucky in love, but no more than the other girls here. I have to sleep with mostly common girls who are always making jokes, but I get on well with them. I am quite friendly with a Staff Sergeant, 26 years old, Scottish, very big and also very nice! But I don't think I am in love with him. I'll perhaps see him tomorrow. Maybe he wanted to come here tonight. Is he in love with me? I wonder. Army life is very funny. I still don't get it.

Born in Breslau in June 1921, Gerda was twenty-two in June 1943. As she says: **Schrecklich alt.** Conclusive proof at last – she was in the ATS in June 1943. Where else would she be playing **Ping-Pong in der Stadt**, or getting friendly with a very big Staff Sergeant? That clarifies the chronology at least, and I can now attend to other matters, such as her emotional state at the time. Fortunately, for one so **very often alone and unhappy**, someone had remembered Gerda's birthday – Miss

Stainton of S.E. 15 – who wrote to her in June, hoping that Gerda would be able to celebrate in some way and not have to work all day. She commiserates with her for having to work so hard: *I'm afraid the life of a Cook is rather hard*. Miss Stainton also thinks it rather a pity that Gerda has been *separated from the other German girls*. She herself is spending *quite a lot of time* picking raspberries in the garden for jam:

Picking them makes me think of you – you did such a lot of the picking for us didn't you. There are not many maggots in them this year, which is a relief.

As to be expected from birthday greetings in June, with raspberries and jam-making still on her mind, Miss Stainton's letter ends on a positive note: *However, the War won't last for ever.*

10

LETTER FROM GERDA TO GUNTER

L Company ATS
Catterick Camp
Yorkshire
England

15th Jan 1944

Dear Gunter

I am sorry you didn't hear from me for such a long time.
There wasn't much news, life was always very much the
same. I am now in the English ATS army and enjoy life very
much. I am very happy here. There is plenty of work and
plenty of fun and entertainment. I am a 1st class cook and
have to cook for over a 1000 men in a big cookhouse with
another 9 girls and a few men. We cooks get of course the
best of everything. I am on very good terms with
everybody. I go to a lot of dances and still like jazz music
more than anything. In fact I haven't changed a bit, and you
would very often have the opportunity to say, "ein Prugler
ist reif" I've learned to swear a lot in English as I mix a lot
with lower class English people. I do a lot of PT (exercise)

and beauty care and sleep. I am in love with a boy called George (I don't think anything will come of it) and now you know all about me. I am so sorry to hear the bad news about Tatta. As for the so-called "goods" Tatta managed to give me, there isn't a Brosel left – because I was in need of it and couldn't get one eighth of its real value, so I'm afraid you've had it. Now please don't think I've been extravagant, because I haven't. Have you heard from Kurt? I haven't heard from him for years and years. How is everything with you? I am sure you get on all right.

So Gunter, I herewith promise you sincerely to write more, I am your loving (ha – ha – ha) sister Gerda

(*Ein Prugler ist reif* doesn't easily translate. Gunter often refers jokily in his letters to making use of his *Prugler* (stick or cane?), especially as regards sexy women requiring discipline. *Reif* = ripe. So I suppose Gerda means that it's high time, as she hasn't **changed a bit**, that she was given the *Prugler* treatment.)

LOOSE PAGE FROM DIARY:

20 Marz 1944

I feel the need of writing again. I am still not married and I am nearly 23 years old! Will it ever come true? Or have I been too bad in my life. I often feel so very lonely, I hate being a Jew. One is despised everywhere. Just now I am sort of in love with a full-corporal called Jacky. I like him an awful lot, I really think he is an awfully nice chap and I will be happy when I see him again tomorrow in the cookhouse. I got a date with him on Wednesday at 6.30 pm. He says he loves me and he thinks I am an angel and he wants to make me

happy, but I am suspicious with every man these days and don't trust anybody. I hope he doesn't turn out to be like the others.

PART OF LETTER FROM GUNTER (FIRST AND LAST PAGE(S) MISSING)

UNDATED. (Possibly May/June 1944 in view of the reference to revolution and election of a new president (in Ecuador) in May of that year, with Jose Ibarra regaining power after the "Glorious Revolution" of 28th May 1944).

. . . When I saw you the last time you was 17 years of age. Now you have grown up to be an "old lady". Frequently I am talking with my friends about you, pointing to your "belleza". We all here are most anxious to know how you are looking. Send me a photo – picture!!! I got pale when I read, "I am on best terms with all men"!! (Hu, hu, ay weh!) Let's hope that you are not imitating the exaggerated habitudes of your brother Kurt. Look at me. I have remained the old boy, still abstaining a little of all enjoyment of love. Later we will talk closer about this matter.

I am most glad to read that Miss Stainton is sending you cake and tea. How would you like it if for her great kindness to you I send her a parcel of some Ecuadorean articles like Panama-hats, money-boxes of leather or straw, or coffee, chocolate?

Instantly business conditions are awful. After revolution and election of a new president, the actual police-chief has ordered . . .

LETTER FROM GERDA TO GUNTER

L Company ATS
Catterick Camp
Yorkshire
England
15th June, 1944

(This letter is a repeat, almost word for word, of Gerda's letter above dated 15th January 1944.)

Dear Gunter

I am sorry you didn't hear from me for such a long time . . .

(This later version ends a little differently, as follows:)

I still always go to Miss Stainton for my leaves. They are ever so nice people and made me a real home, I am terribly fond of Winkel the dog. So Gunter – I wish you sincerely to write more With best regards I am your loving (ha – ha – ha) sister Gerda

LETTER FROM GUNTER

Quito/ Ecuador S.A
Lista de Correos
August 18th, 1944

My dear Gerda:

Already almost 3 months have past that I received your nice letter. To-day I will break the long silence by writing you some lines and I hope that these will reach you though you have changed your domicile.

As you know I was employed in "El Batan". Business was excellent, however my employer was compelled to give it up because his wife was heavily diseased by suffering of liver and kidney. She had been cook and it is a pity that you are not here to replace her. By this you would have had a chance to make good money. Besides of this you would have had a nice and most agreeable time. It's a good idea from you to dedicate yourself to the art of cooking. It makes me proud to read that there in a camp you are cooking for about 1000 soldiers.

I don't know whether after wartime you intend to remain there or to come over to this continent. You will find a good chance to make your living here either as cook or if you have abilitys, as tailor. Not so good would be profession of housekeeper.

When El Betan shut its doors and I was fired I went back to the Boris-Palace where now I am employed, mostly playing the piano, leading a 5-men orchestra including one singer. Besides Boleros, Rumbas, Tangos, we also like to play swings and hot music in the new bounced Booggie-Wooggy style. I would be very much obliged if you would help me to some new, fast hits. I will do you a service in return. Do you ever hear the new sentimental "no love no nothing". It is so exciting and thrilling that always when I hear it I am so overwhelmed by ague and I immediately begin to cry. I am so fond to listen to the music of the broadcasting company in London by means of my nice Victor-Radio set. Very attractive also is the station voice of the United Nations located in New-York. When I am listening to the station of London I understand each word.

Last week I got a cable from Guayaquil. A job as trumpeter has been offered to me from the "Lido-Bar". Payment extremely good. Nevertheless I am resolved not to give up my position in the Boris-Palace until has come the day of victory of the Allies.

Now the Allies-troops are marching on with giant steps. I suppose the day of victory no more is far. Later in peace-time I will realize my round-trip to Colombia-Peru-Venezuela-Mexico. I hope you will accompany me. Then also I would be inclined to manage with you together a restaurant or bar. More details and suggestions I will make you next time.

Your brother

Gunter

When Gerda wrote to her brother on 15th June 1944 that she is **now in the English ATS**, it gave the impression that she had only recently joined up. However, an almost identical letter – but dated *January* 1944 – then surfaced, ie it had only just come to my attention. Why she did not send him this earlier version remains a mystery, but the most likely explanation is the diamonds. Gerda was afraid to confess what she had done with them. Her gas mask, I notice, does not feature in this version of events. There is nothing about hiding the diamonds in the lining of her gas mask, which was then collected by an official while she was out. Such an account of what happened to them perhaps seemed improbable even to her when baldly stated in writing, and if it really did happen like that, then at the very least it might have come across as rather careless of her to lose the entire family fortune in that way. In her draft letters of January and June 1944, Gerda's rushed explanation is that she was in need of the money, could not get **one eighth of the real value of the diamonds - so I'm afraid you've had it**. Not the best words for her to pick in the circumstances.

This is what I think actually happened. She drafted her letter and confession in January 1944, at which point she had been in the ATS for well over half a year already. This was wartime – a time of interruption and disconnection – and I appreciate how world war might interrupt and delay letters between England and Ecuador. And I can appreciate, too, that Gerda would not want to give her brother the impression that she wasn't keeping him up to date with big changes in her life, given that they were the last of the Lewinsohns to keep in touch. So I can see why, at the start of the new year, she refers to the ATS as if she had *only recently* joined up. But that letter was never sent, and she went back to it in June to draft an almost identical letter. By June 1944 she had been in the ATS for a year or longer, so her big news – **I am *now* in the English ATS** (my italics) – sounds odder in June than it did in January. Evidently Gerda overlooked this in her haste to confess.

There are other oddities here. In January 1944, Gerda was still **in love with a boy called George**. By 20th March, she is **sort of in love with a full-corporal called Jacky**. Apparently unaware of this, George is still the object of her love in the June letter. Had Gerda forgotten to delete him? She might have been *in love* with both of course. **I am on best terms with all men**, she had written to her brother, who was greatly tickled by her remark. **Hu hu, ay weh!**

Maybe the truth is that she loved George in January but had, some months later, stopped loving him, and had deleted him from her thoughts if not from the June draft of the still unsent letter to Gunther. There is another oddity. Why does Gerda draft virtually the same letter in January and June – not just to tell her brother that she is in the ATS and about her love life there – but to express her sorrow on hearing **the bad news about Tatta**, when Gunther had given her **the bad news** two years earlier in April 1942? Is it likely that Gerda had not responded to news of her father's painful and protracted death, had not even acknowledged it, and was still struggling to do so by June 1944?

It is very likely, I think.

And this was not because she thought so little of him, but so much – or so I surmise. It is hard to know what Gerda was thinking about around this time (1943-1944); there is a dearth of diaries, and the few letters extant are from Gunther. To discover two letters of hers in the same year seemed quite a find, until I saw that they were virtually the same letter, word for word, and that she was simply repeating herself, as she was wont to do. So there is not much evidence available of what was on her mind, but I do know one thing about her. Gerda was afraid to face – recoiled from – difficult things. Dreaded them. What happened to the diamonds was one such difficult thing; what happened to her father another. I have only to go back to those pre-war photographs (they are still on my phone) to appreciate this. Tatta was her sole parent, her protector. Gerda was seventeen when she left him. Had she felt abandoned even though she had done the leaving?

Here he is: her Tatta in his light-coloured suit, portly in those high-waisted trousers, some kind of arch behind him, and in the background women too distant to make out in any detail in their long, dark clothes. The sunlight is bright, and he is casting an oblique shadow on the road. Here he is again, in the same or similar suit, his braces visible, and he has a striped tie this time, and his daughter is with him. The doors of the black car with the number plate 1K 13327 are open, and they are casually leaning against them. The next one is a snow scene: Tatta in a thick tweed jacket and plus fours, Gerda wearing a hat and dark jacket with contrasting wide lapels of a light checked pattern; both holding onto the ropes of their toboggans; and as I enlarge the photograph, I see more clearly now that he is laughing so much he can hardly contain himself, which is unusual. I pause here – taking in the four rows of bright buttons on her winter jacket, her fur gloves, the white house with dark shutters behind them – then flick through the rest. They are so familiar to me now, more familiar than my own childhood. Fat Tatta in his stretched trunks on the beach. Gerda lolling on top of a striped shelter, a matching upholstered striped straw seat inside. The 1926 photograph of Tatta in his great carved, leather upholstered chair, half looking at her while she, five years old and astride a clawed arm, half looks back at him; and here I see something I haven't noticed before: how he rests his left arm on his great knee, how massive his hand seems in the foreground. Finally – on the beach again – arching corporeally above her in his dark trunks, belly thrust forward, legs splayed, while she crouches on her hands and knees in the sucking surf; behind them, the wide white margin of breaking waves, and the darker water beyond.

They remind me how much her Tatta meant to her, and as I find them on my phone, I could forgive her almost everything. She found life always so difficult. Those two difficult things – her father and the diamonds – were one and the same thing. He *was* the diamonds, and in that way he stayed close to her when she went to England. And then she lost them, or sold them for next to nothing, if she can be believed. I recall, without needing to check, the exact wording of his last letter to her, and its date, 20th January 1942, which also happened to be the date of the Wannsee Conference: *What is the matter about the goods I gave you the other day? Did you sell or are you still in possession?* She never replied. She did eventually write (though probably without answering that specific question) but too late, for as Gunther subsequently informed her, their father died on 30th April 1942.

That was a month before Reinhard Heydrich – whose nicknames included *The Hangman, The Butcher of Prague* and *The Blond Beast* – was assassinated. Having already noted the coincidence of Elkan last writing to his daughter on the very day of the Wannsee Conference, I check some dates and find that the *Reich-Protector* died almost the same time as Herr Lewinsohn, within the following month, May 1942 – albeit in a different way, being killed in his Mercedes Benz 320 Convertible in a Prague suburb. And here is another coincidence:

Heydrich was interred in "Invaliden Friedhof", a cemetery located at *Scharnhorststrasse* 25. Admittedly that Scharnhorststrasse is in Berlin, while Herr Lewinsohn's address – Scharnhorststrasse 31 – was in Breslau; but I can't help noticing these odd correspondences.

Heydrich's death was a year old, and the Wehrmacht's defeat at *Stalingrad* was over, by the time Gerda joined the ATS. As Gunther, who noticed such things, wrote (letter above of 18th August 1944), the war was coming to an end: *Now the Allies-troops are marching on with giant steps, I suppose the day of victory no more is far.* If that was the case, 1944 was also a year of great progress for Germany. Auschwitz continued to be improved – with a new arrival area or "ramp" at Birkenau completed by late spring and gas chambers installed on the same level as the crematorium ovens – enabling 150,000 monthly murders. Recruitment of *Sonderkommando* to work in the crematoria more than quadrupled, and the heaps of hair cut from female heads and the jewellery found in orifices no doubt added to the war effort.

News of the gas chambers was also reaching London and New York in 1944, with a BBC broadcast on the subject in June. It was decided for strategic and other reasons that the bombing of Auschwitz was not an Allied priority.

But as Gunther wrote to his sister in August, the end was approaching. In the previous month there had been an assassination attempt on the Fuhrer, bloodying his trousers, which he then sent, with the rest of his splattered uniform, to Eva Braun at the Berghof – their idyllic Alpine retreat and stronghold. Eva was beside herself with concern. This must have been a low point for her. The assassination attempt, the Allied bombing of German cities, and other indications that things were not going so well, encouraged Eva to draw up her will on 26th

October. Even then, she would not have forgotten some of the good times at the Berghof in 1944 – including the celebration of Hitler's 55th birthday on 20th April, when her Fuhrer was on good form, getting his beloved Alsatian "Blondi" to sing as they sat round the fire: "Blondi, Sing!" Both of them then singing and howling in unison. Eva sorely missed Hitler when he left the Berghof for the last time on 14th July, though she had her beloved dogs as well as her young cousin staying with her. There were still summer days of walks over Alpine meadows, picking strawberries, and swimming in the Konigssee. And I have read that a tanned and cheerful Eva had her favourite bathing place there, where she swam in the nude and climbed the waterfall. Maybe this was her way of shutting out the bombing of Munich in April 1944 and again in July. Munich was her city, where she was born. There, age seventeen, she had first met Hitler, or "Herr Wolf" as he was introduced to her, at Hoffmann's photographic shop and studio where she worked.

Thinking about Eva Braun's situation in 1944 is not the digression it seems, for there are links with Gerda. On the face of it, they could not have been more different – Gerda's hair much darker than the darkish blonde of Eva's. As for clothes, though both liked to dress stylishly (Gerda in that ankle-length coat of hers with its wide leopard-skin lapels, Eva in a white ski jacket), Gerda would never have worn the traditional Bavarian costume Eva can be seen wearing sometimes as she served drinks on the sunny terrace of the Berghof, or photographed him with mountain peaks in the background. Different, yes, yet linked (at least in my mind). Both seventeen years old at critical junctures in their lives – when Eva meets Hitler, and when Gerda leaves Germany and meets Joe. Both went skiing in Kitzbuhel, albeit at different times. Both were married in April 1945.

Mentioning "Herr Wolf" reminds me of – oh yes, the restaurant in Gunther's undated letter of probably summer/autumn 1939: *All my dishes I take here at Mister Woolff, who is known to you by his restaurant in Breslau on the Tauentzienstreet corner Anger.* An entirely different Mr. Woolff from the "Herr Wolf" (or "Herr Wolff", as I've seen it spelled) introduced to seventeen-year-old Eva Braun in Munich, but still – these odd coincidences keep coming up.

11

LETTERS FROM JACK TO GERDA

Sunderland
Co Durham
No date

Dearest Gerda
Really Darling I hardly know how to begin. I suppose I must tell you about my journey home. Some chap kept on talking, no one could get a word in, I just wanted everything nice and quiet so I could think of you. When I saw you this morning at breakfast, honestly I hated leaving you. You have certainly grown on me. I suppose its because you are so very different from other girls. You have ways all your own and everything you do, even when you talk, is so very delightful, I just could not help falling in love with you xxx. I have looked forward all day to writing this letter. I can imagine you reading it, and I can see already those lovely dimples when you smile and the twinkle in your eyes.
You asked me to send you a photograph. I have looked through all the photographs at Home and cant find one of myself except when I was about two or three. Dont I keep on, writing about myself, I do find it hard work writing letters, I wish I could tell

you just how much pleasure I find writing to you. - if only you can understand it and dont keep looking for mistakes especially in my spelling. You know its really time I went off to bed.
Jack.

Luton,
Beds
No date

Darling,
What a terrible place this is. We arrived here at teatime, we have to sleep in a chapel and wash in a Church graveyard, can you imagine it. We are herded together on little wooden beds with only three blankets and I have to use one to lay on. Am dreading my wash in the morning amid the tomb stones, but I suppose I shall get used to it. Never mind, you certainly dont need to worry about me, I am still crazy about you and wildly in love with you.
Lights out now. Goodnight Darling. With All My Love xxxxxx
Your Jack

NO ADDRESS
UNDATED
PART OF LETTER:

. . . you are my Dream Girl. I know I am very lucky and certainly dont think I really deserve such happiness. Can't you feel my love for you even though we are so far apart. Dearest one you are my whole life, without you I dont live just exist, nothing matters nothing is of any interest without you. You must be just mine you must Love me with the burning passion I feel for you.

You have given me my Darling the hope and longing to live of which I never dreamed. I could not feel for anyone what I feel for you.

Now my Sweet, Cheerio sleep well and Love me even in your DreamsYours All my Love Jackey

xxxxxxxxxxxxxxxxxxxxxxxxxxxxxxxxxxxx xxxxxxxxxxxxxx

NO ADDRESS
UNDATED

My Dearest Gerda

have just received your letter, you make me so very happy and I want to be with you more than ever. Am afraid I was getting very very miserable but your letter made everything much brighter, and I feel as though I shall be able to carry on here much better knowing that I am allways in your thoughts. Thank you so very much for your special big X.

You must be careful Darling when you are out by yourself. There are such a lot of men without any scruples, and they would pick on you because you are so, what shall I say, desirable. I keep on telling you how beautiful you are but you wont believe me.

You must excuse this writing as I am laying down sunbathing while I write to you. Der Himmel ist blau and die Sonne ist sehr Gut. Ich liebe Dich. I love you and need you darling.

I have got you a couple of bars of chocolate, hope they wont make you. . . I dont think I had better finish that, you may be angry with me.

I hope you dont forget about your hot water bottle. Dont worry about what you spend, you must enjoy yourself and have a good time. All my Love to You Yours

Yours Jack xxxxxxxxxxxxxxxxxx

NO ADDRESS
UNDATED
PART OF LETTER:

. . . wonder if I shall have a letter from you in the morning. Do you still Love me, I wish I could write you more interesting letters, I want to say ever so much but when I begin it just fades away and I sit wondering what to put down and wishing I could talk to you instead. Your hot water bottle has not turned up yet, I begin to despair, storekeepers look in surprise when I ask them, they think I ask for the moon, but I shant give up, surely there ought to be one somewhere.

Have I told you how much I am in Love with you, it gets worse and I am terribly scared. You have done such a lot for me, it will take a whole lifetime for me to repay you. To make you happy is my one ambition in Life. I know we shall be happy together. Am really missing you Sweetheart, always love me unless you want to break my heart. I keep on wondering what you are doing with yourself. Afraid I am terribly jealous, one of my bad points. Perhaps I shall have a letter from you tomorrow. You cant imagine how much I am looking forward to hearing from you, something like water in the desert you know. Always yours Jackeyxxxxxxxxxxxx

NO ADDRESS
UNDATED

My dear Gerda
Please don't be wild at my letter writing. Its been a marvellous day, plenty of sunshine no rain at all, I have thought about us a lot today. I think it must be the nice weather, its really lovely, it all looks so grand with the sun shining and making everything look so beautiful. I dont know my writing seems to

get worse and I know my spelling is terrible. I want to write you such nice long letters. This Love Darling must be the real thing, its all such a very nice feeling but it certainly hurts me a lot at times. You perhaps will understand my feelings by now, if only the war would finish and let us do what we so want to. You know Darling I am not happy at all while I am away from you. Will say cheerio for now.All my Love to you Dear Yours Jack xxx

Keep you chin up and shoulders back. How I Love You. It hurts

NO ADDRESS
UNDATED

My dear Sweetheart

Sunday evening, have been to the Gym tonight and saw a grand picture. Deanna Durbin in Hers To Hold. I think that she is one of the finest singers on the Screen.

So far Darling I have not been out of Camp since you went away. You cant possibly know how much I have missed you. I dont know what day you shall be coming back, anyway I hope that you receive this before you leave London.

And if you are glad to get back to me, then I shall know that you are just as much in Love with me as I am with you. Its been grand weather this weekend.. I could spend more time laying out in the sun, I love to lay out in the sunshine, its an obsession with me now. Back again to work tomorrow.

No letter from Home this week, I hope everything is OK. Its nearly time for lights out so I must finish. It comes in quite dark at nights but still quite warm, I do hope that you shall not forget your hot water bottle. I think that you will need it. All the Girls keep on asking about you and they do attend me at meal times. We had shell eggs for breakfast this morning I did enjoy it. Must say Cheerio for today the lights are going out now. I love you and love you for allways. Ever yours with all my Love and tons of xxx big long ones Yours Jack xxxxxxxxxxxxx

**NO ADDRESS
UNDATED
PART OF LETTER:**

. . . You ought to manage quite nicely in London, I suppose you shall go round all those big stores seeing whats new and wishing I bet that you were in Civie St and able to buy just what you want. Never mind Darling it wont be long now before the war is over, and then we shall both be quite happy. Shall have to say Cheerio for today
Dont forget to keep your shoulders back. All my Love and tons of xxxxxxxxxxxxxxxxxxxxxx

Your Jack

**NO ADDRESS
UNDATED
PART OF LETTER:**

. . . You know its quite a job this letter writing. I really do feel such a stranger to it. When I read it over its not half of what I wanted to say, perhaps I talk better, what do you think. Never mind I do my best. I know that it must bore you always hearing me talk about my work. Its about all that keeps me going whilst I am away from you. But I think you ought by this time to have a good idea of my feelings for you. They are strictly on the level and I know that I shall indeed be very happy when we are able to be married. Perhaps we shant have to wait much longer. Roll

on the end of the war.
Well Dear time for work again, so will say Cheerio for the
present. Take care of yourself Darling.All my Love to you and
millions of XXX Just yours Jack
P.S Dont forget
Shoulders well back.

NO ADDRESS
UNDATED

My Dearest Gerda

Thank you so very much darling for your two very charming
letters. You know I was becoming ever so worried about you
and I am glad to hear that the flying bombs have subsided a
little.
The Girls in the dining hall were asking if I had heard from
you, and I told them yes and that you were having a grand
time. I suppose you go to the pictures three or four times every
day. I bet you look simply grand in your Civies.
You must write and let me know what train you will be on and
what day, and I shall try my best to meet you. You have a grand
time and really enjoy yourself. Now where was I? Oh yes, I am
as always. Just Yours. All my Love

xxxxxxxxxxxxxxxxxxxxxxxxxxxxJackxxxxxxxxxxxxxxxxxxxx
xx

Sunderland
Co Durham
UNDATED

My dear Gerda

You are such an Angel to write me such a charming letter, at first I could hardly believe it was from you and I kept putting off the pleasure of reading it until I was quite alone, and then I made myself comfortable in a nice big chair by the fire, lit up a cigarette, and thoroughly enjoyed reading your letter. I am so glad you are missing me. I have felt hopelessly lost without you, and I shall be glad when Saturday comes along so that I may see you again. It seems ages since we last saw each other, and well Darling I must love you a terrible lot the way I miss you. You are all I think about, and I am so very sure that I can make you happy. We have lots in common and we ought to have a perfectly wonderful life in front of us. Please Dear don't think that I want to rush you. I know you forbid me to talk of these things when we are together, but this is different somehow, and if you so desire I can wait a long time for your answer because I love you so very much.

I am glad you are going out a bit and I know it will do you good, and also it helps pass away the time. Half my time here I dont know what to do with myself. I go for long walks and do a show now and again. I seem quite lost without you. Have ordered some table tennis balls, hope I get them OK. Think I have got fixed up with a cycle for you, its going to be quite a problem getting it through to Richmond but will manage it somehow. Am so looking forward to the summer, we are going to have memorable times together just we two. Are you bored yet, Dear? I do go on. I was going to write you such a nice long letter, but I am about dry now. Your tooth, I do so hope you are not going to be troubled with it, they can be so very painful I know. Thank you again Sweetheart for such a nice letter. Roll on Saturday. All my love to you Dear, and keep well and happy. Ever yours. Lots of love and Kisses

Jack xxx

S.O. BOOK 135 SUPPLIED FOR THE PUBLIC SERVICE (USED BY GERDA AS DIARY)

UNDATED

I just came home from Sunderland with Jacky. I was at Jacky's sister's wedding. I thought it was very dull and boring, not like I wished my wedding to be. There should have been more life in the party. English people are really awfully dull and uninteresting. I don't like them much, except my little Jacky of course who is really one of the best fellows in the world and don't you ever forget this Gerda. He'd do anything on this earth to make me happy. And he has to bear a lot of me really. I make his life really sometimes uneasy. I'll try to make him quite happy. He doesn't deserve it, I'm really awfully selfish. Dear God please help me to become a better person. Please help me to be good. Forgive me all my sins and help me to correct my mistakes and please make me happy and satisfied. Make me strong and give me power to resist temptation. Please make me beautiful, slim and rich. And please always show Jacky and me the right way to go. Show the Jews the right way too and please help them.

LETTER FROM GERDA

NO ADDRESS
UNDATED
PART OF LETTER

Dear Miss Stainton,

Well it's all over now but we are keeping it secret! I had the best leave I ever had in all my life and Jacky's people are ever so kind and nice. I bought myself a nice green hat and wore the costume and the coat, so I really looked quite smart. I don't like Sunderland very much though. I think it's a rather dirty town because of all the shipping business. I wouldn't like to live there for good. Well as long as they don't send my little Jacky to Burma, I shan't grumble at anything. It is ever so hard to bear Army life now after all the comfort I enjoyed in Jack's home. I am getting proper fed up with the cold and discomfort. . .

S.O. BOOK 135 SUPPLIED FOR THE PUBLIC SERVICE (USED BY GERDA AS DIARY)

1 May 1945.

Jack and I are married and I couldn't find a better husband anywhere. Only I don't love him as much as I loved Joe. It is more a calmer peaceful love, I love him to make love to me and Jacky spoils me terribly. That is very nice too. He does anything I tell him to do. He is mostly always the same, never changes his moods much. I am still in the army. Hope to get out soon though. I am not at all happy any more. I used to like the army once very much. But not now. I am afraid of all sorts of things. I must try to slim. Nobody will like a fat Jew girl. If I had only more strength to resist food. I am easily hurt these days and not happy. So please roll on better times. I'm tired, so good night for now. I work in the bakery and have to get up early tomorrow. I like baking very much. But I don't like the girls I am working with, at all. They are all bossy, jealous creatures. I don't like girls really at all. They are all mean or catty, or perhaps it's me. I know I'm funny and get on very hard with people and I just can't change myself. I wonder what will happen on our next leave. Where will we go. I don't want to go to Sunderland, I hate it there. It's dirty and awful and all dirty proletariat there. I'd hate to live there and Jacky knows this and promised me we would never live there. I wish we'd get a room or little house soon.

The marriage was to last longer than the thirty-six hours Eva Braun enjoyed underground in the *Fuhrerbunker* in Berlin before biting into the ampoule of cyanide Hitler handed to her. Gerda and Jack still had their whole lives ahead. He may not have been a lover like Joe, but considering the extremes to which too much love can lead (as in the case of Eva who promised to follow her Fuhrer to death) that was probably a good thing. Even with Joe, Gerda was incapable of such love, since by the end of the affair she was thinking of her Berliner with revulsion as the **asshole** who **stank so much** that she **felt nauseous**. That was what she recorded in December 1939 – a few months after the start of World War Two – and now as war was ending, Gerda had found a **calmer, peaceful love**. Just so long as it did not end up in his home town, Sunderland.

That they met at all was more than unlikely – she from one country, he from another, both countries at war with each other; he from one class, she from another. Only war could have temporarily closed the distances between them. They met in the camp "cookhouse" where she had favoured him with bigger helpings. But I can tell from his letters that it was more foreignness than food that brought them together – *her* foreignness. Jack had never been abroad (that is, outside Tyne and Wear) before the war, and after training as a tank driving instructor he was apparently of more use to the army by staying put in England and leaving giant caterpillar tracks in the camp mud than by dying at the front, unlike the friends who never came back. Staying put gave him a big advantage over other soldiers sent abroad. Jack might not be **the Great Love**, but he did not leave her – if he did, it was only to another army camp in England. She did not have to say a permanent goodbye to him. In years to come he must still have wondered how he had managed to catch such a woman, *so very different from other girls* with ways all her own, and a delightfully different way of speaking. So delightful that even he – unused as he was to words spoken or written – tried it out for himself: *Der Himmel ist blau und die Sonne ist sehr gut. Ich liebe Dich.* So different, and yet they have so much *in common*.

Looking back over this last paragraph, I pause at *they met in the cookhouse*. Curious how one phrase can so resonate through a life without being scrutinised (until now). When I heard about this meeting (exactly when, I don't know) it seemed a sufficient – a complete explanation of their past, requiring no further detail – no background, no back story, nothing. It was a comforting word, *cookhouse*, suggesting warmth and dinner and home, and much later – coming across an old book of hers, *Wie koche ich in England*, in the home-made oak bookcase – I questioned nothing, but again felt reassured. Gerda was a cook – inasmuch as she worked in the *cookhouse* – in Catterick Camp in Yorkshire, or somewhere near Newcastle. More recently (2021) I found that her trade on enlisting was recorded as "Housekeeping" and that the testimonial (in the *Release Leave Certificate* which I just happen to have in front of me now) described Gerda as "a very good cook" who "has carried out her duties conscientiously" and is "reliable and trustworthy". So as well as catching a foreign girl with a delightful accent, Jack caught a very good cook.

The end of the war (almost): 1st May, 1945, V.E day a week away, the death of Hitler (whose suicide was probably yet to be announced), and marriage. As Gerda wrote: **Well it's all over now but we are keeping it secret.** It is not clear why it had to be kept a secret. Eva and Adolf also kept their marriage a secret – a secret from the German people, if not from *Fuhrerbunker* occupants like Magda Goebbels, who may or may not have been present at the ceremony, though husband, Joseph, was there as a witness. Magda did see them before their joint suicide on 30th April, after which (on 1st May) she arranged ampoules of cyanide for her six children, who were also too good for this world and who were later found dead in long white night gowns.

As Gerda and Jack were looking forward to married life and civvy street, much was already behind her. Not only the Germany she had left in May 1939, but world war and the remains of a Germany Hitler bequeathed to the remaining *Volk*. Behind her were the death marches and the liberation of Auschwitz and Bergen-Belsen. By 6th May, Breslau was also finally behind her. Whether she was thinking of Breslau at that time, I don't know; whether she had given it a moment's thought earlier in 1945 (20th February) when old men and Hitler Youth fought the Red Army in the city's *Sud Park*, where as a girl she had walked with her brother – is also unknown. With all the other broadcast news of war, and Gerda's impending marriage, street-by-street battles in Breslau, extending down to the sewers, probably passed by unnoticed; and if she had noticed, it can only be conjecture that such news reminded her of home. It is unlikely that any of the people she had once known were among those who fought and died for "Fortress Breslau", since its last defenders were old men and Hitler Youth. Most likely the destruction of Breslau escaped her notice, if only because it was the irrecoverable past and she had her future to think of. All of this is surmise. Doubtless Gerda did sometimes revisit that other Breslau where her father was a respected merchant and where shop windows were not broken glass. If so, any such thoughts she kept to herself. In May 1945, the worst thing she could think of was having to live in Sunderland with Jack, among all the **dirty proletariat there.**

12

LETTERS FROM GUNTER

Boris – Palace
Quito
Ecuador S.A.
Cascilla 781

May 8th 1945

My dear Gerda:

*To-day I write you these lines just in the exciting moments
where victory in Europe is announced everywhere. I hope that
you are enjoying of good health and will find opportunity for
celebration of this very expected V.E day. I am sorry that our
correspondence during the years of war had been interrupted
and nearly completely ceased. This time I must ask you again
for a photo from you because no more I can imagine how you
are looking. When I saw you the last time you were a child, now
you have grown up to a real lady. Maybe that meanwhile you
got married or engaged. Make up your mind and tell me exactly
which progress you have made in these seven years of exile.
Have you the intention to come to Ecuador? You would find
here a job very soon and also you would have a chance to get to
U.S.A. Maybe you are resolved to remain in England, going as*

private soldier, waiting until the defeat of Japan?

I am still in the Boris-Palace and give too piano-accordion lessons to some nice girls. Though in the meantime I have become an old fellow I must confess that still neither I am fallen in love nor I have the desire to marry.

Though this day is Victory – day it is absolutely silent here. I can imagine that there in London this event will be committed with the greatest joy and more enthusiasm than here. Nevertheless me and my friends to-day will find together in the Benifiencia – Israelita for a modest celebration taking a cup of coffee and enjoying some good pieces of cake. Here in Ecuador are living many Americans, Englishmen and Suisse. If you would be here doubtless you would have a touch with them. As I never found a chance to go to war I was obliged to spend the years of war here. Life here is agreeable though not as noisy as London and Quito has no character of a huge city. I find here all kind of entertainment, movies, theatre, speeches and radio-transmissions. Last night listening to the British Broadcasting Company, London, I heard for the first time of the unconditional surrender of Germany and really I got mad by joy. Then followed a brief announcement that the City of Breslau had been captured by Russian troops. What about Schonfeld & Co? I am convinced that we Jews have lost all chance of living in Europe. Just to-day I got a nice letter from an American friend. He advised me not to leave this continent and to try to forget Europe forever! Please let me hear from you. Many kindly regards and kisses (hu! Hu!) Your old brother, Gunter.

Guayaquil/Ecuador S.A.
Roxy – Night – Club

24 de Agosto 1945

My dear sister Gerda

probably you will be astonished that your last comfortable letter remained unanswered such a long time. But just when arrived it, I had much trouble with my boss, gave up my job in Quito and moved again to Guayaquil. Here I have a good employment in the Roxy – Night – Club and have some other jobs too. I still rent a furnished room in Quito, because perhaps in winter time I will go back there as the climate here will become unbearable. War is finally over now and I hope that soon I will find a chance to meet you somewhere. I have enjoyed very much your last letter. Naturally the news that you got married shocked me tremendously. Your enclosed photograph was the greatest surprise for me. All my numerous friends in Quito who saw it said that I can be proud to have such a nice sister. It is a pity that you don't pay a visit to Ecuador to present yourself personally to my friends who are admiring you by a glance on the photo. But now as you have become the wife of Jacky it is very questionably whether you ever will. I would be glad also to have a picture of your husband, because not yet I have a chance to make his acquaintance. What do you intend to begin now peace has come back? Now I am brother in law I would be very much obliged if you would give me some details of your lucky marriage. I unfortunately could not yet find a girl who would be worth to be my wife. I need a woman who either has a little fortune or earns some money. As here the choice of under 400 immigrants is not good and I can't resolve to marry a native Ecuadorian, there remains only a single chance that you there look for some girl who would be inclined to marry your bald-headed brother.

Here I am enjoying life as good as I can. In this hot climate everybody is compelled to say, "Take it easy". I always have plenty of time to go to the movies, to listen to the BBC of London, and to spend much time in the nice swimming pool. I do not like to ride a bicycle like you, I would prefer some of the nice pastries you make there. You will imagine that I spend much money for ice-cream and chocolate. Here there are many Czechoslovakian bakers who make excellent cookies and Tortchen. Come here with Jacky, I invite you, you will have here a nicer time than perhaps there in Europe!

In the Roxy we play mostly difficult syncopated American arrangements of the latest hits, as for instance "I Wanna Boog it" Boogie Woogie. My favorite piece is "I could not sleep a wink last night" - a very soft and sentimental hit. Dear Gerda, it has no value to send me the words of hits. That what I need are either sheet music or orchestral pieces for entire orchestra. Maybe that you have some music friends there who can help me to this I ask for.

Momentaneously here take place good demonstration of peace and special Victory dances. Everybody here is most satisfied that peace is restored. In spite of this fact it must be said that we have to complain the loss of all our relatives in Germany. Though no information and no lists with regard to survivors of Jews in Germany I have in hands, it can be said that Aunt Bertha and the rest of the family who lived in Brandenburg have perished and must be included to the Axis-victims. I am very, very sorry. I have done the best for father and I would have done also the best for them, if they would live.

Expecting your prompt answer I remain with best regards to you and Jacky

Your brother Gunter.

Guayaquil/Ecuador S.A
Lista de Correos
2nd of November 1945
(FIRST PAGE ONLY)

Dear Gerda:
To-day I will answer your lines of 20.9.45. With great pleasure I received the included foto-picture. This picture like the other one you sent me find generally here the greatest approval. I sent the foto to my close friends in Quito and I hope they will admire it incessantly, just as I did. We always here appreciate it very much to hear from you and to know which experience you make in England now where peace has restored. The war is over! All services of war had been done. I am very glad to read that you and your husband have contributed so much for the Allies sake. I always had the desire to take part in the war, but here in the forgotten angle of the world never I found a real chance to participate.

Meddling more to the content of your letter I must confess that you are a little awkward. On every sheet is your question more or less: "Little man, what now?" After having been pleased to read that you had so much fun to be in the army, now apparently you begin to complain of too much work - "Down to the knees and not fit to do anything". I got nearly crazy when you revealed that your work-hours are from 4.30 am to 6 pm, and above all in a disgracefully hot Nissen-hut. When you announced me that you got married I believed that it would mean a step to a better and more comfortable life, but instead of this it seems that poco a poco you are gliding to misery?! Look at the scar of your back and you will find that it points to some trace of severe illness you had as a child and it is recommended to you not to make experiments with your health. In one of my former letters I suggested to you to go to South or North America because I previewed that after the war will come an economic depression in England, a stagnation in whole . . .

Guayaquil / Ecuador S.A.
Lista de Correos
1st of March 1946

Though I was going to answer your nice letter of Sunday 30th Dec. 1945 months ago I must stop writing because I was heavily attacked by a sick liver. Swelling of liver is a typical tropical disease and at my belief it was caused by taking too much Quinine to prevent Malaria. Indeed climate here in wintertime has turned nearly unbearable. While dropping you these lines temperature has more than 31 degrees. I am sweating awfully and the penholder glides from my fingers. I always guessed that, as soon as war is over, I will find lots of facilities to initiate my round-trip as outstanding expert of my squeeze-box and trumpet across this continent. I supposed that after the war there would be a boom and prosperity at all. But not at the least! In the contrary here for instance there are spreading symptoms of inflation. Some money I saved is losing in value absolutely. I fear if there is not given help from some of the powerful democratic nations to eliminate the tremendous economic depression, fascism and anti-democratic feelings will spreading more and more. Look at the Argentine.

Not yet I am in a position to send you gifts of more value as those I sent you formerly. I intended to send you some nice Ecuadorian-made bracelets, or good-shaped finger-rings. But instantaneously I must abstain to do it because of the too high duties. Nevertheless I will find an easy manner to send you, if you want: a coconut, silk-stocking, all kind of real good leather-goods for instance letter-cases, money-holders, straw-made Panama-hats, straw-slippers, etc. Naturally I advice you to choose only goods which are of small volume. You did me a great favour by sending me both the Violin-Cello strings I needed urgently. Also the hit: "It wont be wrong" had been orchestrated by myself and we play this old-timer with great success. I personally at present am so fond of, "I'll be seeing you". It is hammered in my brain, and even walking along the street I whistle it unconsciously. It makes me so sentimental, it must be swell to hear it sung by Bing-Crosby.

I am glad to read that your "Chubby" is growing-up nicely, preparing you much fun. But particularly I am most disappointed and angry because nothing from the home-made cake, maltloaf, butter and jam, came to me! Ay, caramba! I got pale, when I read of such good, delicious dishes. Never mind!

The next 3 days of Carnival I will spend in a nice hotel in the beach, playing with the Costa-Rica Swing Boys to whom I belong. There finally I will find a chance to swim in the open sea, Pacific-Ocean, but I must be careful that the sharks will not swallow me.

Now it is up to you to write me.

My best regards to you and "Jacky"
Your brother
Gunter-H

Guayaquil
Ecuador S.A
Lista de Correos
(TWO SHEETS WITH CORNERS MISSING)

29th of September 1946

My dear Sister Gerda:

I am very glad to be in possession of both your letters containing nice pictures. I must confess that your last letter was a little strange. You asked me to send a Panama Hat to your landlady to get rid of the trouble you have there.

Naturally I am always ready to send you all kind of gifts if they would be supposed for your personal use.

Scarcely you had changed from London to Oxford and you dropped me your letter, which gave some impression of the poorness of your living conditions there. But now, while writing these lines, glancing to the marvelous pictures of you and your husband I am convinced that you are all right and still nicer than ever before. Probably you are using "Schonheitscreme" which helps you to your beauty!? Your pictures passed again to the view of my friends and found everywhere full approval. Indeed your husband must be a clever man for he looks like a R.A.F. Pilot . . .

. . . I go on with my employment as Violin – Cello teacher in the Conservatoria – Nacional del Ecuador. If my pupils not obey, then the distiguido Profesor Gunter Heinz give them also a "Pringler" with the stick. Ha, Ha, I have my fun!

Well, next year is finished my contract and I told you the other day that I decided to leave this country. Either I go to Colombia – Venezuela or to the United States. After I have spent more than seven years in this country I consider Ecuador nearly as my home, but I must be careful. Generally here in South America people are living only by "cheating". The economic crisis has increased after end of war. I am by special restrictions not in the position to send you gifts which represent great value. Nevertheless I will forward to you a small parcel, which as the former parcel "will disappoint you" again.

Finally I give you notice that my endeavourments to investigate what has become of the fate of our relatives in Germany remained without any success, so we must pass in sorrow that Aunt Bertha and the relatives in Brandenburg have become victims of the Nazis, and I expect from you that you will remember their names with the greatest reverence.

Please let me hear from you.

With 1000s of kisses . . . (hu, hu, hu, ich werde verruckt!)

I am your brother . . .

(A *"Pringler"* with the stick: In later letters Gunter writes *"Prugler"*. *"Pringler"* does not translate, and the closest I get (in a dictionary) to *Prugler* is *Prugel* – a club or cudgel, and also a beating, a thrashing. This must be what he was thinking of.)

Both sheets of that last letter of Gunther's are torn, with the larger corner missing from the first, so that – after comparing Jack to an RAF pilot (if only!) – the lines that follow are incomplete sentences. I can just make out phrases such as *because I have turned out a niggard, a real avaricious bachelor,* and . . . *money-box, ha, ha, ha* . . . The paper is tissue-thin airmail, five years older than me, and I reflect that I have also reached the age when I am prone to tear. It is an apt metaphor, I reflect, for what Gunther has gone through: a corner or two of the family torn off. It seems he is admonishing his sister at the end of the letter, and I – at this great distance from the Holocaust – feel somehow included in his admonition, as if, like Gerda, I also am inclined not to remember *with the greatest reverence* those Lewinsohns (unnamed apart from Aunt Bertha) killed by the Nazis.

Still, it is odd how Gunther, after stating almost as a reproach what he now expects of his sister by way of remembering the *victims of the Nazis*, then sends her *1000s of kisses* followed by apparent chuckles (*hu, hu, hu*) and *ich werde verruckt* (I'm going crazy). What is all that about? Actually I have noticed similar endings, when Gunther makes fun of his own extravagant affection for Gerda. Is there a sexual suggestion here of something illicit, or am I just reading too much into it? Women are often on his mind, or in his letters, in a half serious, half mocking way, eg when he keeps going on about his little sister finding him a young woman, and how he is an old bald-headed bachelor disinclined to marry. His disinclination never stops him thinking about it.

By the side of my laptop is a single page of a letter from Gunther. The previous page is missing, as is the next, so I have no idea of the date or even the place. It might have been written well before the above letters from 1945-6 –

or after. There is nothing in the text to give me a clue. I mention it now because of the following passage halfway down the page:

Now a "gelistige" surprise!!!! Guess who has written a comfortable letter to your brother Guenter ?????? Hurrah, oh ein Liebesbrief!! Watch the included picture and you will find it out! She wrote me a letter of full 4 pages. Oh, I'm so proud and simultaneous foolish! However I am an honest man and therefore I will confess that she is no more the type for which I am interested. She looks too old fashioned European, but I am now accustomed American make-up. Strawberry with whipped cream! Besides of this, though I would like to marry, really I have not the desire to marry but I was curious to see what such girls have to offer. No, no, it is better to remain single, free without any obligation. The marriage of E. Preiss to Oschinsky is most funny! Now I have to take a damp-bath of chamomile for my nose.

Gelistige translates as "cunning", but it remains unclear (to me) how this *Liebesbrief* is a cunning surprise, unless he means that *she* (whoever *she* is) was trying to trick him into love. As the *included picture* is missing, I'll never know. Who *E. Preiss* is, I don't know either, though the name *Oschinsky* sounds familiar – the Ada Oschinsky of Gerda's pre-war Breslau diaries? Aside from such questions, I mention this fragment of a letter now because it seems to reveal something about Gunther to be found elsewhere in his letters: some defining characteristic or predisposition. After returning this fragment to its blue folder marked *Incomplete letters – Gunther,* I then notice another even more interesting fragment and these words:

I now expect that the old "quarrel in the house – Lewinsohn" has been buried. Aunt Bertha was never my friend. She was always disturbing the rest of the house. The mother was hating her and I too !!!!! Many of the unforgettable "Freitagabendhuhnchen" would have tasted still better if Aunt B would not have so very often provocated strife.

This from a man who must *pass in sorrow* that Aunt Bertha and other Lewinsohns *have become victims of the Nazis*. Now that I subject this fragment of a letter to closer scrutiny I see that it must be earlier than the above letters, perhaps written while he was still in New York, as indeed the above reference to *American make-up* suggests. He could surely not have written about Aunt Bertha in this way *after* she was killed. Could he? Whatever, it comes as a shock that avuncular Gunther could think of her like that – that he could actually *hate* her to the extent that unforgettable Friday evening chicken was not as tasty as it should have been because of Aunt Bertha provoking strife.

Now that I have started to think about him differently, there are other discoveries to be made. It is no surprise that Gunther would have liked to participate in the war against Germany, the country he had lived in for the first twenty-seven years of his life, because he had no reason to be grateful to the Reich after 1933, and his own sister had fought against it in the cookhouse. It is equally no surprise that he liked cakes and cookies, ice cream and chocolate (especially *the sweet chocolate balls or Rum-Kugeln*, whose recipe he details lovingly in another letter). The surprise comes in his letter of 2nd November 1945 and his view then of her situation: *poco a poco you are gliding to misery*. That *is* perceptive of him, even prophetic. I pause to consider. He is being protective of her, if patronisingly so, that is also apparent. Gunther always the big brother, and Gerda always the little sister in need of advice. From the distance of Ecuador, he is still there to guide her, reproach her when required, warn her before it is too late. Gunther *the bully* is how Gerda came to describe him. There is no evidence that she considered even for a moment joining him in Ecuador, as he wished, but there is evidence (in later letters) that she never wanted him to visit her in England, as he kept threatening – but here I risk getting ahead of myself. Going back to the war and the early post-war years, I see that this not simply a story of siblings separated by convulsions on a scale previously unknown. Gunther went to all the trouble of arranging his father's *Auswanderung*. Gunther alone looked after him through the ravages of cancer. With no help from Kurt. None from Gerda. It was Gunther who admonished his sister to remember the names of the exterminated Lewinsohns *with the greatest reverence* as she might otherwise forget. And it was Gunther who looked down and warned her that *she was sinking*. Gunther had turned into Tatta, and Gerda was the girl needing direction and even saving.

But enough for now of such Gunther-like pronouncements. Here, in another undated letter fragment, is that recipe for *Rum-Kugeln*:

Ah, how fine it tastes! Come here on weekend to try my sweet chocolate-balls. Quarter pound cocoa, quarter pound smashed chocolate, quarter pound butter, three tea spoons rum, pound of sugar. Do you know this recipe?

Aside from this useful information, there is something else in this undated fragment worth mentioning. I say "undated", but there are clues to its possible date, firstly in the following reference to *Carnegie Hall*, a film released in February 1947:

Last week I saw the picture "Carnegie Hall" and I recommend to you to see this film. It is overwhelming exciting. You know that my body is equipped with a good heart and when a movie – picture becomes sentimental I begin to cry and loose my brain by shedding tears.

Another clue is in the reference to Kurt:

Did you hear something about "your brother" Kurt? The other day I made an application to make a trip to the Argentine but I failed in my endeavourments because of the restrictions imposed by the Peron – Nazi – regime which still admits discrimination to the utmost in respect of races.

That is all Gunther has to say about Kurt in what has survived of this letter, and he seems to erase him from any further thought by going on to ask Gerda if, in her reply, she can send him some sheet music so that *your favourite hit will be played by my orchestra.* As the Peron regime, to which he refers, was from June 1946, this letter must date from some time after that, and there is what could be another clue to the date: a reference to *the American Presto – Cooker,* which he also recommends to his sister:

Now everywhere have become a fashion to use in the kitchen the American Presto – Cooker. By this for instance a chicken may be prepared and ready for the table with half hour. Or beef – tongue which generally needs a 2 days cooking may be soft cooked in that time. These Presto – Cookers are available here, and if you are interested to have such cooking – machine which helps you to safe time, I will send you prospectus and catalogues.

But as these wonderful cooking machines were on sale from 1939, Gunther's admiration of this time-saving device does not help pinpoint the date of his letter. He might have been writing from Ecuador, or from Pittsburgh where he would soon be living, and where he would change the spelling of his first name to Gunther, and shorten his surname to Lynn. There is no evidence of Gerda taking him up on his thoughtful offer of a Presto – Cooker prospectus and catalogue. In fact there is little evidence of Gerda at all during this period, other than that Gunther's letters were addressed to her. She was doing a *Kurt,* i.e. vanishing. In his case the vanishing had lasted much longer (from 1939) and I see from Gunther's reference to *your brother* that on the whole he wanted Kurt to stay that way.

What Gerda thought of her missing brother is unclear. What she thought of Gunther was clearer. As well as being "a bully", which came first in the list, there was his baldness. After that: "leader of a band". She said little about Kurt, other than that he too was musical, played piano, spoke languages. He was also handsome, by which it was clearly understood that Gunther was not. Apart from those key attributes, Kurt was a blank, vanishing into the blankness of Argentina.

And now here is Gerda, in the immediate post-war years, doing a Kurt. There are two khaki diaries for 1945 and 1946 with most of their pages torn out. Why? Days, weeks, months, years torn out. While momentous things were happening in post-war Britain – the welfare state; the NHS; industries nationalised; a million or so council houses built – all I get from Gerda is this:

Marz, 1947. Ich lebe in Oxford auf der Argylestrasse 53 in einem Zimmer mit Jacky. Ich bin 25 Jahre alt und werde 26 im Juni. Jacky is 31.

There is more, another four pages – but they are illegible, indecipherable. If that prickly script of hers conceals anything worth reading, if it reveals totally unexpected things about her life, I'll never know. There is one thing to note: instead of **1947,** she had actually written **1937** by mistake. As she was **gliding poco a poco to misery,** was her mind on other things? There is no way of knowing, no discernible shadow of *her* Breslau in any diary entry, though its shadow may be there in the spaces between words. If so, it could only have been the Breslau of ten years earlier that she sometimes remembered, and not the Soviet occupied post-war city of collapsed buildings, fires, rubble, rape, looting. Apparently pianos were in particular demand by post-war looters in Breslau. There may have been one left behind at Scharnhorststrasse 31. Gerda was probably not thinking of pianos in 1947. Whether she got any news of the destruction of her city is unknown. She had other things to worry about, such as making ends meet, Jacky getting a good job, and placating her landlady through some other means than the Panama Hat she had asked Gunther to send her, and which he had declined to do. If news about Breslau did reach her, what might she have thought? That the German civilians remaining there got what was coming to them? That it was their turn to be evicted, expelled, packed into cattle-wagons?

As for **gliding to misery,** there is evidence to the contrary: a photograph, undated, but probably 1946 or '47, given that she is on holiday and not yet pregnant. This photograph shows her looking happy and slim in swimwear on the beach. Studying it again, I wonder why it stands out from other photos of the post-war period 1945-1951, and decide it is because she looks so relaxed on that sunny beach, her knees together, her head propped against a sun-warmed stone wall. The thick black shoulder-length hair half hides her face, but you can see she is smiling at the camera (held by an invisible husband). I wonder, was she thinking of other beaches?

QUE SERA, SERA

13

LETTER FROM GERDA TO GUNTER

51 Billingdon Road
Oxford
NO DATE (BUT BEFORE 20 JULY, 1947)
(UNSENT DRAFT)

Dear Gunter

As you see I am in Oxford, the famous English university town. Jacky has got a job with Morris Motors here. Oxford is a very nice clean town with plenty of cinemas and nice shops and imposing buildings. We live in lodgings here. The housing problem is very bad in England and you have to take what you can get. Jack and I would love a home of our own, but there is no chance. We even thought of buying a caravan and living like Gypsies by the river. I put in for a house at the town hall but they consider big families first, so we might have to wait another 3 years. I should like to go out and work as I have time on my hands (and there is plenty of work) but there is Chubby the dog. I wish now I wouldn't have got him as he is a constant worry to us and I have to look after him all the time. A baby couldn't be more bother. But I got attached to him and I hate to give him up.

Our landlady is a terrible nagger and makes our life a misery. We are not allowed to have a fire in our bedroom so it's blooming Iceland upstairs. We are allowed to use the kitchen, but she is terribly stingy with the gas and we live chiefly on sandwiches. To have meals out costs such an awful lot of money . . .

LETTER FROM GUNTER

Guayaquil/Ecuador S.A.
Lista de Correos

August 5, 1947

Dear Gerda:

Just this moment I picked up your letter of July 20, '47 and I am mostly glad to have news from you after months of complete silence. It is very satisfactory to read that you are o.k. And of course I have been largely shocked by the communication that you are going to get a baby. I have you still in my mind like the 12 years old school – girl when we walked with a bag of "Borxel" and "Pussy" through the Breslau "Sudpark", and indeed I can't imagine that now you have become 26 years old and probably I will become "uncle". Though your childhood has gone I must pointing to the fact that you have become nicer looking than ever before. Gazing to the foto you included, nearly I got pale seeing you dressed with pants. Hu, Hu, I get mad! Are you not ashamed? I hope that Jacky is going on all right with his job in the famous plant of Morris – Works, and I hope that payment is so good that soon all your wishes will come true and will afford you at least the desired prefab and wireless set.

Now as war has ended and peacetime has restored, awaked my idea to go to the U.S. Already in one of my former letters I pointed to the fact that I got a good affidavit, and by means of it I would find easily entrance to the U.S. Meanwhile also I made an application for immigration. But the trouble is that now I am a little afraid to make a step to U.S.A. because the general situation of employment is not good. Some close friends of mine who showed themselves most happy to have found the chance to go to U.S. now are disappointed and even a great number of them are returning. Here in South America it is very easy to make a living. If I would be finally resolved to U.S. I would take with me only a small unimportant quantity of dollars, because the change in my fortune in "sucres" would be very low. That means that with 36 years of age I would have to start again there. But otherwise there I would find convenient climate conditions and live in a civilized world. I would like to hear your opinion.

Also I made some other efforts. Namely to go to the Argentine. But this seems to be most difficult. I made in the Argentine Legation an application for immigration, pointing to the fact that my brother lives there, but I doubt that I will be successful because the immigration office has got some antisemitic directions.

Now in summertime days are not so unbearable hot like in winter, where I am compelled to go up to my room in Quito. Actually here take place lots of festivals and I have many contracts to strike up the band. I go on playing in the "Costa Rica Swing – Boy – Orchestra" and just I have returned from a round trip to the beach of the Pacific coast where many dance parties took place. These parties not only assist the natives but also Americans and Englishmen who work for the big Oil mines. Sometimes I go to the movie – pictures but not as often as you because here the cinemas have not yet airconditioners. Always when a picture is too sentimental I begin to cry and the spectators begin to laugh about me. You are the same as me, I think, and love the pictures. Are you still the old "Bucherwurm"?

The other day I intended to send you some nice Ecuadorian – made bracelet, but I could not get a permit to send silver goods abroad. So if you make some excursion with your bike don't forget to pass by Ecuador to call for my gift!

Should you have relations to any dance – orchestra please ask for old orchestrated foxtrots or Boogies which we always need in great quantity. Dear Gerda, are you lucky to be married? I am still looking for a girl, but I can't find the victim. Perhaps you can help me to some nice girl with much "brosel" When finished these lines I go to the Conservatorio de musika to teach my silly pupil. What is doing with Ada Oschinsky? Have you still a touch with her?

I got last week a letter from the Jewish Community in Quito asking for some support and funds to reform the cemetery where father is buried. Donkeys are entering the cemetery and it is necessary to provide it with a fence. Should you be able to meet at the disposal of the "Kultus – Gemeinde" some amount, please let me know it. Here again my best thanks for your letter and foto.Let me hear from you as soon as possible. My best regards and kisses, Your brother Gunter.

(*Kultus – Gemeinde* translates as religious community.)

LETTER FROM GERDA TO GUNTER

53 Argyle Street
Oxford
England
15th Sept. 1947

Dear Gunter
I received your letter and was pleased to hear that you are getting on all right. Your English has not improved very much, do you use it a lot or what language do you use most?

I should love you to write me a letter in German some time, as I never get an opportunity of keeping my German up and have nearly forgotten it all. Well I'll be having my baby (if all goes well) on the 23rd of April. I haven't been feeling at all well and was sick all day long. Food made me sick.

I'm afraid I can't send you any money for the cemetery as we have an awful lot of expenses. Things here are dreadfully expensive. We have to get all the baby things and a pram, cot, blankets, an electric fire, an ironing board, an electric kettle, maternity clothes, etc. You won't believe it but a baby costs an awful lot of money. I get quite frightened at times. If we could only get a house. Then we could let rooms to get an extra penny or so and we could keep chickens and a dog. I would so much like a golden retriever. Our landlady is not so keen on my having a baby. I only hope it won't cry too much or dirty too many nappies. Jacky is of course thrilled at becoming a father and he does everything to make me comfortable and happy. Well as soon as baby is big enough I'll send you a photo.

Have you seen any good pictures lately? Tell me all about yourself again. I think I'd stick to Quito if you can stand the climate and make enough money. I sometimes feel I want to be out of England but I might be worse off somewhere else, so I hold on to what I got. It would be nice if you could send your nephew or niece a little present for April but I expect you got too many difficulties.

I take plenty of milk, orange juice, vitamin pills and fruit. So it ought to be an A1 baby, so please wish me luck Gunter. I feel I still need it.

Hope to hear from you soon

Lots of love, Jack and Gerda

LETTERS FROM GUNTHER

Quito/Ecuador S.A.
Calle: Francisco Pizarro 1060.
29 de November 1947
(ONLY FIRST PAGE OF LETTER)

Dear Gerda:

Though your last letter of Sunday July 20th '47 had been answered promptly, not yet I got some further news from you. What is the matter with you that you are absolutely silent? In your last letter you mentioned that soon you will receive a baby, so that I suppose that meanwhile you will have become mother. I would be glad to have your information in this concern. Is your husband Jacky still employed in the Morris Motor works? Are you working too or enjoying the time by hiking in the University Park with the landlady's dog?

As you can see I am living again here up in Quito. This time I must reveal that in the end of October I got immigration – visa for the U.S. What is your opinion, it would be good to go to the U.S? I am a little afraid because friends of mine who are living there are emphasizing the fact that life there is unbearable expensive. It is suggested to me to remain here in South America. Besides of this the change in the Sucre in $ U.S. dollars is very low. In this country I may be considered as a man in good economic position but my immigration to U.S. would mean to start again. I believe I am not skilled enough for the U.S. and perhaps too old. But if I would move there I would doubtless find a chance to help you to some affidavit to follow me with your husband.

Momentaneously I am complying a 3 months contract in the "Derby – Night – Club", playing the piano and the squeeze-box . . .

Gunther Lynn,
3119 Beechwood Boulevard
Squirrel Hill
Pittsburgh/Pa
May 3, 1948
(ONLY FIRST PAGE OF LETTER)

Dear Gerda:

Just coming home from my daily work I was surprised by your announcement of the arrival of a baby – girl. I am mostly glad to have become uncle and I guess that my niece looks nice and probably has blue eyes. I hope that some day we will meet and there will be given a chance to me to admire her.

I always had the desire to write more comfortable but my new experiences here and by much distraction I found no chance. Here in the nice place where I am living 3 radios are playing and the two daughters of my landlady like it to have noisy here, every minute rings the telephone, and furthermore I have to take part in the house parties playing the piano – accordion and dancing jitter – bug.

You wrote me it would be "unwise" to go to the U.S. You are right. I feel it. But the last years in South America I had much health trouble, liver – sick by heat and too thin air. After each meal I was vomiting, my body swelled and other diseases I had to complain. A medical doctor suggested to me to go to a cold climate, and so I did. I went to Pittsbugh because it is a very industrious city . . .

LETTER TO GERDA
(ONLY FIRST PAGE OF LETTER, WRITER UNKNOWN)

27, St. John's Road
Orpington, Kent
10th May 1948

My dear Gerda,

I was so pleased to have your letter this morning and to know that you are getting strong again.
It's a pity you had such a bad time but you will soon forget about that when the little discomforts have gone. I had stitches too so I know how uncomfortable it can be. You, must have patience and plenty of rest and you will soon be yourself again. Actually you will probably be even better than before. What a good thing Jacky is so helpful – it makes all the difference I know.
I am sorry and rather angry to think they did not take better care of your nipples. I know how painful they can be. I used to get some stuff from Boots which kept them soft and yet firm at the same time. It is made of two things but I can't remember what it is called. However, if you asked for it and told them what it is for I'm sure they would know. It was very soothing...

PART OF LETTER FROM GUNTHER
(FIRST AND LAST PAGE(S) MISSING)

NO ADDRESS, BUT MUST BE PITTSBURGH.
UNDATED, BUT MUST BE AFTER 3 MAY, 1948:

... I have found a steady job as caps – blocker in the Penn – State – Caps Co. My salary is only $25 for 40 hours week. I have

additional income making music at weddings. I am making a living but I must change my room. I will move now down – town. It takes about an hour with the street – car, and fare is expensive, each ride 10 cents. Yes, I am a "stingy" guy and here I will safe up against depressions. Also here I would still find a chance to get married, and I would hurry up to become father like my little sister has become mother. Still I can't believe that little Gerda who got always a "Prugler" in the "Sud – Park" now has become mother.

Now I will close up sending you my best congratulations to the happy event. If you would be here you may be assured that we would commit celebrating this event with a fine bottle of brandy, beer and lots of "borxel". Here again I am shouting across the ocean . . .

(There's that *Prugler* again, to which little Gerda was apparently quite accustomed.)

His letter of 29th November 1947 confirms it: Gunther obtained his immigration visa for the USA in October, and by May 1948 he was settled in Squirrel Hill, Pittsburgh and enjoying the peace and noise of his new home. And his name has changed as well as his country. At one time, when the world was a different place, he sometimes signed his letters with the additional middle name "Israel" inserted with ironic inverted commas. For that addition to himself he had the Third Reich to thank. There is now a silent "h" in his first name, Gunter becoming Gunther. As I had not previously imagined Gunther existing before the Pittsburgh-Pennsylvania years, *Gunter* (with an umlaut) or Guenter (as it was also spelled) was foreign to me. And I had never known him as a Lewinsohn. As a mark of his entry into the country of the self-made man, he discarded *Lewinsohn*, or rather compressed it to *Lynn*. In his letters from this period I find no commentary on this change, no mention of it, as if it came courtesy of his immigration visa: *Now that you are here, Herr Lewinsohn, let us unburden you of your name.* Another surmise: back in the US, he wanted his surname to take up less space, attract less notice. *Lewinsohn* was too German, or too Jewish. Whatever the reasons for the name-change, he has evidently arrived at his final destination. South America was all right, he made a good living, he was a man *in good economic position*; but it was too hot there, the air too thin, the cinemas lacked air conditioning, his liver and body were swelling, he was vomiting after every meal. He needed to emigrate to a *civilized* country. The USA had taken him in before, in 1938, but then it had not wanted to keep him. Now he was in for good.

His was not the only arrival to celebrate in 1947: his little sister was to be a mother, and he an uncle. On first getting news of her pregnancy, he is *largely shocked*, remembering her as *the 12 years old school girl* who walked with him through the Breslau *Sudpark*, with *Borxell* and *Pussy* (whatever they were) trying to avoid his *Prugler*. As previously noted, this is not the first time he has mentioned the *Prugler* (which springs to mind whenever he thinks of girls and young women) and it won't be the last, but he invariably brandishes it with good humour. His nostalgic remembrance of the *Sudpark* also reminds me of something: this could be the park in *Breslau–Sud* (Breslau–South) visited by Elkan through 1939, along with other Jews, to hand in their forms to the Financial Office which had been set up there specifically for the purpose, so that they might put questions and seek guidance concerning assets and contributions to the *atonement penalty* required of Jews.. It was the same park where, in February 1945, the old men and the Hitler Youth of the Volkssturm battalion attacked Red Army positions. But in August 1947 *Gunter* (not yet *Gunther*) remembered *Sudpark* differently, and he remembered his sister differently as just a *12 years old school girl* in 1933. Although pregnancy is good news – and she is *nicer looking than ever before* (Gerda would have read that with pleasure) – her *childhood has gone.*

But I cannot let the moment pass without further comment. Gunther considered emigrating to Argentina, referring in his application to *the fact that my brother lives there* – but neglecting to mention that there had been no contact between them since before the war. It is noticeable that he can't bring himself to refer to Kurt by name. There is more that might be noteworthy at this point, such as his excited response to the photograph of his sister *dressed in pants (Hu, Hu, I get mad!),* or on the *Prugler* he so likes to swing in his letters. Actually, I find his reference to Gerda as a "Bucherwurm" more interesting. It is not the first time he has called her that. I never thought of her as a *bookworm* – unless popular women's magazines of the 1950s and '60s, of which she had stacks and stacks, count as books.

One other thing: in his letter of 29th November 1947, he referred to her *last letter* of July 20th. Had he not then received her letter of 15th September in which she announced the expected birth date? *You are absolutely silent*, he complained. It may be a case of transatlantic letters getting lost in the distances. Most likely it was never sent. Indeed, how could it have been sent if I have just read it?

Gerda's letters are the missing ones. In a letter dated February 1949, Gunther opens by referring to his previous letter of December 12th 1948, which *came back with the mark, Gone Away, undelivered, not known.* Much to his relief he then received her letter of 7th January 1949, *by which I learned that you are doing all right.*

Of course I am a little disappointed because you are moving around and it leaves the impression as if now you would live in some distress. What is the idea to live in a hut without bathroom in the neighbourhood of "filthy people"? I guess that at least the "Kinderchen" should have helped you to some comfortable housing!

So there they are again – the missing diamonds, here referred to as *Kinderchen* – five years after her bold confession that not a "Brosel" is left of them. His February letter continues: *Dear sister, you always made your own decisions in your life, neither you paid attention to my opinion or suggestions nor you cared for your daddy who loved you so much. Your husband is earning some money and you perhaps too, why do you not live like a – Mensch???*

And there I pause and ponder. That word *Mensch* (person). So what was Gunther actually saying to his sister the year after the birth of her first baby? That she is not living like a person, a human being, because a respectable young woman with her background would never *live in a hut without bathroom in the neighbourhood of filthy people,* and that to do so risks becoming "untermenschen", subhuman. I notice too the sly way he brings up the diamonds. Even then he's not quite done. There is this further observation: *Nearly I forgot that you are 26 years old, just old enough to know how to behave!* Evidently he forgot that in February 1949 she was actually twenty-seven.

Re-reading what remains of this letter (only the first page, which ends with the unfinished line, *I am surprised that...*) I am reminded of an earlier letter, and after again picking through the unsorted heap in front of me I find it: 2nd November 1945. It was then that he referred to a 1932 novel by Hans Fallada, *Little Man, What Now?* That is the question Gunter heard on *every sheet* of his sister's letter of 20th September 1945, visualising her (from her own description) as *down to the knees and not fit to do anything.* When I first came upon this literary reference, I didn't know that it was a novel by Hans Fallada, or that it was first published in Germany as *Kleiner Mann – was nun?*, or that it was a best-seller with two films of that title out within two years, or that Fallada was imprisoned in 1933 for anti-Nazi activities and in 1935 declared an "undesirable author" by Nazi authorities. I did not discover any of this until much later, but now – having since read the novel – I see what Gunther was getting at. The Lewinsohns were a successful business family. In fact, Elkan Lewinsohn owned the kind of business (Gentlemen's Outfitters) that employs the salesman, Pinneberg, the powerless *little man* of the story, who knows he is a *nothing* but can do nothing about it, and who sinks – with his *Lammchen* of a wife and their little *Shrimp* of an infant – to the level to which Gerda appeared to be sinking at the end of the war. Gunther's reference to Fallada's famous novel was therefore a warning to his sister: *Remember who you used to be. Don't sink.*

There is no evidence that Gerda heeded his advice, then or later, though the further warning, in his letter of February 1949, that living as she did risked her becoming *untermenschen*, subhuman, must have upset her to judge by her subsequent silence. Gunther's next letter (undated) begins by expressing astonishment that he has had nothing from her for almost half a year:

Peter Thornthwaite

LETTER FROM GUNTHER

Gunther – H. Lynn
404 Jackson Street
Pittsburgh 12/ PA
? 1949

USA

Dear Sister Gerda:

I am very astonished that almost half a year I could not receive any news from you. What has happened, or what the idea that you are "eingeschnappt"? The other day I sent you a comfortable letter which remained unanswered. How are you and Jacky coming along, how is doing your daughter?? Are you at good health and making good "Brosels"? I just take a look again at the nice picture you sent me months ago. On backside is written: "Jacky build that little porch to stop the draughts". I hope that your winter was not as tough as mine, but now spring feelings are warming me again and I am looking round for a girl friend to have more pleasant time!

The last 6 months in Pittsburgh have been many strikes, esp steel and coal idled thousands here, but I am still the slave of H.J. Heinz Co without interruption. Also in music I keep going. Recently I participated in a Radio contest and won $25 as best accordion-player! Ah, Goldbrosel in schone Dollars machen mich ja so glucklich! Saturdays I play organ in a beautiful saloon, and I wished you would see to your brother surrounded by nice people applauding him.

I guess it was a good inspiration to go away from the tropics to this country with a European climate. But many newcomers are here disappointed in Pittsburgh because life is too tough and the city too dirty and smoky. Many come from Ireland and England. My close friends in Los Angeles/California are mad

223

that I don't join them there. Former friend of father, Mr. Wolff, restaurant owner, arrived in Los Angeles. Another good friend from Quito, Mr. Sachs, will come there in June. Mr. Sachs is always teasing me. He emphasized that in Breslau when I came to his house with the little Opel to collect the money for a cleaned hat, I accepted 20 Pfennig tip to put it on savings account.

How do you enjoy life in your hut and what is new? Do you possess your own furniture? How is doing your little daughter? Does she get a Prugler once a while?

Did you hear anything about Kurt, your lovely brother, and find where he is hidden? Is he alife at all? You know Kurt always had something strange in his mind regarding politics. Maybe he has become a victim of some agitation?

It is quite possible that in few months I get married. Hu, Hu, ich werde verruckt! I am getting crazy. Well, that is all for today.

My best regards for you and Jacky and daughter

In love and with sweet kisses(Hu, ich werde ganz rot im Gesicht)

Your "guter" brother Gunther

(1000 kisses – hu, hu, ich kriege eine Fausehaut!)

Which translates (his last words after *1000 kisses*) as: I am getting pimples. Goose-bumps, I suppose he means, ie what a brother gets when he thinks of his sister in that way, as well as getting all red in the face. Is he lavishing her with affection, sensing that he has previously offended, even hurt her? *Eingeschnappt* initially translates as snapped, but he can't mean that exactly, more that she is cross with him, peeved, sulky. Now he merely asks: *How do you enjoy life in your hut?* A genuine inquiry. No insinuation there of degradation. And he pleasantly inquires after her little daughter as to whether she gets the *Prugler once a while*. Gunther is always in a good and placating mood when he thinks of the *Prugler*.

Gerda did not need Gunther to carefully avoid mentioning that she had fallen among the *filthy people* in the camp of Nissen huts in countryside outside Oxford. For her and her new post-war family, this was the beginning of a time in her life far more degrading than her domestic service in S.E. 15 in 1939. Within ten years of fleeing Germany, she would find herself among what she described (in a diary entry) as **the poor and the proletariat,** and what could be worse than that? Gerda, quite as much as Gunther, no doubt considered a Nissen hut dreadfully *common*, though it was less the hut itself than the kind of people accommodated in such camps that she feared – ie all her neighbours. Those ex-military, prefabricated half-cylindrical corrugated iron huts were utilised as family accommodation, and for her it was an improvement on single room lodgings in Oxford – especially after giving birth to a daughter against her landlady's objections. It meant more living space, with a garden for chickens, though I have just read that these iron huts provided less usable space than at first appeared, as it was difficult to fit angled furniture into a house with rounded walls. It also meant countryside, though that was less a blessing than a burden, as it was a long bus ride into town and an even longer bicycle ride to the factory for Jack. And countryside meant mud throughout the camp, which might explain Gunther's description of the people living there as *filthy*.

Those years, from 1948 to 1955, were the *Nissen hut* years. Shameful though they were (to her, to Gunther) there is much photographic evidence of them in her albums. I must admit that she does not look her best there with her black hair tangled as barbed wire, and no smile. She is not in the photograph in front of me now (though her existence is implied by the big black old-fashioned pram outside the front door); that must be Jack looking out of the window, a diminutive Jack viewed from a distance. It is unusual to see him at all in these family photographs, since he was the one taking them. Expanding the image on my phone only further blurs his face, but it could only be him looking out of the open window of a rounded Nissen hut which looks like a hobbit house. Below the face in the window is a tin coal bin and next to that a tin dustbin, and what appears to be earth or rubbish piled up against the white painted hut wall. When enlarged, the white number 10 can be made out on the black painted front door.

But the *Nissen hut* years could not have been as bad as I once supposed, as evidenced by Gunther's next letter fragment (final page(s) missing):

Peter Thornthwaite

LETTER FROM GUNTHER

GUNTHER H. LYNN
404 Jackson St
Pittsburgh 12/PA
U.S.A.
May 22, 1949

My dear Sister (ein Kusschen first!):

Probably you will be very disappointed that your last comfortable letter had not been answered yet. My new job and other additional work keeps me so busy that scarcely I have time to sit down for writing.

I was pleased to find in your last letter lots of beautiful pictures of your family. I always glance again at them and sent already one of them to friends in Los Angeles. It makes me proud to have such a nice sister, always smiling, and a good looking brother in law. And my little niece, how cute she looks. I guess she must have blond curly hair and blue eyes? I am right?

I am glad to read that you feel all right in your "hut" and actually have no reason to complain.

Now to tell you that by slowing down the production at Heinz Co I got laid off, but then the private secretary of Mr. Heinz asked me to work as a gardener, so now I am working in his garden in wonderful surroundings! After quitting time at 4.30pm I teach my numerous pupils, and at weekends my squeeze-box keeps me pretty busy. I guess it was a good idea to leave South America. Pittsburgh is named "the dirty city", but I feel pretty good here. It is a shame that I don't have a girl friend yet. Frequently I have the desire to give a kiss to some nice girl (hu, hu, ich werde verruckt!) I am getting old and it is time now to get married. Besides of this I need somebody to give a Prugler! . . .

There is this further partial letter (first and last page(s) missing), undated, but written sometime after her birthday in June:

. . . Is the hut you occupy your own property? If so, then it makes me proud to have a "wealthy" sister. Even poultry you keep there. Probably you will do some gardening, like I do.

Delayed but cordially I remit you my congratulation for your 28th birthday. I hope you celebrated by having a delicious chicken dinner and as desert "Erdbeeren mit frischen Schlagsahne" Huh, das Wasser lauft mir im Munde zusammen. My mouth is watering!

How do you judge the very critical situation in Korea? Though until now nobody paid too much attention, today I heard much talking about it. I am depressed that again we have to look at the monster of war. As displaced person still I have in mind those days of fear, days of concentration camps and persecution, and now again the outlook for the next future makes me fear.

From time to time I take a look in a published paper from New York, in German language, to find out whether anything is mentioned about the fate of Kurt.

Get you enough food and stuff to buy? Here the grocery and department stores offer a wonderful choice, and I wish you and Jacky would live here to be a witness of this.

What are you doing for fun? Go you to movies? Once a while I go to see news-reel picture with some Mickey Mouse films.. Also I enjoy it to pay visits to the typical American amusement centres, with wild horses from Texas, racing, scooters, etc. Oh, and there I have lots of fun eating Pop-corn, milk-shakes and frozen custard.

Dear Sister, auf den beiliegenden Bildern siehst Du zunachst den beruhmten Accordion teacher Gunther Lynn instructing little Bobby, 12 years old, whose father is foreman at Carnegie Steel Corps . . .

This last line, if I translate it correctly, directs her to the photographs enclosed, one of which shows her brother, *the famous Accordion teacher Gunther Lynn instructing little Bobby*. I don't know what opportunities Gerda had, in her mud camp of corrugated iron huts, to get away to amusement centres, marvel at wild horses from Texas, eat popcorn and custard, etc, but life couldn't have been too bad if her brother is correct about her birthday celebrations including roast chicken, strawberries and fresh whipped cream.

One further undated fragment of a letter has appeared. It seems to be from the early Pittsburgh period, as there is a reference again to his good fortune in having left "the tropics". It is evident from its tone that Gunther is still feeling unsettled following the move – which may explain why he appears to be having a go at Gerda:

Finally, dear sister, I have to reproach you that nothing you had contributed to the expenses of father's sickness and not yet you have given me explication what happened with the "kinderchen". I worried much all the after time that my request for a little contribution for the settlement of father's hospital bills had absolutely been ignored by you and it gave me reason enough to show you the cold shoulder. Neither I received a formal invitation to your wedding. Last, not least, not even a congratulation to my citizenship! But let forget about this! Since I wear woollen underwear my aches have disappeared completely . . .

Well, Gunther is not getting away with that. As previously noted, Gerda did provide an *explication* of what happened to the diamonds: **As for the so-called "goods" Tatta managed to give me, there isn't a Brosel left – because I was in need of it and I couldn't get one eighth of its real value, so**

I'm afraid you've had it. That was in her letter of 15th June 1944. Admittedly it was an unsent draft letter, but she must have sent him some letter around that time as his reply of 18th August 1944 refers to her communication: *Already almost 3 months have past that I received your nice letter.* Yet in subsequent correspondence there is never any acknowledgement of her previous explanation. Then suddenly I understand what must have happened. Gerda did write to Gunther in May or June 1944, but the actual letter she sent made no mention of the diamonds. Had she done so, it is unlikely that an incensed Gunther would have acknowledged her *nice letter.*

Confrontation was not her way, and probably she hoped that Gunther would eventually forget about the *Kinderchen.* Fat chance of that. As he would write in a later letter: *the Elephant never forgets.* As for his accusation that he never got from her *a congratulation to my citizenship,* it might not have occurred to her that congratulations were called for.

14

Hut 10 Site 5 Chalgrove Oxford
24th May 1949

I am now 27 years old, nearly 28. Jacky is on Night work and earns good money, but we had so many expenses lately, so had no chance to save up. But we got about everything now so I think we ought to start saving now. But we are still paying our furniture off, there is still another £40 to pay. It seems a lot of money. Wish I hadn't lost my diamonds. I still dream about them an awful lot. I don't think I'll be ever able to forget about them.

The first year was an awful trial and I have decided to have no more babies. It's too much trouble. Please dear God keep her safe and well and healthy. Be good to her. My next door neighbour is Mrs. Docherty. We don't talk. I started it. It's a long story. We were once good friends. But she wanted to rule my life for me. Then she told me my nappies wanted boiling. Well I thought that was about the limit. She is too anxious to tell people their business. I used to like her and she's got her good points but it's fini-now. Then I was friends with Mrs. Smith. I got tired of her too. She is now friends with Docherty. Our other two neighbors are a filthy couple, and a very noisy big-mouthed couple who are jealous of our bit of wire netting. Well a nice crowd I must say. I don't want to fight with anyone, but people are so difficult to live with. I seem to be always in trouble. But I keep on fighting.

LOOSE NOTE BY GERDA, UNDATED

Jacky, I want you to take the gate down completely. It doesn't work out at all. Both neighbours went for me last night. I told Thomson to argue it out with you. She said something like, "Damn your husband". Mrs. Next Door was too scared to take her bike through. I gave everybody dirty looks who came through. Thomson said, "We've been much too good to you. There isn't any room for Malcolm to play". Bobby was very spiteful too. Local girl. Mischiefmaker.

It's not worth it.

LETTERS FROM GUNTHER (LAST PAGE(S) MISSING)

Gunther H. Lynn,
404 Jackson Street
Pittsburgh/PA

October 13, 1949

Dear Gerda:

You almost will believe that I'm dead because your comfortable letter of May 29 had not been answered yet. In fact thrilling life in the U.S. offers so many distractions that I forget to write!

I am glad to see that you are getting on all right in spite of the most troublesome economic situation in England which actually form headlines in American newspaper. I can proudly point to the fact that here the average standard of living is the highest in the world. Nothing is subsidized or restricted. In the contrary, you would be astonished to see the big choice of goods offered everywhere. Of course Uncle Sam hangs the grapes very, very high, and who wants to reach them has to work "like hell".

Now is worthwhile to buy a car. Originally I thought to buy a little Jeep, but friends of mine told me to buy a bigger car like Chevrolet, Ford or Plymouth. Besides it was told to me that my girl friend would not like to ride on a Jeep.

I am corresponding with close friends in Chicago, Los Angeles and Ecuador. By the horrible earthquake situation in Ecuador, it has become nearly unbearable there and I can give thanks to God that I have settled in U.S.A.

I am very glad that your little daughter made her first steps. Soon she will run around to find out where "the rich uncle of America is hidden" . . .

Gunther H. Lynn
404 Jackson Street
Pittsburgh 12/PA
U.S.A.

July 16, 1950

My dear Sister:

Just back from the swimming pool where I cooled off a little from the heat wave. Today I will take opportunity to answer letters, and of course I will pay attention to your last letter from a couple of months ago.

You know here in U.S.A. I have to keep moving all the time to make a decent living, and with regard to the fact that I am not owner of a car I always arrive home lately to some advanced hours. Yes, your stingy brother namely hopes that you will give him an automobile for nothing! You should support a little your "poor Bruderchen".

This time I have not to tell any kind of "exciting" or "thrilling" news like the other day where I wrote that I will get married pretty soon. Ha, ha, I only was kidding! I guess I will be condemned to remain an unlucky bachelor. I am disappointed failing to find among American – born girls somebody who would fit me. A great part of women drink "Schnapps" and smoke cigarettes in mass. They play cards, eat chewing gum, and like to sit in night-clubs. If I would get married with such type of women, she would get "Pruglers" every day.

I must confess that in spite I am invited everywhere, not yet I have a circle of close friends like I had in Quito. Life here is pretty rough. In the factory I work much, I eat with haste in some cafeteria, and then I fall like dead in my bed. I have fun by eating some chocolate or ice-cream. My friends in Los Angeles are always teasing me because they know me as big sweet – tooth!

I am still the old slave of Heinz. Some threatening strike and new job classification brought a boost in wages for about $1.30 an hour. Once a while when I am supposed to operate a crane with attached dumper, this promotes me to higher classification. Mostly it is my duty to work on conveyors and pull baskets with caned goods to the labelling machines operated by girls who earn about $1.02 an hour.

I was not successful yet in finding more refined position . . .

FROM GERDA'S DIARY

Hut 10 Site 5 Chalgrove
Oxford
Jan the 3rd, 1951

I should so much like to have a lot of nice friends and be popular with everybody. I did have six friends in this camp but have fallen out with all of them. I feel an outsider, not belonging anywhere. I do wish something nice would happen, or we would win or get left a lot of money. Please dear God let something nice happen.

Thursday the 4th January 51

Another dull and slow day is over. Nothing happened. Jack won 2/- on the football pool. I wish it was £2000. I got a cold and my back tooth bothers me. I think it might have to come out. I still haven't got any nice friends. Penny from next door was here nearly all day. Quite a nice little girl but she talks common and has very common parents. Her mother had her by an American before she was married. I am still looking forward to my baby but am scared of all the work, worry and trouble. But it is such a dull life, anything to make a change. Hope I am going to be lucky and it will be normal in every direction. Hope my cold is soon better. Just now I have a big fat tummy. It's too nasty to go out. I hate wind, it always gives me tooth and ear ache. I am going to bed presently. It is about 6 and Jacky will be off to work in a minute. Pressed Steel night work. He gets about £10 a week. Very good money really. But we never seem to get anywhere. If I could only win some money. It would give me great pleasure. But how many people want the same? It seems funny to think I should never fall in love again or there should never be any romance in my life. But I expect I had my share. Gunther still writes to me but he is a dreadful old miser. Wish he'd leave me some money some day though.

Saturday the 6th Jan, 1951

I scratched myself in the face with my fingernail and look a sight. I get older and uglier looking every day.

Wednesday the 10th Jan, 1951

I seem to get more and more buried in misery. Jacky gets on my nerves and the less I see of him the better. Everybody and everything seems to have turned against me as if I have done a crime. Why am I so completely friendless and people ignore me and turn the other way when they see me? There must be a reason! I mustn't let go, I must hold on. If I could only be content with my quiet uneventful life. If I think I'd have to stay here for more years I'd go barmy.

Monday the 15th Jan, 1951

I went to Oxford with the bus and first talked to Mrs. Docherty. Two people gave Rachel a smile and greeting, but they always ignore me and hardly ever say hello. What is the matter with me? Is it because I am a foreigner, or is it me? It was the same in the ATS. I felt left out of it and the girls treated me as if I was poison. Dear God can't you help me. Please help me to keep going. Give me some nice friends.

Tuesday the 16th Jan, 1951

Well I am definitely trying for a baby again. How often will I change my mind about it? I have changed it already 100 times. I am dead scared of all the pain and inconveniences again. After all I got lots of time to myself now. But I am not happy or at peace. If only we could move from here. Why can't we win some money? I hope I won't be too sick with the baby.

Wednesday the 17th Jan, 1951

In the morning we had another heated discussion about Australia. We have decided not to go but have another baby. I hope it won't be a miscarriage.

Thursday the 25th Jan, 1951

I am dreadfully annoyed about the dog next door (Penny's people). Yap Yap Yap all night long before their door and the blasted people won't let him in. They are the most ignorant and inconsiderate people. If I should have a baby that dog would drive me barmy. In fact I was quite against a baby all day because of it. I've taken that puppy next door in our hut, it's better than that constant barking. I just feel frightfully restless and unsatisfied and am looking for a miracle. If we could only win some money. I should like to get on in the world. Every day I see the same blooming old silly faces. Mrs. Docherty seems very hostile lately. I have to be careful. I don't want any trouble her way. She begrudges me any friends, always tries either to belittle them or snatch them away. I am sick to be always among the poor and the proletariat.

LETTERS FROM GUNTHER

FRAGMENT OF LETTER
UNDATED: POSSIBLY EARLY 1951 (OR EARLIER?)

. . . How did you enjoy the movie "Snake Pit"? Meanwhile I saw the film "House of Strangers". Edward G. Robinson. You should see the picture, it will remind you of your parents-house. Movies got a new competitor – television. You find it here now in every place, specially bars and restaurants keep big screens for entertainment and stimulate people to drink – viel Schnapps. My boss of the restaurant where I play bought a big Zenith television set and I hope he will not fire me! Besides of "separating pickles from cucumbers" in the factory, music keeps me pretty busy. Last week I played for a Jewish wedding.

I enjoy very much the pictures you sent me of my niece, her nice curly hair and how cute and lovely she smiles. Particularly my friend in Los Angeles, Dr. Brucker, who was in Breslau once like us, enjoys the pictures.

Here in Pittsburgh live quite a whole lot of Breslauer, even people who worked for Schonfeld & Co, and last not least in this neighbourhood lives (name illegible) whom you know pretty well in days of childhood.

Meanwhile my health has improved a lot in spite of the cold since I wear in winter my woollen underwear to help the penetrating ache of arthritis . . .

Gunther H. Lynn
4041 Murray Ave.
Pittsburgh 17/PA.
U.S.A.

September 30, 1951

My dear Sister Gerda:
About 8 months ago I received your last interesting letter and it is a shame that I did not drop you an answer. Not only you would have reason to complain about my reckless silence, but my closest friends too. My strenuous life here, the heat waves, the rush and daily struggle take away the appetite to write letters. Right now I have not the slightest idea how you are coming along, but I guess everything is OK or I would have heard.

Regarding me, I am glad to tell you that everything is just fine. Still I keep on at the food-processing factory and also with my music business in spare time. Meanwhile I found a nice chance to join some musical – combo as accordionist. It is a 4 piece polka and jazz orchestra band established here for years. We get engagements, mostly picnics, weddings, parties, and clubs, and provide A1 music. Of course we cannot compare with Guy Lombardo or Woody Herman, but we get a nice kick out of it.

My gosh, I'm just thinking that in June you became 30 years old. Hoo, ich werde verruckt! And I will become pretty soon 40 years. I have turned into an old stupid bachelor, but still I have hope to find a wife. The first day after the wedding she would have to expect a Prugler!

My friends here always are teasing because I did not buy an automobile yet, necessity No. 1 in this country. They all say that I would be too stingy to draw some money from the bank for such purpose. Would you join their opinion?

Have you realized your idea to buy a motorcycle? Be careful! On one single day yesterday we had here in Pennsylvania 190 persons dead on account of traffic accidents. There is no doubt that a motorcycle is twice as much dangerous than an automobile. I hope that Jacky and you changed their mind in this regard.

What about a visit here to Pittsburgh? You will enjoy it to see your lovely brother again before he wears a white whiskers. Please write at me without delay.
Your old brother Gunther

Zenith television sets were first sold commercially in the USA in 1948, so Gunther's reference to one in the fragment of the letter above – plus the two films mentioned (*The Snake Pit*, released November 1948) and (*House of Strangers*, in July 1949) – prove that it was written some time after the summer of 1949. Then there is the reference to his niece as having *nice curly hair and how cute she smiles in the pictures you sent me*. Finally, there is the reference to his woollen underwear (to which, as I recall, he draws attention in other letters) and the *penetrating ache of arthritis*. This must be winter. As for the films, *The Snake Pit* concerns a woman who finds herself in an insane asylum and cannot remember how she got there. *House of Strangers* follows a family held together by hate and (as Gunther informs her) *will remind you of your parents-house.*

Not for the first time I reflect how doors to an inaccessible past appear where you least suspect them. That film, unknown to me until now, but which I could order from Amazon today, is a way back to Scharnhorststrasse 31, Breslau, if that is the house Gunther had in mind. *It is all there on film.*

And as a matter of fact that's what happened – I ordered it from Amazon. It seems you can get almost anything off the internet these days, including intimate family history. *House of Strangers* is not an exact representation of Scharnhorststrasse 31, but I take Gunther's word for it resembling the old parental house. Whether Gerda subsequently saw the film, and remembered how things used to be, is not recorded, but those lit chandeliers and glowing lamps, those great branched candelabras and cherubs holding up single candlesticks, and those darkened vast rooms stuffed with massive dark wood furniture, the heightened shadows of bannisters on the papered wall – did they take her back?

Watching *House of Strangers*, it was almost as if Gunther was sitting next to me (just a little too close for comfort), pointing out this and that to his nephew. *Look at the old world décor, boy, that was how it used to be, but not so dark. None of that fancy film noir chiaroscuro. It was light, more light than dark. Such a shame you'll never see it as it was.*

Gunther – and this is one of the things I like about him, and dislike about his sister for lacking it – was nostalgic. Though, by the end of the war, he had put Europe and the old world behind him, every so often he couldn't help going back. Probably he was remembering his own father when he saw *House of Strangers*, and the loyal role he himself – he alone – had played. Gunther had something to be proud of. Kurt had nothing. Gerda had nothing.

Something in the later letter takes me back, too – its date, 30th September 1951. When he writes of his *strenuous life* in Pittsburgh, its *rush and daily struggle*, and admits having *not the slightest idea how you are coming along*, he is obviously unaware that his little sister was at that very moment giving birth to twins. Maybe it wasn't that exact moment, and allowance must be made for the time difference between Oxford and Pittsburgh, but certainly that was the day I was born.

The date has a wider significance too, being the last day of *The Festival of Britain*. Indeed I have a commemorative tie, not one of my favourites (a guardsman in a red tunic with raised sabre astride a grey horse against a wide maroon background) but the narrow end proclaims *Festival of Britain 1951,* and it still hangs, unworn, with the rest of my obsolete vintage tie collection. I don't know if whoever wore it in 1951 had only to look down his front to be reminded of the bright colours of the Festival. I have read that many people then, still in their demob clothes, saw the Dome, the Skylon and the fountains as an escape from the ubiquitous grey of post-war Britain.

If pregnant Gerda witnessed the rebuilding of Britain between May and September 1951, there is no written reference to it in diaries or letters. Britain was for her a hobbit-like hut with a corrugated iron roof in wet countryside a long bus ride from Oxford. Still, for all I know, she visited the South Bank that summer, and looked across the Thames at the lights and colours, the olives, scarlets, yellows and blues of the Festival streaking the river, and shared in the optimism and euphoria, the promise of future happiness visible in the twenty-two pavilions celebrating Britain and its citizens. It is unlikely. Yet some of the South Bank wall slogans might have reached her – those to do with every home demanding space, and space being limited and costly in this crowded country, and every housewife and mother wanting more.

Due to a shortage of conventional building materials such as bricks and slates, designers made use of steel and glass for the temporary pavilions that, by the end, had to be smashed and removed. Something similar was happening in Wroclaw. Rather than rebuild the city, it was looted for bricks for the reconstruction of Warsaw – bricks not just from rubble but from intact buildings. In 1951, the bricks collected in that way amounted to 165 million. Whether news of this reached a Nissen hut in Chalgrove is unknown. Breslau was no doubt far from Gerda's thoughts then – further even than the South Bank. I have read of a *systematic reign of terror* in Stalinist Wroclaw, its jails full of political prisoners, but as can be seen from Gerda's diary entries at this time, she was more concerned about the reign of terror organised by her neighbours and heralded by the constant barking – **Yap Yap Yap all night long** – of the puppy next door.

As for Gunther, things were looking up. Things were usually looking up for Gunther – despite factory *slave* work, filthy winter in the steel city, penetrating arthritis, and the absence of a wife to beat with a *Prugle*r. For Gunther on 30th September 1951 (while Gerda was splitting with twins) *everything is just fine*. He has his accordion, his polka and jazz band, his ice-cream, his chocolate (*big sweet tooth* that he is to his friends). He has his visions of American women drinking schnapps, smoking cigarettes, chewing gum, playing cards, and sitting in night-clubs, and his mental picture of the *Prugler* they deserve and he would so love to give them. It is not a bad life for an immigrant with a German accent, now American citizen.

Until this moment in my investigations no evidence had come to light of Gunther actually informing Gerda of his American citizenship. As already noted, in one letter he indignantly referred to having done so in previous correspondence. Now another partial letter has emerged from the pile, in which he does exactly that: *I am proud to tell you that 4 months ago I have become Citizen of the U.S.A. I look at my citizenship paper, singing the actual smash hit: Little things mean a lot!* As the first and last page(s) are missing, this truncated letter is undated, but a little detective work reveals something surprising: *Little Things Mean A Lot* was a "No 1 hit" by Kitty Kallen in 1954. Which suggests Gunther did not obtain US citizenship until six years after emigrating from Ecuador. Much later than I had supposed.

So that previous undated letter, reproaching her for not congratulating him on his citizenship, must be out of narrative sequence. It is not from the "early Pittsburgh period", as I had initially supposed, but from a later period – the mid 1950s.

As for the song he was moved to croon on receiving his citizenship paper, irony is surely implied in that Gunther hardly regarded US citizenship as a *little thing*. Looking more closely at the lyrics (thanks, internet) I'm struck by their relevance, as in: *"A line a day when you're far away/Little things mean a lot"*. And then there are these lines: *"Don't have to buy me diamonds and pearls. . . I never cared much for diamonds and pearls . . . Show me you haven't forgot . . ."*

15

LETTERS FROM GUNTHER

Gunther H. Lynn
5844 Beacon St.
PGH. 17/ PA.
U.S.A.

August 26, 1954
LAST PAGE(S) MISSING

Dear Sister Gerda:

After marvellous days of vacationing in Atlantic City summer resort, I am back again in Pittsburgh, the Iron City. Having your lines of August 20th I am really pleased to read that you are all doing fine.

I beg to apologize that I had overseen to congratulate you to the arrival of twins and your great blessing of children. In the last months I was distracted heavily by my own worries, namely my health was shattered by enlarged prostrate glands and arthritis. Now again I am in tip – top shape.

After reading your nice and clean shaped letter I am really proud to have a lovely sister and decent relatives in Europe.

My goodness, already you're 33 and I myself 42. Do you remember when you was "sweet sixteen" and we went with

Tatzel, Tante Bertha, and Pussy in the "Lotte – car" to the Zoblen – Mountain? It is said that after 30 start the best years of our life. I see that you are going to improve your beauty by having removed moles, and probably still using "Schonheitscreme" (Ha, ha, ha).

I am glad to read that Jacky sticks at Pressed Steel. Here I must confess that the general situation is not so good. Numerous strikes are spreading. A prolonged street car strike forced me to buy an automobile. Poor Gunther had to draw $600 for a 1949 Chevrolet Coupe De Luxe. If you and Jacky would be here, I would drive you to all interesting points and you would be convinced very soon that this country is . . .

5844 Beacon St
Pittsburgh 17/ PA
U.S.A.

November 8, 1954
(FIRST TWO PAGES)

Dear Gerda:

Following the impulse of the fast going American life I never find a chance to handle my correspondence. Mostly I'm on the go and distracted from writing.

In your letter of October 8 I'm pleased to find that everything is fine, and the photos you kindly enclosed gave proof that your children grow up nicely. They look nice and clean and I believe that frequent sickness hasn't shaken their huskiness.

Of course I have to confess that you could have looked nicer! Your hair is not combed a bit, you look like "Struwwelpeter". Without any extra cost you should fix your hair with bobby – pins like they do here. You complain that your hair is turning to silver.

Never mind. Brush your hair nicely, keep smiling, then you will look like a million! I personally got my first grey hair 12 years ago when I had to take care of Tatzel in Ecuador, paid surgery and hospital bills etc, and "nobody" gave me a helping hand, in spite of the "Kinderchen" which would have been available to you that time. The Elephant never forgets! The only advice I got was to stay in Ecuador – it would be unwise to go to the U.S. But by great initiative I found the way to this great country and I'm proud to be citizen of it. Besides of this, on account of my ambitious, diligent life I succeeded to save up a fortune.

In all the past years I did not get an engagement announcement from you . . .

START OF AN UNSENT LETTER FROM GERDA NO ADDRESS (BUT STILL THE NISSEN HUT IN CHALGROVE)

November 25th, 1954

Dear Gunther

Received your letter today and it put me in rather a bad mood. No. 1: My hair: I tried curlers and I had a perm, I tried to wear it cut short, in fact I tried it every way but it always looks the same. I think the damp climate makes it so unruly. I brush it hard every day. But I don't dare to play about with it too much as it has gone very thin in places and I don't fancy to be bald. The woman opposite me has hardly any hair left and she'd gladly change places with me as regards hair. No. 2: "The Kinderchen". I wish I would never have had them. I haven't had them for 15 years now. I either lost them or they got stolen, I don't know which, during an air-raid in the war. I always tried to hold on to them, but I just had bad luck. Altogether they were only worth £100. I am sorry I couldn't help you as regards to Tatta but I just hadn't any Brosels. Neither have I now, but we get by and that's about all. If we would ever win some money I should like a little bungalow on my own ground not too near other people ...

FROM GERDA'S DIARY

25 January, 1955:

Our first month in the new house was not very successful. Jack and I had a real bust-up. We haven't made any friends yet. I don't want any trouble with the neighbours. Keep aloof of neighbours. Keep yourself to yourself. It pays in the long run. I only get tired of people and I am quite happy on my own.

LETTER FROM GUNTHER

5844 Beacon St
Pittsburgh 17/ PA
U.S.A.

February 14, 1955
(FIRST TWO PAGES)

Dear Sister Gerda:

I am very pleased to read that you moved to your new residence in Wood Farm Estate. The name sounds very romantic. The scenery probably shows lots of woods and farms. You maybe are enjoying villagers' life, while I live in this Iron City. This area is invaded by a cold wave with subzero weather. I shiver when I get up early for work and I hate to go out playing in the club at nights. If you would have come here, I would probably sit down sometimes, but being condemned to lead a lonely bachelor's life I keep hustling all the time to make always a dollar more!

Right now I am repairing an old Steinway Grand piano which had been partly destroyed. Piano tuning and repair is pretty good trade. I am proud to say that I have become one of Pittsburgh's top experts. I am really sorry I did not get a chance to give you proof of my skill by repairing your piano you meanwhile sold again. I cannot imagine that woodworm in the instrument should have done so much damage.

Music season is all right this year, and since I bought the Chevie I am coming around much easier. Right now I don't have any pictures on hand to show you the big car and your beloved brother. When taking picture I will put a big cigar in my mouth to have the right title for the snapshot: "Der reiche Onkel von Amerika".

I am glad that you are getting on all right and even Mickey the black dachshund is gobbling up hot chocolate

I guess that in few months in May 21 will be your 33rd birthday. My birthday in January passed pretty quiet. I got a lot of candy from my friends in Los Angeles – and ate it all up in 2 days! I am still the old sweet mouth. I get lots of fun by eating Kuchen with self made instant coffee. My landlady who is wonderful to me says always: "Don't be stingy, drink another cup of coffee, have another Kuchen" . . .

FROM GERDA'S DIARY

12 March, 1955:

We are back where we started from. We might as well not have moved at all. I don't get any peace here. Let children go out front if they want to, but don't encourage them. They are less trouble in the garden, don't need constant watching, won't get me into trouble with the neighbours. Wish we'd win some money and could get away from here.

25 June, 1955:

Jacky stayed up in the morning to please me, but was tired and exhausted. Took children to a fete in the Quarry Road. We enjoyed it. They had lots of lovely junk, only wished I could have spent longer there! -

26 June, 1955:

My birthday. Got lots of presents of Jacky = 1 Blouse, 1 pr Slippers, 1 pr Nylons. Talc Powder. Bath cubes, shrimps and mushrooms. Jacky finished swing for children. Burned my finger. Gave 2 old coats to Ragman. Found moth in old Fur Boots.

22 October, 1955:

Met Mrs. Stickland. She never once asked how the children are. She seems to be very stuck up lately. I wonder whether she is annoyed about anything. I still feel very out of things, still very much the outsider, but as long as the children don't suffer – Why oh why must I be so out of things, but I expect it's my fate. I eat too much lately. Must try to eat less.

3 November, 1955:

Been eating too much lately. Must start slimming again from now on. No more porridge. No more meat pie. No more onions. They don't agree with me. Diet tomorrow! I must get down to 8 stones. That means losing 9 lbs.

21 December, 1955:

Went to the market, bought a carpet remnant for 17/6. Also got 2 pieces of lino for 3/9, but they are no use to us just now. My hair is getting dreadfully thin on top. I hardly dare to wash it. I cut it with a sort of fringe to hide it. Am getting balder every day, and very old and ugly. I wonder whether I look very poor. Had a dreadful nightmare last night.

FROM END OF 1955 DIARY (MEMORANDA FOR 1956):

No more market.
No holidays.
No stray animals.
No dog.
No more looking into windows.
No large sausages.
No children in garden and house.
No neighbours in for tea, and talk to next door as little as possible.
No trouble and gossip.
No more expensive toys.

No more out the front for the children – it brings nothing but annoyance and trouble.

I said, No more jumbles, but I am definitely going to jumbles again – Reasons:

No. 1. I get extremely touchy and depressed without them.

2. I am tempted to spend a lot of money on new things.

3. I must try and control my greed.

4. I must have some change and entertainment or life is just too boring and pointless.

5. I must stick to the rules about jumble sales.

6. Don't buy things I have got a lot of.

7. Don't buy things I don't really need.

8. Don't draw attention to yourself, don't haggle too much.

9. Keep an eye on your purse all the time – beware of pickpockets!

10. Don't take any risks. I've got too much to lose and it's not worth the trouble - Disgrace to all the family.

LETTER FROM GUNTHER

5844 Beacon St
Pittsburgh 17/ PA
U.S.A.

December 26, 1955

Dear Gerda:

The great silence of Christmas gives me chance to settle down and answer correspondence which had been neglected tremendously.

Life in the U.S. goes fast and I have always to keep on the go. I just realized that your last letter of June 8, '55 is still unanswered. I am glad that you meanwhile moved into your new house and you're going to buy a refrigerator. After years and years in furnished rooms I know to appreciate to have a house of my own. Right now I have not to complain, but there is always a struggle about the bathroom, which mostly I find occupied, something what burns me up! In your letter you pointed to the fact that I could get too fat. Never mind! I am 100% OK. Thanks to God!

In the picture you sent, standing with your children right by the house, everything looks nice and clean, though some lines in your letter contain complaints. Probably they all go to school during the day, and you are discharged of your heavy duty. How is Jacky? He never writes a line! My friends in Los Angeles are always asking about you. Two of them know you from Breslau. They ask me in their letter to move to Los Angeles. But as I am OK here and could save an undetermined amount of "schone Dollarchens" I cannot make up my mind to go. It is not impossible that sooner or later I will follow the call of my friends in California.

I still keep my job at Heinz, play in clubs, tune pianos, and give plenty piano and accordion lessons. You should take a look at my drawers – all filled up with Christmas gifts! I still make efforts to find some woman to marry, but I guess the American girls are too particular. I would like rather better somebody from Europe. I find that people in Europe have more sense of fun.

Here people all live in a rush. Everything is hurry – up, and even in leisure hours people know only pleasure in racing the highways with their push – button cars at 80 miles a. h. speed. Living in this whirlpool of "money – hunters" I show myself ambitious too to make a dollar more. To have a car here has become necessity because Pittsburgh's streets are not level and I lost much pep when I had to climb steps and hills. My Chevie gives me good service when I give music lessons or tune a piano.

Right now also I have 2 violin students, and you probably will be puzzled because I never took a violin lesson myself in all my life. Also the art to repair and tune pianos and accordions had never been taught to me. Is that not really something?

By the way, I would appreciate it if you could give me that recipe how to make "Rumkugeln". Yes, I am still that old sweet mouth. And eat "Borxels" in mass. It don't even affect my teeth, I did not lose one single tooth yet. If the "senoritas" here would be as sweet as the candy, I probably would be married.

In love and kisses (hu, I get goose pimples!)

Your brother, Gunther

FROM GERDA'S DIARY

20 January, 1956:

Have been eating too much. Haven't been on the toilet for 2 days. Wish my skin wouldn't look so old and wrinkled. My hair is still frightfully thin on top. Didn't see anybody interesting today. The women round here don't like me and just ignore me. Is it because I am a foreigner? Never mind, I shall try to get hardened and ignore it. As long as my children don't have to suffer. Our TV is OK again.

10 March, 1956:

Went to a smashing jumble sale. Got about £2 worth of stuff. I couldn't carry it all, and Jacky had to fetch the rest. It was one of the best sales I have ever been to, and there were hardly any people there!

13 March, 1956:

That woman in the Post Office definitely doesn't like me. She lets me wait for a long time before she serves me. She treats me like a bit of dirt. Last week it was that big fat baker woman. She gave me a most contemptible look. I have done nothing to hurt her. I am scared stiff of people like that. There seem to be some really nasty women. Is it because I look and seem stuck up? Is it because I never chat and smile at them? But then I can't go against my nature. I can't help being what I am. Things are coming so much to try me lately. Please dear God, hilfe me not to get hurt so much. After all I am now 17 years in England and I don't want any more upsets.

Peter Thornthwaite

LETTER FROM GUNTHER
(LAST PAGE MISSING)

5844 Beacon St
Pittsburgh 17/ PA
U.S.A.

May 16, 1956

Dear Sister Gerda
Today I get a chance to answer your very fine letter. Of course I am pleased to read that everything remains satisfactory in your residence. I enjoyed it to have your nice family photos. Everything looks nice and clean, and it seems that Gerda takes extremely fine care of the children, dressing them nicely and doing some good cooking. I was very pleased to see the pictures with Sandy, the doggy. I feel fine when I see you in excellent shape in your backyard.

A friend of mine who just come from New York tells that the people's only pleasure is T.V. and automobile. He said that almost nobody anymore goes to Movie – Theatres, and they close up one after the other. New York has over 14 T.V. stations with good comedians and actors. I have the feeling that the piano business is not anymore as big as it used to be on account of recording – machines and push – button devices.

This summer I intend to go again to Atlantic City but should you have in mind to visit me here in the Iron City, you would all be greatly welcome. It is about time that you come to see your old brother. Maybe you would like it here at all!

Now I will put on my "Ausgeh – Anzug" and have a good dinner in a down – town restaurant. Today's menu: Chopped Liver or Fish, Matzo Ball Soup, Duckling and Cucumber Salad, Sherbet, Pastry, Coffee . . .

(*Ausgeh – Anzug*: going out suit.*)

FROM GERDA'S DIARY

17 June, 1956

I must get away from here. First the upset with that man opposite and the police, then that Drayton boy next door who attacks Peter every day, sometimes with a knife and spat at me today three times and stuck his tongue out. I tried to make the best of it, the constant dirt – throwing, but I have got to get out of here. I shall definitely not let the children out the front door anymore! Some people treat you like a bit of dirt.

FROM 1956 DIARY
LAST THREE PAGES (INDEX TO DIARY ENTRIES)

Only take pills when I am really worried about something.
    Excess work instead of exercises.
    ARBEITE! ARBEITE!

(The end pages are covered with drawings of faces, presumably hers – crudely done, with wrinkled brows, and bulbous, mostly bald heads, against which is written: *Ich bin*. I am.)

The correspondence above, or what survives of it, and intermittent diary entries, are all I can find (as evidence) of their lives around the mid-1950s. The letters are Gunther's – apart from that unsent letter of hers dated 25th November 1954, drafted in response to his letter comparing her (her hair in particular) to *Struwwelpeter*. Perhaps not everyone can visualise what Gunther had in mind with that comparison, but I can because *Der Stuwwelpeter* (Heinrich Hoffmann, 1845) was the book of my childhood. No doubt I identified with it because its title translates as "shock-headed Peter" (I wasn't "shock-headed", but I was Peter), but above all else I loved it for the usually violent and sadistic endings of the stories. In *Struwwelpeter* every bad child comes to a worse end. For me the best/worst story is that of *Suck-a-thumb*, who was finally cured of his habitual sucking with the snip-snapping entrance of the *long red-legged scissor-man* who cuts off the boy's thumbs with his shears. *"Snip Snap Snip/ They go so fast/ That both his thumbs are off at last"*. The rhymes are like those shears. But evidently Gunther and Gerda had not that but a still more shocking image in mind – *unbrushed hair.* As her unsent reply shows, it needled her despite its inaccuracy. Far from her hair resembling the haystack of *Shock-headed Peter's*, it was **very thin in places**, to the extent that she worried about going bald. What with that, and getting fat, she might yet end up looking like her brother.

That was Gunther for you. He had to set her right. It was the role of the older brother: to get her to change direction before it was too late. She needed to take a good look at herself in the mirror, and if what she saw (with his help) was *Struwwelpeter* – or a sister who lost or wasted the family fortune – then she had to change. If a little chastisement was mixed in with the guidance, that was good for her too. Concerning the diamonds, it was already years too late to change her behaviour, so his intention here – in bringing them up every so often – was not to guide or correct her, but to punish. That inheritance, the family fortune turned to stones, shadowed her adult life. From an old habit of concealment, they were usually referred to as *the Kinderchen*, the *little children*, but I think there was another reason for this euphemism. Gerda was almost still a child herself – and she remained one to her older brothers – when she fled Germany in 1939. The *little children* were in the care and safekeeping of a child, so what else could be expected of her than to lose or exchange them for a fraction of their worth? Though she could not have been expected to act differently, still it was necessary to remind her from time to time where she had gone wrong. If she ever forgot about them, he was her memory.

Die Kinderchen. In Gerda's case, they kept coming back with a vengeance, *the little children*, and would not go away, for they were everything: assets, shops, property, everything the family had amounted to financially. What really did happen to them, I wonder, those dark stones tucked inside the lining of a gas mask? Lost or exchanged? It's strange that she could never quite remember. As she said, she **just had bad luck**, and anyway **altogether they were only worth £100.** So no great loss.

Not to her maybe, but Gunther (*the elephant*) never did forget. In less important matters he could be forgetful enough, repeatedly forgetting the date of her birthday, for instance. In his letter of 26th August 1954, he correctly noted that *already she is 33.* Six months later (14th February 1955) he wrote: *I guess that in a few months in May 21 will be your 33rd birthday.* In fact, it would be her 34th birthday on 26th June 1955. This is not the first time I have had occasion to note his repeated error in confusing the year of her birth with the day (she was born in 1921), and getting the month wrong as well. And there is something more than a little odd in Gunther congratulating her on the *arrival of twins* almost three years after they were born. I wonder, did he actually pay attention to her, or was he always too distracted by the *rush and hurry-up of fast going American life*? Too preoccupied with himself maybe. Going back to his letter of 14th February 1955, I look again at that *snapshot* of his: *Right now I don't have any pictures on hand to show you the big car and your beloved brother. When taking picture I will put a big cigar in my mouth to have the right title for the snapshot: "Der reiche Onkel von Amerika".* There you have him, Gunther, *the rich uncle from America.* Yes, he is making fun of himself, he loves making fun of himself, but he swells with every word.

The letter dated 16th May 1956 also strikes me as noteworthy – not so much the letter as the date – for it is the exact date of the release (in New York) of *The Man Who Knew Too Much,* a Hitchcock film with James Stewart and Doris Day. It is the film in which Doris Day sings *Que Sera, Sera (Whatever Will Be, Will Be)*: Gerda's favourite song of all time. There is no evidence in her diary that she went to see it. Gerda went to the pictures a lot around that time (as the diaries reveal) but frustratingly she never named the films, except just once: *Lady and the Tramp.* So if she did see *The Man Who Knew Too Much,* and came back singing (not as loudly as Doris Day) *Que Sera, Sera* – and if it reminded her of anything – remains unknown.

In search of possible clues, I watched the film recently and made a note of the plot. The McKennas are holidaying in French Morocco, travelling from Casablanca to Marrakesh, when they find, or rather lose themselves in an underworld of false appearances, espionage and assassination. Finally, in London, popular singer Josephine "Jo" Conway McKenna, after saving a foreign prime minister at the Royal Albert Hall by screaming, then sings loudly enough, in the foreign embassy finale, for her kidnapped and about to be killed son to hear her and whistle along to the song. At the end I too found myself accompanying Hank, but with words not whistles:

When I was just a little girl I asked my mother, what will I be?
Will I be pretty? Will I be rich? Here's what she said to me . . .

RESTITUTION

16

I can't stop thinking about her diary entry of 10th March 1956, about that **smashing jumble sale,** when she got so much stuff she **couldn't carry it all,** *and* there were hardly any people there. It's that last detail, the absence of other people, that gives it idealised, iconic status; sets the standard to which subsequent jumble sales could only aspire. That particular jumble sale was her equivalent of the high grapes referred to by her brother in an earlier letter – the grapes that *Uncle Sam hangs very, very high.* She could only ever reach up, again and again, for such pickings. By March 1956 Gerda had lived in England for as many years (seventeen) as she had previously lived in Germany and had reached her zenith, as far as jumble sales were concerned. It's a shame (I can't help thinking) that she could not have stopped there – 10th March 1956 – and lived the same day over and over again, editing it as necessary. In time she might have improved it (if the ideal can be improved) – with piles of jumble heaped up just for her, and no other calloused female hands reaching out, snatching at bargains. Gerda's idea of heaven.

There are moments I keep returning to, as she kept going back to jumble sales. They are not my moments, but hers, and I have rummaged through suitcases and trunks to find them. Mostly they are not moments that lit up her life, or mine, but are rather where the darkness collects, and where I can only imagine what she was thinking or feeling at the time. When she learned of her father's slow death, for example. Whenever Gunther mentioned the diamonds. When the puppy next door yapped and yapped. When other women crossed the street as they saw her coming. When her hair reminded Gunther of *Struwwelpeter*. There were good moments too – a few. That **smashing jumble sale** in March 1956, for one. But even her jumble sales let in the dark. Never Again! That stern warning to herself can be found everywhere in her diaries from the mid '50s on. **Do not go to any more jumbles – they are bad for you. No more! Never again! They only make me spend money I don't have. And they are degrading.** In a 1st April diary entry, she wrote this: **It is infectious, it wants me to spend more and more and it all adds up, so give it up altogether**. Though **it** is not specified there, **it** obviously refers to jumble sales, though more generally she means the **spending bug** which had bitten her by then and never stopped biting and infecting.

Gerda might have sometimes had other things in mind with her **Never Again!** and **Degrading!** and **It is infectious**, but what exactly I'm not sure. From the mid 1950s onwards her diaries – seldom very notable for the depth and range of her introspections – turn into lists of things purchased, or to be purchased, amounts spent, **bargains** and **blow-flies** bought. If I hadn't the earlier diaries to go back to, I would never have bothered with those from the mid '50s to late '60s. They make for depressing reading. She visibly shrinks in them, reduced to endlessly repeated lists of this and that. At the time of course (around the mid 1950s), she was not the incredible shrinking woman. She was big. She was *Mum*. And I was in the habit of burrowing under her bed, looking for a place to hide. Under her bed (even then it was *her* and not *their* bed) was *the* place to go – a dark, dusty maze of narrow passages between old brown suitcases with their scratched and peeling evidence of foreign travel. They were a huge draw, those heavy suitcases, with their evidence of transit – London, Paris, Berlin, St Petersburg, New York – and under her bed was the only space with the right mix of dark and dust. After worming around, it was then simply a matter of waiting for the voices: *Peter, where are you, come and get your . . . I won't call for you again.* No one called. I wasn't missed. Life went on without me. It was strangely comforting to have it confirmed. She would go to bed at last (the ceiling of black bed springs creaking above my head) and fall asleep, not knowing I was there and with no memory of my existence . . .

I am reminded of that passage in *Speak, Memory,* when as a small child in a country estate near St Petersburg (a far cry from a raw council estate in the mid 1950s) the author of *Lolita* creeps on hands and knees along a narrow passage between a big cretonne-covered divan and the wall of one of the drawing rooms – a hidden tunnel of dust and dark, where he listens to the voices in his ears. We had no drawing rooms at 27 Chillingworth Crescent, no cretonne-covered divans, and we were some distance from Tsarist Russia, but the underneath of her bed was *my* St Petersburg.

For some reason, this memory leads on to another. They are both bedtime stories, I suppose. This later one comes with Ladybird pyjamas, which locates it anytime between about 1957 and 1960, when shops like Woolworths were selling Ladybird clothing for children in huge quantities. I have read that, by 1957, 850 workers for Adolf Pasold & Son were producing a million garments a month. 1959 seems about right for this memory, and 1959 or thereabouts also fits in with its other conspicuous feature, *Sergeant Bilko*, as *The Phil Silvers Show* was watched on TV sets, even in new council estates (if you were lucky enough to have a TV) between 1955 and 1959.

It was bed-time, I was in my Ladybird pyjamas, they were covered with red ladybirds. She is saying, to my surprise – as it is way past bed-time – *This is something you should see*. She is twiddling the knobs on the bulbous TV set in the living room, which usually means she has a treat in mind, but by her expression I worry that this time a treat is unlikely. We sit on the new settee in front of the television, the three of us, and the coal fire is burning, though I shiver and curl my toes against the cold.

You should know about this, she says. *This is what happened to the Jews*.

The film she is making us watch all the way through is a documentary, but in my Ladybird pyjamas I am not too familiar with the genre and was hoping for Disney. It may be first footage of what was found when liberating the camps: the heaps of nude bodies, all jumbled together, and others with shaven skulls and also wearing pyjamas, pressed up against the barbed wire, caught on camera.

I don't want to look.

This was not the treat I was still half expecting. It was not the *Sergeant Bilko* I had been allowed to stay up late to watch on another special occasion when a toothache had kept me awake. I remember thinking for a long time afterwards that she could be very cruel, my mother, especially when she was in one of her *funny* moods.

You have to look.

17

LETTER FROM GUNTHER

5844 Beacon St
Pittsburgh 17/ PA
U.S.A.
January 7, 1957

Dear Sister Gerda:

Months passed since I received your last letter. As always I have too many irons in the fire!

I learned of your intention to purchase a 2nd hand car to travel around. I hope that meanwhile you realized your great wish to buy an automobile (a la "Lotte" from Breslau days) and get out all the pleasure you always pine for.

Christmas-time and New-Year passed by smoothly. Though I was plagued tremendously by a head-cold with fever, still I kept going, doing my work in Heinz's and played to many parties. Still I have a reddish nose.

Dear Gerda, there is a special reason I write to you. Namely, right now I make the greatest effort to recuperate some of our beloved father's fortune and property which under pressure of the former Hitler-Regime had been lost. According to the new German law with regard to "Wiedergutmachung" we are entitled to be compensated for the huge fortune father had to give up.

We both are the only inheritors and we should not delay to make our claims in according with the existing law.

Please write immediately in German language to Dr. L -, Dusseldorf (see address at end) about the following. Of course it is up to you to make additional remarks at your convenience. I offered Dr. L - 10% commission, deductible from the amount handed us from the German Government. No advance payments will be made. 10% commission will be allowed as soon as he has accomplished something. . . **(REMAINDER OF LETTER MISSING).**

FROM GERDA'S DIARY

1 February, 1957:

Went to the pet shop to get some dog meat and the man in the shop was very rude to me. That just shows how old and unattractive I must be getting. People are so unkind to me, and I seem to get more and more sensitive. I wish we could win a lot of money soon.

18 March, 1947:

I want to lose 9 lbs in weight quickly, so I shall try the following method: I start the day with coffee and toast, then just only have drinks of orange juice until I get very very hungry, then have more toast and coffee, then continue again on the same lines. Just coffee, toast and orange juice. That should get rid of the unwanted 9 lbs.

15 April, 1957:

Had a front tooth pulled yesterday. Was glad to get rid of it. Afraid I am losing my teeth. This week Jacky had to go to doctors with double rupture and a lot of pain. More dentist appointments. Will have to have more out.

LETTER FROM GUNTHER (LAST PAGE(S) MISSING)

Gunther H. Lynn
5844 Beacon St
Pittsburgh 17/ PA
U.S.A.

April 25, 1957

Dear Gerda
I am sorry that I answer your letter of March 7 with delay. In these early spring days I am always on the go, lots of things to be done, I just do with nobody's help.

Also my state of health was shaken by a virus infection in my stomach, which left me extremely weak.

I was shocked to read that your children, especially Peter, were plagued by measles, and I imagine you had a rough time. I myself struggle ahead through life with the same impulse as always. Though I have in mind to send you a $10 remittance, I have to pay a tremendous amount of taxes, and I had to give up some of my activities because my health was shaky.

Mr. Levi who lives in Baltimore and who helped me come over to U.S, and even helped father to his immigration, wrote me. Mr. Levi has a straw and felt hat factory in Maryland and travels a lot by plane. I met him about 19 years ago and since then he helped me in awkward positions of my life. This summer a trip to my friends in Los Angeles, California is planned . . .

271

FROM GERDA'S DIARY

29 June, 1957:

Extremely upset today. Went to hospital fete to the jumble sale and somebody stole my handbag with £1. 10/ - in it, my powder compact and lipstick and comb. I am really down and out. I shall not go to any more jumble sales for a long time. I wish I wasn't so greedy and depressed about things. They let me have the cot mattress for the dog for nothing at the fete, but they got very fed up with me there.

LETTER FROM GUNTHER

Gunther Lynn
5844 Beacon St
Pittsburgh 17/ PA
U.S.A.

July 2, '57

Dear Gerda:
I am sorry that your last letter has not been answered. The tremendous rush of life and the heat wave mostly vanishes all my intentions to write.

I was very pleased to see the nice pictures with Sandy, the doggy. I feel fine when I see you in excellent shape doing exercises in your back yard.

However there was the discouraging news that Jacky has rupture. You pointed out that he will get operated. I myself struggle on making a living. My income was diminished by the Suez Canal crisis. Right now I cannot make any promises to visit you there because I am tied up till September. Actually I make efforts to get out of the food factory job and build up a business of my own. My close friends want me to visit them in California, but this would be too much of spending and I need a new accordion. My old one is all beaten up. I played hell out of it.

Enclosed please find a small birthday gift of $5. That is all what right now I can afford. I still hope that you saved up some of the "Kinderchens" with which father provided you.

I must state that while your former letters were always full of joy, now the content switched to bitterness. Never mind!
In love
Your brother
Gunther

FROM GERDA'S DIARY

14 July, 1957:

Nobody brought my bag back. I am going to see how many days I can go without buying any clothing. For every day I am not buying anything I am going to make a star.

(Big yellow stars have been drawn for this and the following three days, then stop.)

July 17, 1957:

Felt a bit low about not going to the market, but am determined not to spend any money on clothing unless I really need it – and then I am going to go to some jumbles or second hand shops before I buy it new. I wonder what I will need first in the line of clothing.

July 22, 1957:

I am going to give this star business up. I don't seem to get any fun out of life any more. Sandy has been an extremely naughty dog. I could just about kill him. He made a mess of my kitchen and bit my petticoat to pieces. He'd better not do that again – So on with the fetes and jumbles, but watch that handbag! Enjoy life while you can -

5 September, 1957:

My hair is getting thinner than ever. I can hardly hide the baldness in front. Wonder how long before I have to wear a wig. Am going to try a new cure for £3. 17/6 at Christmas. I am from today never going to cut it again. Every bit of hair shall be precious to me.

October 2, 1957:

Been to the market. Thought I looked very old and got treated like a very shabby poor person. I am really growing old with a vengeance. I have decided not to go there any more, for at least a year. So goodbye market - WILLPOWER!

October 3, 1957:

I am going there after all. Must have some fun in life.

November 23, 1957:

Been to 3 jumbles today. Bought a lot of clothing, a

gramophone, one electric fire, and quite a lot of ornaments and shoes.

Jumbles MUST NOT interfere with strict Budget!

December 18, 1957:

Been to the market today. Bought pair of shoes and cardigan for Jacky. They both were very desired so I had to make my mind up quickly. Spent 22/-. I really must stop going there. It's too much temptation. I might try not to buy any more clothes for a whole year, until next Christmas. That means no market, no jumbles for a whole year! See how I get on. I get a star every day I don't spend on clothes.

December 26, 1957:

My new set of teeth spoiled my Christmas. I just can't seem to get used to them. I shall definitely not sleep with them in. They still feel a mouthful and make me sick.

1957 DIARY: LAST PAGES (NOTES): HAND-DRAWN (BLACK INK) PORTRAIT OF A HUGE CORRUGATED HAIRLESS HEAD WITH HORNS, A BARBED WIRE SCRIBBLE OF A FACE, AND UNDERNEATH IT:
That's the devil in me.

As at the end of 1956, the last pages are covered with multiple crude doodle drawings of shorn heads with staring faces.

That old pine trunk of hers, with its faded gold initials GRL, houses the photograph albums, and I have to flick through decades to find the Gerda (or Gerdas) I am looking for. There are few that interest me from the early '50s onwards, except one of the Nissen hut where the pram outside the black door, and the man looking out of the window, only frame her absence (she must be holding the camera). There are photos of babies from 1952, babies with identical fat smiles and combed hair, rumpled bibs and bare shoulders as they turn in their pram to squint at the camera, while a little girl with Shirley Temple hair and bright eyes stands coyly behind them. In all of them, Gerda is noticeable by her absence, which is perhaps just as well because when I scan the matching diaries they make dismal reading, with the same complaints, repeated almost word for word, of things **going all wrong lately** and **old age creeping up on me with a vengeance.**

Better to flick back ten years at a time. Summer 1947 finds her on a beach, relaxed and slim in her swimwear, reclining against a white sun-warmed sea wall, her hair full, lustrous, dark, and though she is too far away to disclose her features in detail, you can see she is smiling.

Then to 1937 and the start of **the beautiful Prague time,** the sudden passing of which she mourned. Here in sunshine, on an apparently cool day, Gerda and three friends perch (two of them in in warm coats) on the back of a bench against a sunlit, tree-shadowed wall. This must be the classical front of Victoria College, the boarding school for young women, where she flourished for a year before returning to Germany in time for the worst pogrom to date.

In another photograph from 1937, she is looking down intently at something. It could be sheet music, or a document of some interest, and she seems unaware of the camera – her expression too serious and absorbed to be a conscious pose. You can see the ruler-straight parting in her pulled-back dark hair. That must be Gunther next to her, looking down at the same thing. It looks like him, with his premature baldness, bow tie, double-breasted striped suit with the sharp wide lapels of the period. And at the other side of her and to the back, is another man, looking down, dark-suited (it could be formal evening wear), also intent on whatever they are studying. .

Back to 1927, she is six years old – my age in 1957 – and I pause a moment to reflect on that number – 27 – repeating so often in my life. It stood out in the address of the new council house, 27 Chillingworth Crescent – and in the registration number of that black tank-like 1954 Rover 90, **MTM 727**, which Jack would one day hand down to me, only to see it scrapped within a year. The above are just a sample of the 27s that crop up everywhere.

In 1927, Gerda is sitting sideways on a high-backed wooden chair and holding a picture-book almost as big as herself. With her head-phones and sleepy-eyed, abstracted expression, she is looking but not looking at the camera. That I have already described this photograph (with the date 1927 written underneath it as proof of provenance), I know. Such repetition is necessary if anything previously unnoticed is to emerge. John Berger observed that photographs don't *preserve meaning* but *offer appearances*. If so, then *appearances* sometimes seem to shift and mutate, offering up something new each time you look, and each time they seem to add another layer of meaning...

Photographs are one thing. The written word another. Gerda's later diaries weary the eye with their word-by-word repetitions. Was she aware of it? Maybe not, for it is unlikely that she read and re-read them as I do, and anyway her standards were perhaps lower than mine. Gerda just let it all out. Whatever was on her mind at that moment, out it shot, no matter that the same things were on her mind and she could never get away from them. Such circular thinking – did it never weary and even nauseate her? It must have done. There is a particular German word which reappears now and again: *Verseuchung. Die Verseuchung* – meaning: contamination, infection, infestation. This was how Jews were depicted – as an infestation, an infection. Yes, I'm sure of it, it reappears often in her later diaries, though unfortunately I made no note of the places at the time and can't bring myself to go through year after year and pick them out again. Whenever she scribbled that word she was thinking of jumble sales, charity shops, the bug that had bitten her, the itch she had to scratch and scratch. *Buy buy buy spend spend spend. Jumble jumble jumble.* There was no end to it. But she also had something else, something deeper, in mind.

How many times this past year have I gone through her diaries and (finding nothing new) returned them to her dark trunk with its faded old gold initials, *GRL*? It might appear a wearying and Sisyphean task – except for one thing. Eventually, I notice something I have previously missed. Her trunk, for example, with its old gold initials. Had I really not noticed before? All that time it was staring me in the face. Insert an *I* into *GRL*, and you have *GIRL*. *Remember who you used to be*, her father had written in July 1939. Whenever Gerda opened and closed this trunk, was she remembering? One discovery leads to another. The khaki-coloured Boots Scribbling Diary ("British Manufacture Throughout") for 1952 – I was about to add to the other decades in the trunk when I noticed that it was splashed with what looked like old blood, but was actually something I could never have guessed if she hadn't scrawled the explanation on one side: **These red spots came through water dripping through the roof everywhere.** Turning over the khaki cover, I saw that her address in 1952 was Site 5, Hampden Estate, Chalgrove; so that was rusty rain dripping through the corrugated iron roof of the Nissen hut, just as the young mother was about to write something of great note in her diary.

18

FROM GERDA'S DIARY

MEMORANDA AT FRONT:
RULE for 1958: Don't buy things just because they are bargains, but because I need them or think I shall need them soon. Don't buy so far ahead, I'll only get the moths into things, and I haven't got a lot of space to keep them.

1 January, 1958

Our TV doesn't work properly, I am fed up with it. My teeth made me feel sick a lot today. Wish I could get used to them. I have been eating a lot today, I shall get fat if I keep on like that.

3 January, 1958:

A man brought us another TV, I definitely don't like it. Our best bet is to get our old set back and just have the aerial altered, and later on a new tube put in. Our old TV is OK and I hope we get it back. I have taken a dislike against this new set.

8 January, 1958:

Couldn't even go to the market today. Felt extremely sick in the night. Think it was my period and danish blue cheese and onions and kidney soup and pancakes combined. I just can't get used to my false teeth. They irritate me every minute of every day.

11 January, 1958:

Got a letter from my brother about some money we might get. I am not at all hopeful. Jacky has high hopes. I only hope he doesn't get too disappointed. He thinks we are going to get a load of money. I don't think so for a minute. If we should ever strike rich, Jacky wants to buy a bungalow and a new car. Well, we shall see as we shall see. It's up to Kismet now. No jumbles today. Wish there was one on soon.

13 January, 1958:

Our TV is absolutely dreadful just now. Hope they come to fix it soon. Wonder what's going to happen about money. Will we get something or not? To be or not to be, that is the question.

24 January, 1958:

I am spending much too much on clothing. Going to a jumble on Saturday. We haven't got a reply from Germany yet.

1 February, 1958:

Jacky and I have been discussing again what we shall do if we get any money. I think we shall stay on here for a bit, we shall buy a new Standard 10. We shall be able to afford good holidays and have a bit of security for the future. Also I shall have a bottle of health wine every week and a nice big chicken, and if Jacky and I are ever ill, we shall be able to stay in bed. So please dear God let us get a nice substantial sum of money.

LETTER FROM GUNTHER

Gunther H. Lynn
5844 Beacon St
Pittsburgh 17/ PA
U.S.A.

February 2, 1958

Dear Gerda:
Today I want thank you for your letter of Jan 5, 58.

My birthday passed by quietly, there was not much celebration. Yes, I have turned to be an old bachelor, and I rather feel it. I have not anymore the elasticity as in years before when I was driving "Lotte" through Sudpark in Breslau. Also my visibility has diminished. My nieces and nephew in England will pretty soon exclaim: Oh, what an ugly uncle we have in the U.S.A. Regardless what even will be, still I stride ahead firmly trying to pile up "Silberbrosels". I never relax, I keep myself always on the go as long as I am in good health and my strength are not vanishing.

Right now there is a stagnancy of business everywhere. I am still employed at Heinz, however the working-hours had been cut-down. Also many night-spots where I played for years and years cut out music completely because of bad business. Of course I am proud to tell you that I have a huge number of students and I teach in the finest aristocratic circles. It helps me a lot to be a good performer of modern music. People prefer Rock 'n roll and calypso style instead of Mozart Sonatas.

Dear Gerda, in my previous letter I asked you to send a report for Wiedergutmachung to Dr. L - in Dusseldorf. Did you send him a detailed report about our wealth we left behind? It is very essential to tell Dr. L - that father was highly persecuted by the Gestapo and urged to leave without money by pressure of the Nazi-Regime. I hope that you wrote meanwhile this letter I recommended you to write in my last letter. Should you not be interested to be compensated for our lost property in Germany, make up your mind. . . (remainder of letter missing).

FROM GERDA'S DIARY

24 February, 1958:

Had another letter from Germany today. A lot of forms to fill out, which I couldn't fill out. I really think it will all be a blow-fly and nothing will come of it. I ought to go on a bread and butter diet from now on and just have one day off on Sunday when I can eat whatever I like. I am getting fat as a pig. Resist temptation! I am starting NOW.

1 March, 1958:

I am building my hopes very strongly on some money from Germany. Please dear God let us get a good amount, enough to buy a business etc. I am still eating too much.

3 March, 1958:

Went to London with Jacky to go to the Deutschen Konsolat again. Hope I don't have to go again. I only hope we are going to get a lot of money for all our trouble. Sometimes I am hopeful and sometimes I think we shall not get a penny. Que Sera, Sera.

(*Wiedergutmachung* – literally, making good again, making amends.)

Something odd has happened here. Re-reading Gunther's letter dated 7th January 1957 – the letter in which he first raises Gerda's hopes with that *special reason* for writing to her, namely recuperating *father's fortune and property* – I begin to suspect the date. Having read and re-read it, alongside the letter he wrote a year later, on 2nd February 1958, I realize my mistake – actually *his* mistake, not mine, for the earlier letter is wrongly dated: *it should have been 1958, not 57*. You have to be a bit of a detective with this sort of research. After checking and double-checking the 1957 diary, there is no mention of compensation for a lost **fortune**. There is much about losing things like hair and teeth (but not weight, unfortunately). There are always jumble sales (sometimes three on a Saturday). There are moths getting into her clothes. Flies during summer walks on Shotover Hill with Sandy the doggy. There are the usual illnesses and incessant grizzling of young children. But nothing about compensation. Or what Gunther calls *Wiedergutmachung*: Recompense, redress, reparation, restitution.

So he never wrote to her on 7th January 1957, or if he did, he wrote her a different letter (now lost) which makes no mention of *Wiedergutmachung*. His letter is therefore out of sequence by a year, and should not have headed the chronology of correspondence and diary entries for 1957. As it was in fact written on 7th January 1958, correct chronological sequence places it *before* Gunther's subsequent letter of 2nd February 1958 with its reminder: *Dear Gerda, in my previous letter I asked you to send a report for Wiedergutmachung to Dr. L - in Dusseldorf. Did you send him a detailed report about our wealth we left behind?*

I'm glad that's cleared up. Now I can get on with assessing her response, which at first (diary entry above of 11th January 1958) is uncharacteristically low key: **I am**

not at all hopeful. As ever with her, it's **up to Kismet now.** But soon she senses that **a change is coming** (she uses this phrase twice), and by 23rd March she is writing: **I shall move as soon as I get some lolly.** By 1st May: **Do wish we'd get into a lot of money soon!** By 2nd September it is her only escape: **There are so many cruel people in this world. They don't really like foreigners at all in England. I seem to make so many enemies and have people against me all because I am not like them. If I only would get a lot of money soon so I could leave this Estate and find privacy and peace somewhere else.**

Whether Gunther knew what he had stirred up with his *Wiedergutmachung*, I don't know. I see now that, as in May 1939 when she boarded the President Harding, this was a turning point in her life. Suddenly a future was possible again. Opening the 1958 diary at a random date (27th May) I read this: **If we get enough money = We must go in for 4 bedroom house in North Oxford near Park, with large garden. I want piano and ping pong table, 2 dining rooms, and definitely another bedroom suite with 2 separate beds.** Yes, it was always **Kismet**, but **Kismet** is always around the corner. You wake up one day and find that you are no longer a stranger in England, instead finding yourself (as in that song) *all lost in a wonderland/ a stranger in paradise!*

More confusion. There are two diaries for 1958, both supplied by *TIMOTHY WHITES Chemists and Household Stores (Branches Throughout The Country)*, but one is an undersea blue-green with dimly visible weeds stirred by the tide; the other red and also with waving fronds of weeds. It is the *red* that I haven't read, and it doesn't start auspiciously, with **No more ice-lollies!** scrawled on the first page. This resolution must have been entered later in the year, I decide, since banning ice-lollies in January is surely no great hardship. As I read on, the confusion of two diaries for the same year is soon cleared up: in the red diary the 1958 has been crossed out and **1959** written above. For some reason she had, or was given, an extra 1958 diary, so (not one to waste anything) she used it for 1959; and even before I get to 1st January, I find (under *Memoranda*) - **NEW RULES 1959** (as follows):

Do as you should do. (Remember all you have learned and use it). Eat what you ought to eat (and don't over-eat). Only buy what you need and think you need. Buy children books (only cheaply). It keeps them amused. Only do exercises if you feel really well and are not expecting the visitor. Don't take any notice if people are rude to you. You can't do anything about it. Ignore it.

FROM GERDA'S DIARY

13 January, 1959:

Bought 2 jumpers in sale 10/- each. One is OK, the other will be a Blow-Fly. Was very keen on brown corduroy slacks for 25/- but I really have no money to spare and also I need size 30 now with all the stuff I wear underneath this cold

weather. Worrying about that jumper for Jacky. I think it is a bit of a Blow-Fly. Wish I had never bought it. I paid 10/- for it. Never mind, I shall have to make the best of it. Lately my tummy hasn't been at all well. I am eating much too much and getting much too fat. Nearly 9 stones. I really need to lose a stone. Wish I could get away from here. I don't belong. I shan't ever make chicken pie or fruitcake or chicken soup again. They are too much trouble to make. No post yet.

27 January, 1959:

No post again. Dreadfully upset stomach all day. Wonder whether it is my visitor. In any case I am going to try a new diet. I can't stand much more of this. There is more antisemitism in Germany. I don't think there will ever be an end to it. Only hope it doesn't happen here. And I wonder will we really get any money from Germany? So far no news. Also no letter from my brother. I am getting dreadfully baldy on the front. I can hardly hide it.

6 February, 1959:

Been sorting letters out lately. Made me think a lot of times gone by, and especially of Joe. I am glad I knew him, but I am also glad I didn't marry him, it would never have worked out. It would have only ended in the divorce court.

7 February, 1959:

Had a letter from Germany today. The first one for a very long time, but it was only more forms to fill out. Went to

two jumbles. One was a Blow-Fly. I only got a pair of panties there for 3d. The other one was quite good. Got a suitcase for 1/-, two skirts brown and green for 1/6, one pr slippers for Jacky 6d, one pr shoes for myself 6d, one roll-neck thing for 3d. I quite enjoyed it. I don't know yet when the next one is—

LETTERS FROM GUNTHER

Gunther H. Lynn
5844 Beacon St
Pittsburgh 17/ PA
U.S.A.

February 8, 1959

Dear Sister Gerda:

Thank you for your nice card from the Radcliffe Camera, Oxford and birthday greetings. I have not had a chance to write for a long time, indeed I have neglected my correspondence because here the impulse of life and the rush keep me always on the go. I cannot settle down so "gemutlich" any more like I used to years ago. Now I have to hustle to help myself to a decent standard of living. In spite of a still increasing unemployment and "recession" all around, I am coming on fairly well. I have in mind to go into business as soon as I have enough "Silberbrosels" saved up. I have not become younger and the early rising to cold waves "burns me up".

I read always your letters with the greatest pleasure, but there is much about sickness and your situation seems to go distressful. I myself go through all kind of troubles and get sick. Nobody cares, nobody would help me, I have to keep smiling!

In spite of my endeavourments to find a girl, I am not

successful. Most American girls are used to a high standard of living with Cadillac and mink coat, and it seems more advisable to meet somebody from the old country. My friends in Los Angeles, who just sent me a very valuable gift for my 47th birthday, want me to come there this summer to meet an attractive girl, but your "stingy" brother is not so crazy about spending a great amount of "Geld" on vacation.

"Die Wiedergutmachung" has not shown any results yet. In my last letter to Mr. L – I pointed out I am "bitterly disappointed" about this.

How is Jacky? Has his rupture been cured permanently?

Please write me about everything!
Mit tausend susse Kusschen
Dein Bruder
Gunther

GUNTHER LYNN
Piano-Tuner
5844 Beaconst
Pittsburgh 17 PA
den 24 Juni 59

Dear Gerda:

Today I will take a chance answering your last letter containing nice pictures of your children. Some of them have their hair really shiny blond "like Germans" and they all look healthy and the boy pretty husky. Also the picture, you sitting on the parks bench with Sandy the dachshund, is very impressive.

Right now I have in mind to visit my friend and family in L. Angeles. I got an invitation to stay in their fancy house. In order not to loose time I will go by TWA – Air-liner. The *round-trip cost lots of "Brosels" about $240 – but I guess I will have a swell time. They will drive me to the Gulf of Mexico, where I will have opportunity for swimming, and also I will pay a visit to Hollywood's movie and TV land. I will take a look at Las Vegas Nevada amusement and gambling centre. I will have lots of fun.*

Next on my agenda is a visit to England. For that purpose I would have to take off at least 1 or 2 months. We will have to talk things over. I wish very much to see "27 Chillingworth Crescent" where you have made your home.

I just received again a letter of Mr. Levy, asking for additional documents. I guess things are moving slowly toward a result because the situation in Germany is uncertain. Nevertheless I hold on and will provide him with all the essential papers. Right now I am worried a little because inflation is gaining more and more and living cost is almost unbearable.

That's all for today. I'll write you again from L. Angeles.

My best wishes and regards from your Gunther

There is then a gap in correspondence with no further letters from Gunther for the remainder of the year, but Gerda continues with her diary through 1959. An entry on 25th February acknowledges his 8th February letter, commenting: **Nothing much new. I wonder if we'll ever get anything from Germany**, and also records her disappointment that his usual $10 was not enclosed and questions **whether he really sent it.** For the remainder of 1959 her intermittent entries are what I now expect, though she emphasizes her usual rules and resolutions with many underlinings, capitals and exclamation marks, as if they have just occurred to her for the first

291

time and require all the fanfare such flourishes can give. So, for example, the entry for 25th March begins: **From today I shall not buy any clothing anywhere for at least 1 year. I am getting much too greedy and am inclined to buy the same things over and over again. Fini! Das Ende!!**

Then this for 25th May:

I really am going to pack jumble sales in for 1 year at least. For 1 thing I can save the money. 2nd reason I might be getting into trouble. 3rd reason I am getting bulked out with clothes. 4th reason I am getting greedy. 5th reason I am getting the moths in. I am starting really and truly today! Verstand tells me so. Know when to stop and the time is NOW. Even if it hurts keep it up and DO NOT change your mind about it. It's Duty! Break with things!

Of course such resolutions were made to be broken. **It's my birthday,** she writes on 26th June, **and I feel rather fed up. No news from abroad yet or from Gunther. I am definitely giving the jumbles up and only go if I need something badly. I shall buy bonds instead. We must get out of here. All the children in the neighbourhood use our fence to sit on. There are 3 jumbles on tomorrow, but I just can't make up my mind whether to buy a bond or more clothes. I am all betwixt and between. Jumbles are the only excitement I get from life.**

There is no acknowledgement in her diary of Gunther's letter dated 24th June 1959, and I wonder if she read with pleasure his announcement: *Next on my agenda is a visit to England* and *We will have to talk things over.* There is no evidence that they ever did talk things over. Her attitude to relatives visiting and overstaying their welcome is indicated by entries complaining about an extended visit from Jack's sister, starting with this:

(18 June): I don't like visitors. Hope Ivy will never invite herself again and cling on to Jacky. She gets on my nerves. If she invited herself here every summer, I couldn't stand it. Hope she won't ever have enough money for the fare to come down here. I shan't send her a penny if I get something. She reminds me of Aunt Bertha. A poor relation clinging on and being a damned nuisance. I shall look out more for myself from now on. If I get any money I shall pay the car off, buy a house, and if there is any left have it under my name. Safety first. Jeder is sich selbst der nachste.

Or: Every man for himself. No, that's not what surprises me. It's the reference to Aunt Bertha. This is the Aunt Bertha, I recall, who wrote to her niece on 5th July 1939: *Do you know, dear Gerda, don't you know a way I could get to England?* The Aunt Bertha, of whom Gunter wrote on 24th August 1945 that *it could be said that Aunt Bertha and the rest of the family who lived in Brandenburg have perished...* The same Aunt Bertha, of whom he also wrote in an undated fragment of a letter: *I now expect that the old "quarrel in the house Lewinsohn" has been buried. Aunt Bertha was never my friend, she was always disturbing the rest of the house. The mother was hating her and I too!!!!!*

The same Aunt Bertha who, as I recently discovered through an internet search, was deported from Breslau on 25th November 1941 to Kovno (Kaunas) Fort X1, and died there on 29th November 1941. This was a revelation, but when I looked further into it, I found that Kaunas in Lithuania had only nine forts, and that the last of these, the 9th, built with reinforced concrete, was the one mainly used for the mass killing of Jews following German occupation in June 1941. I have read elsewhere that on November 24th 1941, 1000 Jews were arrested in Breslau and sent to Kaunas where they were made to dig their own mass grave and undress. Aunt Bertha might have been one of them. The "Fort X1" must have been a recording error, or I misread it – and now I can't find my way back there again. I have since read that four additional forts (10th to 13th) were under construction at Kaunas, but I think that the pit Aunt Bertha helped dig must have been at the Ninth Fort. That was surely where she was shot along with all the others.

19

FROM GERDA'S DIARY

1 January, 1960:

The new year didn't start off well for me. Why, well first there is no money or letter from abroad. 2nd there is a lot of race trouble again here and in Germany. Will there ever be an end to it and where will it lead. I am scared for myself and the children's sake. What good is it to build a future on that. I wonder whether this business will stop us getting any money. Then another thing. I missed a very good coat reduced from £12. 10/- to £2. 5/- in the sales. A real bargain. And I am getting much too fat (9 stones) and I haven't got the willpower to give up food. I shall try to be stronger tomorrow. Should I give the jumbles up from today or not? Just keep decent, tidy, comfortable and reasonably smart (after all I am getting on and I am no beauty) and live according to my means and circumstances.

3 January, 1960:

Had rather a dull Saturday. Had a bad night. There was a mouse in the bedroom. Think I'll go to the jumbles again when they start.

4 January, 1960:

The news couldn't be much worse. I expect I have deserved it, but please God spare my children. Just when I thought we might get to the end of our waiting and get some money from the Germans, the world is starting to hate the Jews all over again. Slogans everywhere = Juden go raus, windows broken, the whole business starting all over again. I thought it might happen one day, but not so soon. I thought the kids might have a chance in life. Dear God I know I have been wicked, especially to my father and Aunt Bertha, but please don't punish me any more. Where could we run to? I never want to leave Sandy. I love him too much. Is there any hope anywhere, any peace and any future? Please dear God don't let the children have to suffer for my mistakes. Turn the Jews into good people so they don't get so disliked. If things get really bad I might try and commit suicide, but only if there is really no other way open.

6 January, 1960:

News is worse than ever today. They are destroying shops and writing threatening letters. History all over again. This has made up my mind for me. We are definitely trying to emigrate to Australia. There are several snags though:

No.1. Sandy.
No.2. Jacky's rupture.
No.3. Will they take me?
No.4. Will we get any money?

The poor children aren't suspecting anything. I am definitely giving up the jumbles as I don't want to accumulate any more junk—

8 January, 1960:

I am just about at my wits end. It said on TV that there is trouble in Australia too, so I don't want to go there either. So that's out! I just don't know which way to turn for the best. If God would only give me a sign. I don't want the children ever to get hurt, and I don't want to get hurt myself. What a future! I live constantly in fear. If only a door would open. One minute I was full of hope, full of a new future, and now—

10 January, 1960:

I took the children to the pictures yesterday and today. They might as well have a bit of fun while they can. Life is so dreadful uncertain and dangerous. It came all so sudden. Please God, destroy the Nazis and all bad people, please help the poor children, they don't know what they are in for. Will they get a chance to grow up? How will it all end? I can't believe the Jews are all evil or a lot more evil than others, that they have to constantly suffer. The children were so happy and loving when we went to the pictures today. I think Jacky and the children really love me, although I don't deserve it. I haven't been a good daughter, but I would act different if I had the same chance over again. I know better now.

13 January, 1960:

That horrible woman in the market stared at me ever so rudely. Wish I'd be grey haired soon. Children got on my nerves. I thought I looked very very old today. No news from abroad yet. What a world we live in and what a time to have children. There is constant fear, fear of persecution and starvation and cruelty, fear of the Atom bomb and destruction and war and being maimed and disfigured for life. There is no end to my fears. Is there going to be a future for me and my family or in fact the whole world?

Can't make up my mind whether to go to jumbles any more. There is one on Saturday, but I don't know whether I shall go. I might do—

There are no further entries for January, and February is blank. Flicking through 1960 I see that much of the year is blank. The intermittent entries are less records of daily incidents than evidence of internal struggle – as manifested in the repeated question, the dilemma she couldn't resolve: to go to jumbles or not to

FROM GERDA'S DIARY

4 March 1960.

No more jumbles!
Be strong.
I am getting much too much junk.
The moths will only come in.
Utilize! Organize!
Resist temptation.
No more jumbles starting NOW!
Remember moths!!!

(Rubbish! I shall go! It's my only excitement).

21 April 1960

> I am making a new start.
> I am starting afresh again.
> Willpower!
> Sacrifice!
> Only buy what I really need.
> Don't take any risks, and don't get into any trouble.
> No more jumbles. Never again! Not at least for 1 year.

15 August 1960

I am going to the jumbles again, but I shall follow the rules. Life is so uncertain, so I shall have a bit of fun while I can. Hope I and my family never suffer cruelty and hunger like so many people have to suffer. I wouldn't mind death straight out. We are buying the new TV today also order ton of coal.

16 October 1960

> Reasons why I shouldn't go to jumbles:
> 1. I might get into some trouble.
> 2. I get too much junk and need a good sort out of suitcases.
> 3. It makes me greedy. Greed was mankind's ruination.
> 4. Break with circumstances before they have broken you!
> 5. I keep changing my mind about it.

Also: I have got a good stock of clothing. I expect to get some money soon.

Otherwise, 1960 was a largely wordless year for her diary. It seems that she had less and less to say with each passing year, and the few words she could spare were for jumble sales. Actually there might have been fewer still, as far as my initial record of them allowed, because (when revising this account of her life) I initially decided to cut out bits in the hope of rendering it less repetitive and mundane. Then I reconsidered. Gerda's life had become repetitive, tedious and mundane, and that should be reflected in the entries. The hopeful seventeen-year-old stepping off the Hamburg docks in 1939 had turned into this thirty-nine-year-old housewife and mother, who had nothing better to write about than jumble sales. But there was nothing so surprising in that. She was, as I recall, always scrimping and saving and counting the pennies, like so many other mothers in her situation. No wonder jumble sales filled her mind. It was a way of buying cheap, of being thrifty, of clothing the family now and for the future; she was fulfilling her role. So when I came to revise my revisions, it took me less than a day to realise that cutting out a few of her written words meant cutting out bits of her, and I hastily restored them – restored to its rightful place in the records every last repetitive and mundane word she scribbled. Let Gerda stand or fall by the actual written record. Entries to do with ordering her winter coal, getting a new TV, going to jumble sales, are back exactly as they are in the original, and in restoring them I have come to realise something vital: if such things were all she had to think about that year, and in the years to come, then so be it. That was her, that was her life, and it wasn't the shrivelled life I had imagined. She wasn't the incredible shrinking woman. Look carefully at her words and suddenly they are writ large on the otherwise largely blank sheets of her later diaries: **I am making a new start – I am starting afresh again – Life is so uncertain – Break with circumstances before they have broken you.** Gerda was a woman who repeatedly ended and began, began and ended. It was the only way she knew of living.

LETTER FROM GUNTHER
(FIRST AND LAST PAGE(S) MISSING)

NOVEMBER 1960?

. . . I am still trying to find out about the fate of Kurt. Don't you have any old addresses of him from France or Argentina? A friend of mine in Buenos Aires could not find any traces of Kurt there! Maybe you write to him (address at end) and give him some helpful hints. The well known paper "Der Aufbau" published in New York carries a column "Gesucht wird", but even there the name Kurt L. had never been mentioned.

Now with winter coming on I am not in the spirit to make plans for a trip to England. Of course I have in mind to realize such a voyage.

Just in these days took place the election of the new president. I am glad that Kennedy for whom I voted was nominated future president. Though I personally cannot complain and things seem to me very prosperous, still there is unemployment all around particularly by the steel mills in Pittsburgh. I hold on to my little job in the Heinz plant in which I have almost 12 years seniority. To get up 4:30 in the morning is not agreeable. But there is still much of energy, lots of pep and initiative in me by which I overcome easily the shady side of life.

Past month I sent $30 to the Funeral society in Quito – Ecuador to set a stone with memorial inscription at father's grave. That money also will be used to maintenance and planting of flowers . . .

An internet search reveals that John F. Kennedy announced his intention to seek nomination in January 1960; he was nominated on 15th July 1960 and defeated Nixon on 8th November. This letter is therefore from November 1960.

The revelation in this partial letter concerns Kurt, who might have been dead for all the space they allow him in their correspondence. *Der Aufbau* translates as the structure, and *aufbauen* as: build up, set up, construct, rebuild, base, assemble. *Gesucht wird* translates as: is searched. So this *well known paper*, to which Gunther refers, had something to do with building or rebuilding, and included a regular column to do with *searching*. Another internet search discloses that *Der Aufbau* was a periodical especially for German-speaking Jews, founded in New York City (1934), subsequently publishing *The Immigrants' Handbook*, a guide for new German–Jewish immigrants in the US and printing lists of Jewish Holocaust survivors. *Der Aufbau's* most famous contributors included Hannah Arendt, who was to witness the Eichmann trial in 1961, and subsequently coined the phrase "the banality of evil".

So in 1960 Gunther was searching for Kurt. This is the brother he described on 2nd July 1939 as *the filthy fellow who help in silence*. The Kurt from whom *any support we have not to expect* (26th May 1940). The brother with whom *I am no more corresponding since about 5 years* (28th June 1941). The good looking one (movie star good looking) as the surviving photographs of him show: the earlier portrait of Kurt in a light coloured homburg; the later one of him in a pale linen cap at a rakish angle, dark bow tie against a white shirt, hands in trouser pockets, posing by an Argentinian classical portico. And I think I can just make out a Clark Gable style moustache there. His movie star good looks might be (I surmise) sufficient reason for a portly, balding brother to resent him, though Gunther had reasons enough without that. The main reason is clear. At a time when everything was disappearing – Breslau, Scharnhorststrasse, the father, the diamonds – Kurt had decided to disappear, too.

If poor Aunt Bertha could be dismissed (after her death) as a provoker of *strife*, how much more might Kurt deserve such an epitaph: Kurt, the eldest, whose absence – before and during and long after the war – was for Gunther a lasting provocation. And I realise that I too have come to think of Kurt as an absence – an intriguing one, but an absence nonetheless – lost to the family more by intention than accident, the only known Lewinsohn to retain the family name). Kurt Lewinsohn, who could be counted on not to be found – not to be found alive at least, as Gunther's words – *fate of . . . traces of . . .* – imply that his handsome brother was probably dead.

LETTER FROM GUNTHER
(FIRST TWO PAGES OF LETTER)

Gunther H. Lynn
5844 Beacon St
Pittsburgh 17 / PA
U.S.A.

November 10, 1960:

Dear Sister Gerda:

I am glad to read that everything is fine over there, with one exception that your husband is still ruptured. Does the steel mill where Jacky is employed not take care of it, by giving him some medical care, operation and hospitalization, like they do it in this country? I myself am often plagued by sickness or accidents, and in all cases the company takes care of me.

I am pleased to have these nice pictures of your children. How fast they have grown up! And among them Sandy and Dinky the dachshunds. I always think how happy you are to be surrounded by your children. I myself am approaching my half century of life and by bad luck I have remained an "old bachelor". Nevertheless I have still in mind to get married some day.

It made me happy to read that you received £390 from the "Wiedergutmachung". I did not get a penny yet in spite of my tremendous efforts. Do you have incidentally an old business letter of Schonfeld & Co where all stores father possessed in Breslau are indicated? Please show yourself a little bit active in this matter so that some guarantee for results in this concern can be created. Write to Mr. L – in English, or better in German. It is about time that you brush up your German a little. Of course don't mention the "Kinderchens". Tell him that father was owner of numerous hat stores and houses and add that you don't remember exactly what happened to father's property!

Momentarily I have gone strictly on diet. I am endeavoured to come down from my 227 pounds and stopped candy and sweets . . .

FROM GERDA'S DIARY

31 December 1960

NEW RULES FOR 1961:
Don't talk a lot.
Don't take risks.
Don't get upset even if I miss the best bargain in the world!
It's a gamble, sometimes you win, sometimes you lose. Take it on the chin.
Don't change your mind again.
So no more jumbles starting 1961!
Stick to the rules.

(Changed my mind about the jumbles. Shall definitely NOT give them up!)
Need some fun and change and excitement.
Life is otherwise so dreadfully dull.

At first there appeared to be no diary for 1961 - a further gap in her recorded life – until I discovered another Timothy White's 1958 diary (this one coloured blue with seaweed) to function as a diary for 1961. As with the previous diary, however, it is largely blank – page after page, month after month, until this entry on 3rd May:

Don't go to pieces. It only makes things worse, not better. Lately at times, especially when out, I thought I am going out of my mind. If Gunther saw me now, he would see a proper mess. All this might have a lot to do with my change of life (menopause). They say it upsets women a lot.

There is just a small chance that we may all live out a normal life, so don't give in to fear and despair.

Eventually followed by this on 20th August:

Had very bad neuralgia and my gums (where the teeth have been pulled out) are dreadfully sore. Life is just not worth living when you are not well. Went shopping to Tesco and took the dogs to the park. Only bought food today and ordered £10. 17/- worth of coal. Please God make my gums and face better – Jordan got 2 months prison. He deserves more than that.

Jordan? Colin Jordan, I discovered after yet more internet research, but as I uncovered more information about him, I found there was something wrong with the date. Returning to the blue 1958 diary (with the seaweed design) she used for 1961, it emerged that in fact Gerda used this diary for 1962. The 20th August entry (above) concerning Colin Jordan was therefore 20th August 1962, and not 1961 as I had at first supposed. This now started to make sense. Colin Jordan, a British Nazi, held a meeting in Trafalgar Square on 2nd July 1962. It led to "a riot". In August he hosted an international conference on Nazis, resulting in the "World Union of National Socialists", with Jordan elected as "World Fuhrer". On 16th August 1962 he was charged with attempting to set up a paramilitary force – the "Spearhead" – apparently modelled on the Storm Troopers of Nazi Germany. He was sentenced to nine months' imprisonment in October 1962. Evidently (according to Gerda's diary entry) he did only two months in prison. It might have given her some small satisfaction that he was subsequently convicted (1975) for shoplifting three pairs of women's red knickers.

Gerda, meanwhile, continued to confuse matters by making use of the blue seaweed design 1958 diary for whatever was happening, or deemed noteworthy (inside and outside her head) both in 1961 *and* 1962. On 16th November 1961 she referred to wearing **loads of junk** and vowed to give it all to the **ragman** and discard for good all the **worn out and shabby clothing**. A year later (but in the same diary) she was freshly determined to **hunt for the things I need in jumbles**. It doesn't much matter if it's 1961 or 1962. She is in the same loop. And as far as diary entries are concerned, both years were pretty empty if the written records are anything to go by.

About a year ago (early 2021), when I was going

through all her stuff – not for the first time, of course, but more methodically than before – I put all her diaries aside for a while to search for more promising material. A large and very dusty old brown suitcase deep under the bed in the attic study contained her old newspaper cuttings. This was no new discovery, I had been there before, but not for quite a while. Emptying it onto the "guest" pine bed (seldom used since Covid) in the attic which serves as my "office" (my "Secret Annexe") and fanning them out, I saw that they date from the late 1950s and early 60s. This paper cornucopia had my undivided attention as winter evening turned to night. Yes, I had been here before, it was all familiar, and yet I hadn't, and it wasn't.

The articles she had cut out and packed into that vintage case, with its reinforced studded leather corners, are from the Daily Mirrors, Daily Heralds, Sunday Pictorials, Oxford Mails she either read at that time or bought specially for the headlines and unusual content. Why she kept them is unclear. As evidence of what happened and could happen again? Yes – but why the need to hold onto them? Did she anticipate a quiet, reflective moment in the time left when, drawn back again - whether as warning or penance - she might re-immerse herself in them? Or was she keeping them for us as our half-hidden inheritance? This heavy case with its reinforced studded leather corners contained everything she could not talk about, everything she had left behind, and there it was again, spilling out. It was soon apparent why Gerda had cut out these headlines and horrors, for they are pretty much all to do with the Eichmann trial in Jerusalem in 1961. Adolf Eichmann, "expressionless in his bullet-proof glass cage in court" – Eichmann behind glass, with his glasses and receding hair and smart dark suit and tie, looking like a manager.

From one article about him I discovered he was a manager, a departmental head at Mercedes Benz in Buenos Aires, when Mossad found and abducted him and subsequently smuggled him to Israel to stand trial for crimes against humanity. At the same time, Mossad agents were also looking for Josef Mengele, the "doctor" of Auschwitz, who had also been doing well for himself in South America, applying his medical expertise and expanding his business interests, but the *White Angel* and *Doctor of Death* had by then disappeared. Turning back to Eichmann, I remembered that Kurt was living in Buenos Aires at that time.

In my attic office, leaning over the headlines, while the dormer window darkened to night, I read again of the millions sent to their deaths, with Eichmann personally watching people queue for the gas chambers. Witnesses at the trial told their stories. A woman, "buried alive" beneath corpses in a mass grave, rose from the dead. A man told of a "tremendous area" over which "were scattered skulls and bones and heaps of shoes". One spoke of sweets handed out to children to prevent panic as they were "herded into the gas chambers". The articles touched on other Nazi luminaries. In one I learned that "a gift" awaited Himmler when he arrived at the camp: "several hundred Jewish women specially chosen to be gassed during his inspection". Dr Mengele had a plank nailed across the goal in a football ground at Auschwitz so that he might more easily select, from the 2000 boys paraded there, the 1000 to be chosen for the gas chambers: the shorter boys were the chosen ones.

And so, as I recall, I read on into the night. A Jewish family walking naked into a death pit. Babies tossed up and caught on bayonets. Photographs of the "barbed-wire barrier" at Auschwitz, and starving people packed into their bunks. Eichmann reviewing prisoners on parade at Maidenek and murmuring, "Take the whole heap away." 1000 Jews rounded up in Random, Poland, and led to a pit where they were stripped and machine-gunned into it. Heads of babies smashed against stone pavements in Warsaw. Like Gerda, I read of right-wing groups rising up again, dismissing stories of Nazi atrocities as "propaganda", and arguing that "there was a lot to be said for Hitler".

There were, as I recall, cuttings from earlier papers, too. In one, entitled "Scenes of Chalgrove", pictures of Nissen Huts "in which families are living" (we could have been one of them!), are set against the "pretty thatched cottages" of the original village. There was a cutting of a 1957 speech by Harold Macmillan, reminding Britons (lest they forget) that "they have never had it so good", and wondering if Mr Bevan had actually seen "any of those six million TV aerials which have gone up since 1951" (Gerda's was one of them!) Then this: the oldest cutting, from The Sunday Pictorial, 30th September 1951. I remember wondering why Gerda had singled out this article about the price of calls from public phone kiosks going up to threepence, although the accompanying photo of the woman in the booth looked more than a little like her. Then I got it. 30th September 1951. My birth day.

After about three or four hours of this I was ready to leave these heaps of cuttings for another day, but then I noticed something else. Next to an account of the Eichmann trial was an advert for a "Cresta" sewing-machine: "for the woman who DESERVES the best!" Sifting through, rearranging the cuttings, even odder juxtapositions appeared. Beneath the article on "shoes" from Treblinka – a "Kiss-in-the-Car" court case unfolded, with the jury witnessing two policemen playing "the parts of the couple". Turning a page of Nazi atrocities, a full-page advert confronted me: "Now I See It In Action! The Revolutionary New Bendix Triomatic". A housewife wearing a flared skirt and high heels happily loading her washing machine. Other adverts of the period then jumped out: opposite an article concerning "the industry of extermination" was an advert for kind and gentle skin cream. "Skin is what covers people!" A random reassembling of her cuttings produced more bizarre juxtapositions: "Polly Jolly the Amazon parrot" squawking on the page immediately after heaps of bodies at a liberated Auschwitz-Birkenau.

Remembering that winter evening of a year or so ago, when I first sifted through all these vintage newspaper articles and adverts, and how they had gripped me as few things do, I find myself again reaching under the attic bed for that suitcase of cuttings. *Genug ist genug*, Gerda repeated often enough in her diaries. Enough is enough. Usually she was thinking about her everyday obsessions, but I think it applies well enough to what I have been doing over the past year or so. When I again empty the great suitcase onto the bed, its paper contents a muddled mound, I find myself repeating the actions of a year before. This time around I notice immediately – even without rearranging the papers – the collisions of word and image on the same page or over the page, the juxtapositions of disparate things. *Nein, noch nicht genug, Gerda.* It is like a bizarre jigsaw puzzle where none of the pieces fit together and yet are somehow connected. So it happens that, next to a 1960 photo of a woman known as "The Cuban H-Bomb" in "figure-hugging mesh", I now notice a 1961 article about the "several hundred Jewish women" selected for the gas chambers as a "gift" for Himmler. And next to a photo of blonde Diana Dors waving from the Venice Film Festival, 1955 – Diana "wearing a mink bikini" as she glides down the canals of Venice, and "although there mightn't be a lot of it, it costs £125!" – next to blonde Diana, Eichmann turns up, bespectacled, dark-suited, behind bullet-proof glass.

20

LETTERS FROM KURT

Buenos Aires
May 11, 1963

Dear Gunter,
I am writing you an answer with all my heart. My dear brother,
I am glad to finally receive notes from you and Gerda again.
The suspense is killing me to find out how you and Gerda are
doing, what you are doing and what you are working on, who
you are married to, whether you have children, etc.
Immediately after the last World War, I submitted an
advertisement for a search to the newspaper Aufbau (New
York) in Argentine daily and weekly newspapers. However, no
one answered. I was not aware of the existence of a Jewish
search service as I am far from religious circles because my
ideas and ideals have remained the same!

As children and in our teens, we unfortunately had quarrels.
I do not want to free you from guilt, but much of the blame lies
on me in this, and I regret it. I am self-critical enough not to
ignore that in my adventurous and raging life I: 1) did many
foolish things 2) played dirty.

All right, everything is fine; I'm in my sixties and my
personality has changed completely (but, as I said, not my ideas).

First, one clarification: when I refused to send invitation to our father 26 years ago, it was not by malicious intent, but because the Argentine government did not allow Jews into the country, and because I was in a bad economic situation at that time.

I was then living in an unregistered marriage with a working girl and the salary was barely enough for us to feed ourselves. (In addition, I will note: if my father came here, we would be in great conflict).

And now I want to tell you a little about my life. 1933 (February) I went to Switzerland as a political refugee, however from there immediately to France, where I was involuntarily lounging for many months; then I worked as a rural worker for 2 years and later I moved to Paris. Then I went to Argentina, where I also worked as a rural worker, later as an assistant cook, but was soon appointed to cashier. At the same time, I started working with light metal goods at my own expense. With increasing success I have been working with light metal products (nails, bolts, hinges, etc) for 16 years now. The Argentine economic crisis has affected me at this moment and I have to work with a rather small capital.

I live with a wealthy brother-in-law, an old bachelor, who helps me and my family with money, otherwise our affairs would be very bad again.

My wife is a Sicilian, by birth she is a Catholic, but like me not a believer. Her name is Elena Italia America Scarfi Messima de Lewinsohn. My children were neither baptised nor circumcised. My thirteen-year old daughter is beautiful as a painting, developed beyond her years and very intelligent. I want her to study, but I feel that she will get married very easily. She has started her period and is already ripe. We have a lot in common with my seven-year old son: he had liver disease but is now fully recovered . . .

(remainder of letter missing)

Buenos Aires
Dec 6, 1963

My dear little sister Gerda!

Thank you very much for your postcard! I hope that you, as well as your dearest spouse and your children, feel good.

As for me, my liver is sick and I have to stay in bed, swallow medicine and get a lot of injections. My illness does not represent anything serious, because maybe in 8 days I will be able to start work again. My family is doing well.

As the economic situation here in Argentina is worse than ever, I have to grapple with great difficulties doing business.

Dear little Gerda, in your letter you told me so very little about your life, your children, work, your husband, your plans for Australia, etc. Please make up for this in your next letter!

I stay in touch with the lawyer in Dusseldorf, and so does Gunter. I will be very happy if you tell me in the near future about your impressions regarding the state of this compensation case.

Dear little Gerda, I wish you, also on behalf of my family, good holidays and a happy New Year.

I hug and kiss you heartily

Your brother
Kurt

LETTERS FROM GUNTHER

5844 Beaconst
Pittsburgh/ PA
U.S.A.

January 26, 1964

Dear sister Gerda:

Today I want acknowledge receipt of your nice letters of Dec 12 and Dec 30, 1963. I thank you for your new year wishes, which I received now as the new year is quite in progress. I was very pleased to read about your experience over there.

What has become of your appearance on TV for Polo-mints? Maybe you will become a celebrity?!

I hope that the winter is milder in England. Here it is milder, though recently we had tremendous snow-blizzards which blocked me the road to go to work. Things are turning out pretty good for me. I am not complaining!. I had been called to play to numerous X-mas parties and still I am doing fine in the musical line, though I am not a youngster any more.

Your German is perfectly OK and found my great approval. Write some more lines in German. Now some more exciting news. Curt is seriously ill in the hospital. As I mentioned already he has a kidney-liver ailment. Things are very grave. He steadily gets shots of penicillin and even 2 blood transfusions. Please write to Curt and inquire about his illness.

My birthday of Jan 12 passed quickly. I received lots of "bosels" from my friends in L.A. I found out that "Lee's" candy of Los Angeles is the best. I don't smoke and drink but still I'm fond of chocolates and fine foods. Oh boy, oh boy!!

My best wishes and kisses from your brother Gunther Please write soon!

NO ADDRESS (PITTSBURGH/ PA)

March 8, 1964

Dear Gerda:

My best thanks for your letter of 31-1-64. I am glad to read that last year the Winter was milder and you don't have reason to complain. Here things have not changed a bit, I still keep working intensively.

Curt left my last letter to him unanswered because I rejected strongly his attitude as "communistic fighter and agitator". He obviously is really proud of this !!!! However on account of this behaviour he should not wonder that the lawyer is ignoring our restitution-case completely already for quite some time, but Curt thinks people are dumb. There is no doubt that the Wiedergutmachung unit will have attained information about Curt's activities, and the West German Government is bitterly opposed to Curt's adopted doctrine.

Nevertheless I hope that Curt will get well soon, so he will leave at least the hospital.

So far for to-day.

Your brother Gunther

LETTER FROM ELENA LEWINSOHN

Buenos Aires
29, 4, 1964

Dear Sister-in-law Gerda

I received your letter and I thank you very much for your sympathy and condolence wishes.

I am sorry to tell you that the death of my husband was not just a casualty; it was caused by heavy drinking of WINE. When I met your brother first he did not have the habit of drinking that much. But the older he got the more he drank. He turned to look much older than he actually was. As a matter of fact, when he was hospitalized people had the impression that Curt would be "my sick FATHER". The lasting alcohol made him look awfully old. Furthermore he had strange ideas in his mind. Crazed by strange political ideals happened then what never should occur: namely, that Curt was out to kill himself by drinking WINE. Nobody could hold him back from this vice; he just got mad when I tried to stop him.

Will you write to me?

Elena Lewinsohn

LETTERS FROM GUNTHER

5844 Beaconst
Pittsburgh/ PA
U.S.A.
June 3, 1964

Dear Gerda

My best thanks for your letter of May 23, 1964.

Meanwhile I filled out all the forms you sent me the other day.

You was supposed to sign the papers first, what you forgot to do. As soon as you receive the forms, please sign them on the backsides, on the bottom where is written "Unterschrift".

It was a terrible work to fill out all these forms. Unfortunately there are many contradictions in the files with regard to father's transactions. It is claimed that father sold his houses voluntary and not compulsory, under pressure of the Nazi-Regime. Even in some cases they gave proof of it. Also I am unable to name witnesses with regard to father's real-estate property. If there should come any more questions, then let them know that you talked over these things with me but that you have not the right idea what happened because you was too young at that time.

Meanwhile Curt's former wife in B'Aires wrote again a long letter in Spanish to me, complaining and denouncing Curt for his misbehaviour and faults he had. She tells me that he had little by little turned to be a "bad boy", but I insist that Curt was always out of his mind, an upset minded intellectual with crazy ideas. And she should have found out about him before she married him. I have other headaches than to start up a long correspondence with her. I know she is distressed, but right now I cannot help her, I have to struggle myself to make a living. I was suffering last time some kind of "nervous stress".

Some time later I'll write more comfortable. Today I want just tell you about the forms. Don't forget to sign them.

My best regards and my best wishes to your birthday. Your brother, Gunther.

5844 Beaconst
Pittsburgh/ PA
U.S.A.
September 27, 1964

Dear Sister Gerda:

I have to apologise that I answer so delayed your letter, but there are some reasons for it. In first place I am still a little suffering of mental stress. I guess I am overworked, overtired. I was under the doctor's care who gave me pills to quiet down my nerves.

I am highly impressed by the coloured picture you sent me. Your children, very nice looking and obviously strong and healthy seem little by little to turn into teenagers, probably the main reason why recently you moved to your more comfortable house. The 2 dachshunds are really looking cute though they're not youngsters any more. I'll get a chance to meet your children and all members of your family personally. I can't stop looking at the picture, because all 4 of you and the dogs look gorgeously. When I saw you the last time about 25 years ago I never imagined that you would build up a big family. I am very worried practically to be alone and not have taken a chance yet to get married. Do you still remember the days we spent in Prague – Victoria College?

No more news about the restitution case which has become completely deadlocked and I don't know what I am going to do. Did Curt's Argentine wife ever write again? Curt and I we more often were of different opinions, but the news that he died

*came shocking to me. Curt was a highly intelligent man, and I
cannot agree with his wife who denounces him as "absent-
minded Wine-drinker". Curt was probably economically so
distressed that he killed himself by sticking to the bottle.*

*Please write again and let me know how you like your new
residence!*
In Love, your brother, Gunther.

FROM GERDA'S DIARY

23 November, 1964:

Today my beloved Sandy died. We had him destroyed. He
was unhappy and in pain and it might have gone on like that
for a long time. I couldn't bear to see him suffer so. He did
not appreciate my help in the end, but snapped at me when
I touched him. I could not have nursed him back to health.
He would not let me carry him. He didn't eat in the end and
would not take his pill. So I thought it would be best for all
if he goes, but I did love him so. He was my best pal, my
best companion, and I do miss him so very much. We had 8
perfect years together. He could be a bit naughty and I
smacked him hard at times as I got a temper and I hate
destructiveness, but on the whole he was a happy
contented dog with the love of us all and the company of
Dinky which he loved. God bless him and thank You very
much for having given him to me. 8 years is quite a good
long life for a dog and I think he would have hated old age.
Dear God forgive me if I've done wrong. I always try to do
my best but I go wrong sometimes. Give me strength to
carry on and forgive me all my sins. Bless Sandy for me. I
miss him so. I miss his love. He never shouted at me and
nagged at me. He was all love. Oh Sandy I miss you so!

As for the death of Kurt (or Curt as he came to be called, presumably to de-Germanize it) I recall hearing nothing at the time, though his moment would come. Nothing was ever said about his politics, so these letters were news to me. When I wrote earlier that Kurt was a blank vanishing into the vaster blankness of Argentina, the words merely reflected what I knew of him. The mirror of her memory – in those odd moments when she held it up to people from her past – bore almost no trace of Kurt, who was at most a shadow man. So for this shadow man to emerge from these previously unknown letters was a surprise. He was the eldest brother who lacked substance, literally lacked substance from March/April 1964. Suddenly there he was, alive and kicking – at least on paper.

Uncle Gunther of Pittsburgh was known, and it was also known that he sometimes enclosed dollar notes in his blue airmail letters. But Gunter without his *h*, Gunter of Ecuador, Gunter of the Costa Rica Swing-Boy Orchestra, Gunter of the Honky Tonk Piano? The Uncle Gunther we knew was *American*, his airmail letters bore stamps of Presidents and the Statue of Liberty – this we knew, and it set us apart from the rest of the council estate, as if through him we were marginally American; American by proxy. Now that I think about it, Gerda might not have always bothered to notify us when she got a letter from her brother, since that side of her life was her own. As for any news of Kurt – anything at all about Kurt – he was at least consistently absent.

And now I want to tell you a little about my life. 1933 (February) I went to Switzerland as a political refugee, however from there immediately to France, where I was involuntarily lounging for many months; then I worked as a rural worker for 2 years and later I moved to Paris. Then I went to Argentina, where I . . .

Kurt's story of his journey from Germany in 1933 was news to me until a year ago, though no surprise considering who became Chancellor that year in Germany. Switzerland was news. Anything about Kurt was news. Reading his translated letters was like uncovering someone long submerged, like a fallen skier whose thawing body emerges as the glacier ice melts

Tracking back to his earliest letter (7th November 1935), I found that he had not seen his little sister since he left Germany, and was thanking her for her letter from the mountains. So Kurt last saw her in 1933, before leaving for Switzerland (which meant that by 1963 he hadn't seen his sister for thirty years.) *I lost sight of you*, he wrote in 1935, *and constantly picture you as a little girl who plays with Gunter or who has fun with her dolls.* That then was his enduring image of her: as a girl in Germany in year one of a Third Reich meant to last a thousand years. Kurt's reference to her letter from the mountains now reminds me of something... I track back, or rather forward, through the piles of correspondence still before me, to the letter dated 26th August 1954 from her other brother (the one who kept in touch), who was asking if she remembered being *sweet sixteen* when they all went *with Tatzel, Tante Bertha, and Pussy in the "Lotte-car" to the Zoblen Mountain.* That *Mountain* is in the Tannheim Mountains of the Austrian Tyrol, and it is likely that Gunther was remembering a skiing holiday there. But checking the dates, I find that Gunther was either remembering different mountains or the same mountains in a different year, because Gerda was *sweet sixteen* in 1937. On 7th November 1935, when Kurt was acknowledging her letter *from the mountains*, she was only fourteen. It is possible that she was holidaying in the mountains in 1935 *and* 1937, despite the Third Reich – and indeed I have recently found evidence of this.

In 1935 the "impractical" and "idealistic" Kurt was in rural France, earning a living by *feeding pigs*, though taking time off from his labours to reply to his little sister's letter and ask her if she has *a couple of cute girlfriends* (apparently one would not be enough). In 1935 Kurt was not yet the angry, alienated son of the 21st May 1939 letter, who by then had become almost as distanced from *der Vater* as from *das Vaterland*. By the time Gerda is about to leave Germany for good (of which Kurt seems unaware) he is mainly brooding on his father, regretting that he can do nothing to help him. It took him a further thirty years to explain why he *refused to send invitation to our father 26 years ago*. It was because *the Argentine government didn't allow Jews into the country*.

While post-war Argentine politics aren't my research area, I have found out enough (from the internet) to begin to understand Kurt's predicament. I have read that, before the Second World War, Peron considered Mussolini and Hitler admirable models of fascism, and that Argentina provided post-war protection for Nazi war criminals – including Mengele and Eichmann. The internet also informs me that Argentina accepted more Jewish immigrants than any other country in Latin America. But in 1939, Kurt may have been right about not being able to help his father, for it seems that Argentina was ambivalent in its attitude. A government can be anti-Semitic and still allow Jews in, if that is to its advantage. It would be interesting to know what Kurt thought of the protection of Nazi war criminals.

About Peron I knew little before uncovering the Kurt correspondence. I had heard of Evita, but only through that song when she asks Argentina not to cry for her. From what I now know, it appears that (despite Argentina later welcoming Nazi war criminals) Kurt became a Peronist.

Workers' rights and workers' pay, social justice, access to health care and social security, kindergartens, schools and housing, a nationalisation programme, the rights of the common labourer, the rights of women – Kurt could well have agitated for all that. Why else would his younger brother, a US citizen, describe him (almost with affection) as *always out of his mind, an upset minded intellectual with crazy ideas*? Gunther disapproved of him, first for disappearing for a quarter of a century, then for reappearing as a *communistic fighter and agitator*, thus attracting the attention of the West German Government and putting the restitution-case at risk. So perhaps it was just as well that Kurt died when he did, aged fifty-four, because his *ideas and ideals remained the same* and he was *really proud* of beliefs that could have only further damaged the restitution-case had he gone on living.

Studying the Kurt/Curt letters again, I can see that, for all his later rationalisations and defensiveness, he remained guilty, even anguished, nearly a quarter of a century on. *Say hello to dear dad*, he ended his letter to Gerda in May 1939. After 1933, Kurt would never again say hello or goodbye to his father.

News of Kurt's death *came shocking* to Gunther, for as Gerda had once observed in one of her few surviving letters, Kurt was *family*. Whatever Gunther thought of his brother, family was family, and I imagine Gunther always saw himself as the responsible one who looked after the family, especially as it was falling apart. Though he might denigrate Kurt, he could not agree with Kurt's widow when she denounced him as an *absent-minded Wine-drinker and bad boy*. Later, Gunther wrote of him: *I never was fond of alkoholic beverages like dear Curt, who drank himself to death*. It was, if not a kind epitaph, a not unkind one, since by dying prematurely Kurt had turned into *dear Curt.* He had also aged prematurely (as his wife described him) into a *sick FATHER,* perhaps unconsciously taking on his own father's cancer-ridden appearance at the end.

Gerda's response to the death remains unknown. About eight years later, she spoke of Kurt's widow with a resentment she usually confined to her diary, but then it was to do with money, and money always brought her out of herself. Over the past year I have sometimes imagined them, the three Lewinsohn siblings, meeting in a room, conversing in the only language (German) they could all still speak, finding out what had happened. That was never going to happen – even if Kurt had not drunk himself to death. Apart from his *distressed economic circumstances* it seems most unlikely that he'd have broken the habit of a lifetime and sought such a meeting. And as for Gunther, despite his repeated wish to visit his sister and her family in England, there is no evidence of any plan to do so. Better perhaps to remember each other as they once were, back in Breslau. And as for Gerda, she'd have done anything in her power to prevent a family reunion. I believe she'd have been ashamed to meet her brothers and let them witness not the little sister, the *Gerdala* of their letters, but the layered woman she had become, whose only enjoyment in life was jumble sales and charity shops. Better to be remembered as a girl in Germany, a wonderful person (as Kurt wrote in May 1939 on the eve of her departure), with *such understanding and subtle taste.*

Being movie star handsome in the only two photographs circa 1939 somewhere in Argentina, Kurt easily turns into a Clark Gable lookalike complete with pencilled moustache. There was something of Rhett Butler in him then, and this is not so far-fetched, since

Gone With The Wind came out in 1939 and was so popular when first released that Kurt might have seen it in Buenos Aires. Gerda saw it – probably more than once – but only the later occasion is recorded in a diary, and without further comment.

Whether Gerda (on receiving that unexpected letter from the widow)) saw her movie star brother through the eyes of Elena Italia America Scarfi Messima de Lewinsohn – with an aged father's hospital face superimposed on those film star features – is unknown. Perhaps news of his death took her back to Kurt's letter to her in 1935 when he admitted having *lost sight of you* and pictured her still as a little sister in Germany playing with her dolls. Did she go all the way back and recall writing to him from the mountains? There must have been many times in the mountains, for there are as many diary references to them, and photographs of Gerda in alpine resorts have also survived. In one such diary entry, in February 1937, she *war vereisst* (was travelling) to Spindlermuhle (now Spindleruv Mlyn in the Czech Republic) where she stayed for two weeks. She was sixteen then; about the age she looks in the photograph before me now, taken in some unnamed ski resort, where she is wearing a dark hat, dark jacket with wide checked lapels, and dark baggy Turkish trousers, and poses with a friend against an expansive unmarked snow scene. They look excited, with their skis and poles, as if about to take off. And in another scene, Gerda is ice-skating, a pine-covered white slope behind her, with her right arm half raised, the gloved hand clenched and thrust forward. The back of the photo is inscribed, *Spindlermuhle 1937*, which confirms it. She was never happier than in those surviving moments on snow and ice. In the same little batch is one picturing the Hotel Belvidere as it must have appeared then, but with no people about, no skiers or skaters, no snow, no ice. With its grand portico and balconies, the hotel (where she stayed?) nestles in a grassy meadow. An internet search informs me that Hotel Belvidere is "closed" and there is a "major auction".

Perhaps those long-past happy times came back to her with the death of Kurt. It is possible, though, that she didn't think of him or of those lost days for very long, as by 1964 she had more pressing things on her mind.

21

LETTER FROM GUNTHER

(NO ADDRESS WRITTEN)

December 25, 1964

Dear sister Gerda:

Today on X–mas day at last I get a chance to settle down and answer your nice letter of Nov 2, '64. As I see, you already are used to your new residence and keep Jacky busy with "21 jobs" around the house. I hope that you like it there! Maybe your dachshunds, Sandy the doggy and Dinky, will be puzzled a little by their new residence? It is now X-mas afternoon and in one of the nearby restaurants I had a lamb-chop dinner. If weather is nasty I stay here in my borough of Squirrel Hill, a high class residential section.

Right now my life goes smoothly. Fortunately my state of health has improved and my spells of jittery nerves and mental stress have gone. Some friends of mine found strange definitions for my nervous condition. Some say it could be change of life. Some others say I am depressed because I miss that income I had at Heinz. You think it must be in the family because you too pretend to be nervous once in a while. Curt in his last letter confessed that he was rather nervous too and he blamed it on our ancestors.

I have not to complain. Actually I am still employed in the Music – Store, I teach children in mass - Piano, Accordion, Guitar, Trumpet, and Organ, I repair and sell instruments, and Fridays and Saturdays I am engaged in a High – class restaurant where I play by myself, alternating piano and accordion, mostly request pieces. I am not on the way to become a millionaire, however my income is satisfactory.

Elena, our sister-in-law in B 'Aires, mentioned the other day that a certain Dr. Lucas, a close friend of Curt, will try to push forward a little our restitution-case. This may bring quick results to my long pending efforts. The greatest difficulty right now is to obtain the death certificate for mother who is buried in Breslau. The date of her death is unknown to me. Nevertheless I wrote to the Polish Consulate in N.Y. City and I hope that I get an answer. I had to send $10.00 to the Funeraria Israelita in Quito and I am expecting the death certificate of father in one of these days.

So far for today!

Please write as soon as possible.

Prosit Neujahr!

Your brother, Gunther

Peter Thornthwaite

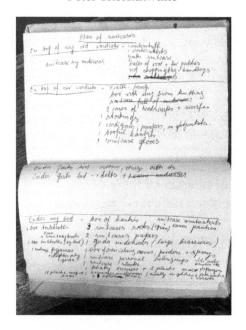

FROM GERDA'S DIARY

January 1965:

Plan of Suitcases:

What I have in kitchen larder – storeroom =

- 1 suitcase scarfs
- 1 suitcase blue children's raincoats
- 3 suitcases socks
- 1 suitcase shoe cloths
- 1 suitcase pyjamas
- 1 suitcase girls' brassieres and silk panties
- 1 suitcase corsets
- 1 suitcase swimming costumes

2 suitcases trousers (Jacky and Peter)
2 suitcases winter skirts

What I have under girls' bed:

1 box belts and warm underwear
2 boxes pyjama wear
2 suitcases jumpers
1 suitcase aprons and plastic curtains
Box full of summer clothing Gerda
1 suitcase skirts Gerda if I get slimmer

What I have under Jack's bed:

Ribbons, strings, belts etc
1 large suitcase fleece long-johns etc
2 suitcases work trousers

Under Peter's bed:

1 large suitcase vests and shirts
1 suitcase underwear
2 suitcases jackets and jumpers
(I have looked at indoor cupboard in Peter's room. It might be big enough for suitcases. In this case buy another wardrobe for Peter.)

Under my bed:

1 suitcase hankies
1 suitcase winter skirts
1 suitcase warm panties
1 Gerda underwear (large brassieres)
2 suitcases papers

1 suitcase personal belongings – odds and ends, photos etc

1 khaki trousers and 2 plastic macs

1 suitcase summer underwear – mostly nighties and petticoats, corsets (Gerda)

1 suitcase slacks

1 box vanishing creams, powders and sprays

1 box toilet rolls

1 box sanitary towels

On top of my old wardrobe:

1 winter stuff

1 winter skirts

Balls of wool for patches

Red shopping bag and handbags

1 suitcase my underwear

Jack's suitcase

On top of new wardrobe:

Health lamp

Box with my brown knitting

2 suitcases of head scarfs and scarfs

1 suitcase of stockings

1 suitcase of cardigans, jumpers, night jackets

1 box of hankies

1 suitcase gloves

Plan for downstairs:

1 bedroom Gerda. Find curtained off space for my suitcases. Need big wardrobe for my coats. Settee for dogs.

April/May/June 1965:

I REALLY must pack it in now. We are deep in debt. Every penny counts.

NE !!!!

Saturday 23rd Jumble – I am definitely going to enjoy myself too much. Must have a bit of fun. But be careful -

Try NE again.

Tuesday 11 May went Spastic shop =

1 pink petticoat = 6d

3 crochet jumpers = 1/6

1 pillow = 3/-

1 brown cardigan = 5/-

1 blue raincoat = 3/-

I vest = 6d

1 shirt = 6d

1 knitted vest = 6d

Coat hangers = 7d

2 rubber bones

Spent altogether 16/6 !

Try NE again!!

Monday 7 June -

NE from now on

2 dressing gowns Spastic shop 6/-

Definitely No more

NE NE NE NE NE

Even if I am bored!

Peter Thornthwaite

LETTER FROM GUNTHER

(NO ADDRESS STATED.)

June 22, 1965

Dear Gerda:

Being always on the go, I never get a chance to answer your nice letter of April 21, '65. Here in Pittsburgh we are plagued by heat waves and not having air-conditioning I feel "beat by the heat".

I am glad to read that you are doing fine over there, however I am sorry to read that Jacky was on strike for 3 weeks, and that you have stomach upsets. I cannot stand fatty food either, it causes too much strain to the liver and gallbladder. Besides of it, right now I try to lose a little bit of weight and come down from my 225 pounds, and I cut out all foods where too much sugar is in it.

In the pending restitution-case I am again sent such a large sheet to fill out, and for the procedure of our case many difficulties have to be overcome. The competent offices ask thousands of questions and want all kind of witnesses and documents which I cannot procure. Years passed by and most of the people who should have been witnesses passed away. Nevertheless let's hold on, maybe something will turn out, otherwise we would be advised to give up. Particularly for Elena's family in Buenos Aires I feel sorry that she lives there distressed and would need some restitution-money badly.

Pretty soon I'll be on vacation and probably I will make a week's trip to Atlantic City, to have some good opportunity for swimming. Maybe then I'll feel like the "King of the Road". I guess that song has also the title "Queen of the House".

I just drop you this few lines to let you know that I am still kicking, and I'll continue another time. Enclosed please find $10.00.

With love Your brother
Gunther

FROM GERDA'S DIARY

SEPTEMBER/OCTOBER/NOVEMBER 1965:

Definitely pack jumbles in now
Verstand =
Got plenty
Degrading
Might get into trouble
Takes up too much room
Might get moth in.

Make do and mend
Utilize and Organize
Massige Lebensweise
Greed = Downfall.

Don't look at adverts anywhere.
Look the other way.
Was Du nicht weiss, macht Dich nicht heiss.

(*Massige Lebensweise* translates as massive way of life. Maybe she meant massive change in lifestyle needed to turn her life around?)

Peter Thornthwaite

LETTER FROM GUNTHER

5844 Beacons
Pittsburgh/ PA
U.S.A.
December 31, 1965

Dear Gerda:

My best thanks for your letter of November 22, '65. Today is New-Years Eve Sunday and I must say that these many holidays with long week-ends are nerve-wracking. I am so used to keep myself busy all the time. Still I gave guitar-lessons in the afternoon and then went to the "Kaffee Klatsch" in the nearby Friendship-Club. I had some good coffee and (yum, yum!) Streuselkuchen. I am still sweet-mouth. Though always engaged in night-Clubs and beer-Joints I never was fond of alkoholic beverages like dear Curt, who drank himself to death.

According to newspapers, chancellor Erhard in Germany wants postpone restitution-payments for 2 years. Let's wait and see because the "nazi-victims" are protesting vigorously against the German decision.

Enclosed please find $10.00 which I promised you in my last letter and use it as ever you want to. My best wishes for the new year and "Gesundheit" to you Your brother Gunther.

Verstand, which translates as understanding, arches over the September–November 1965 entries: Gerda had to understand that, unless she definitely packed in the jumbles immediately and drastically changed her way of life, there would be the direst consequences. **Was Du nicht weiss, macht Dich nicht heiss.** What you don't know doesn't make you hot. Evidently she knew a lot – too much – that made her hot and bothered – worked-up – over-excited – because that's what she felt most of the time. It wasn't good for her to get "too over-excited", she knew, but it was what she lived for. It was *all* she lived for. Otherwise life was **too utterly utterly boring.** Jumbles, charity shops, bargains, packed suitcases – these were the only things that made her life worth living. Without them the world was a windblown wasteland. But she had to give them all up, renounce the only things that gave her life any meaning, because she did not deserve them, and self-denial is good for you. That is my own surmise. Or she may have needed the excitement of such renunciations. How can you know how badly – desperately – you need something until you renounce it? The only thing then left to her was to go back on her word, deny denial, renounce renunciation. Maybe I'm over-complicating things. The fact is – she found life boring. There was no satisfaction for her in it. She liked spending money, and if she had "lots of lolly" (to use her words), she wouldn't have bothered with smelly jumble sales and cheap charity shops. Gerda had precious little else to amuse or distract her in life. So why not go to jumbles etc? It harmed no one. It gave her something to do and look forward to. And, after all, she was doing it for the family, too.

From 1965 her diaries are not diaries in the normal sense, but detailed lists of clothing and other household items, **bargains** or **blow-flies** as she referred to them, with dates of purchase, and amounts totalled.. Where once the word **ARBEITE!** had dominated her diaries – by 1965 **ARBEITE** has disappeared for good, replaced by **NE**, endlessly repeated. **NE** was code, alive with life-changing meaning for her, if meaningless to anyone happening to go through her diaries. Meaningless? Not to a code-breaker. For some time I pondered her repeated words, **Never Again**. Her recurring **Never Again** presented no difficulty. **NE** did. Until I noticed the words - **Nothing Else** – and having once noticed them, noticed nothing else for a while. They were everywhere in her diaries, ending list after list as if, having arrived at such a definite and irreversible decision, there was nothing else to write. **Only buy what you really need. Buy Nothing Else!** Excitedly, I went back to her entry for Monday 7th June 1965: **NE NE NE NE NE**. *I think I understand you now. I get it. Verstanden, Gerda. Verstanden.*

This strict new *penny-pinching* of hers unfortunately coincided with moving to a new and more spacious house; so just as Gerda was determining to cut back on her spending, she suddenly had so much more living space available to her. As Gunther noted in his letter of 25th December 1964: *As I see, you already are used to your new residence.*

This latest (and last) move was to a pre-war house with a vintage butler's and servants' bell indicator box in the *Morning Room,* alerting any servants still around to a summons from *Front Door, Back Door, Dining Room, Drawing Room, Bath Room, Best Bed Room, Bed Room 2, Bed Room 3*, etc. It had a pantry and a scullery, built-in pine cupboards, a vast, overarching attic – all desperately needed storage space. As Gerda's 1965 diary reveals, it was the year of the *plan*.

Her **Plan of Suitcases**, in front of me again, is a

wonderful reminder of just how many suitcases she had accumulated by the mid '60s. Finally, Gerda had the living space and storage space she needed. There were so many spaces for cases: in the pantry; under great mahogany beds; on top of massive Victorian wardrobes, in built-in deep old pine cupboards, and in that vast attic.

As Gunther wrote on 22nd June 1965, he might be *King of the Road*, but she was *Queen of the House*. It was hers to fill. That was really the start of the suitcases. They must have been around before the move, but I associate them with that house. That was where they multiplied. Maybe I do her an injustice – implying that there was something peculiar about amassing, stacking up, hoarding as many old brown suitcases as she did. Personally I like suitcases, especially the vintage cases she collected; I wish I had kept them. And I have to admit that at the time they soon became more or less invisible as we got used to them. They were everywhere in the house, and I stopped noticing. If she was building walls of suitcases, they were walls you could pass through without really seeing them.

What I did not know then was that the diaries were coming to an end. The suitcases were her new diaries, and she put herself into them. The diaries had become too much trouble for her. That's my guess. They were too argumentative. She did nothing but quarrel with herself in them – deciding, determining what to do, only to go back on it. There were decisions to be made with suitcases, but these were simply a question of category – what type of clothing to pack. In suitcases, she had finally found useful work. These were the clothes the family would need one day. **ARBEITE** was coming back as her byword, and she had finally found a job to occupy her: packing clothes as security against an uncertain future. This was **UTILIZE and ORGANISE.** This was a five-year plan: a **Plan of Suitcases.**

Her Plan of Suitcases required simple classification of the type of clothes to be found within: Pyjamas. Vests. Socks. Shirts. Trousers. Blouses. Underwear. Skirts. Jumpers. Woollens. Etc. There were sub-classifications: Winter Skirts. Warm Panties. Etc. Classification by name: Gerda, Underwear. Jack, Fleecy Long-johns. Etc. Further refinements helped such as: Skirts Gerda, if I get slimmer. Now that she had room to expand, she could feel happy in her work. This was far from being a labour of love, though. Folding each item into its satin-lined case, remembering the struggle involved, the snatching hands of other women, the nagging question, *bargain or blow-fly*? What had at first seemed an absolute bargain could not be trusted; on closer inspection it would turn out to be a blow-fly. It was never the other way around. Most bargains were really blow-flies in disguise, hiding in plain sight. It was a fearful task at the best of times. Pennies turned into pounds. Spending, *the only fun I ever have*, turned to recrimination and guilt. Gerda must have turned these things over and over in her mind, as she packed her suitcases, and I do not belittle or denigrate what all this meant to her. With the suitcases packed and stacked and stowed, the family's future secured at last, she was doing what was still in her power to achieve. She needed to be vigilant, though. Her enemies were out there and had to be exterminated, or they would lay hundreds of eggs and turn into white and yellow larvae and live for years in their little woollen world, leaving only holes behind.

22

LETTER FROM GUNTHER

5844 Beacons
Pittsburgh/ PA
U.S.A.

April 10, 1966

Dear Sister Gerda:
*Today on a quiet Easter Sunday I will settle down and drop
you a few lines. My birthday passed by quietly. I just received
a fine box of candy from my friends in L.A. Unfortunately in
the last few months I am persecuted by bad-luck. I crashed
several times with my car and just a week ago a drunkard,
going on the wrong side of the road, collided with my car. I was
in a state of shock, but thanks God nothing fatal had happened
to me.*

*Still I keep myself busy and I have not to worry. Are you still
suffering of colds and fibrositis? I just read in the newspaper
about Cystic Fibrositis. As a child you had a very serious
operation performed by Dr. Steinitz, maybe some traces have
caused fibrositis.*

*The lawyer sent me another mountain of documents to fill
out. I am very disappointed because I am left with empty hands*

in spite of all the efforts I made. I am not a youngster any more and I myself am expecting a restitution pay to have life a little more comfortable. I am getting a little old now and I cannot get around so fast any more like I used to.

Enclosed please find $10.00.

In love, your brother

Gunther

FROM GERDA'S DIARY

APRIL 1966:

Really NE now.
No more Spastic shop.
No more Thalidomide.
No more second hand shops.
No more market stalls.
No more jumbles.
That's the thing to know when to stop!
Enough of everything.

JUNE 1966:

Ate too much today.

I am back to 9 stones 4 lbs. I want to go right down to 8 stones 1 lb. So I have to lose 17 lbs. If I could lose 1 lb daily I could do it in 17 days! So eat very little.

Try the small amount diet.

Peck like a bird.

Liquid diet didn't work. Wanted food too much.
Bought grey cardigan for my birthday. Sehr teuer! Es war drei Pfund zwolf und sechs.

Liebes Gott, ich habe mich sehr grosse Angst.

Next year for my birthday I want a pair of Moccasins. If I have a win or get a lot of money I shall buy them before that.

No more Spastic shop now!!!

Went Spastic again.

I must not go anywhere anymore.

NE

Allzu viel ist ungesund.

(*Sehr teuer* – very dear; *drei Pfund zwolf und sechs* – £3 12 shillings and sixpence; . . . *ich habe mich sehr grosse Angst* – dear God, I am very frightened; *Allzuviel* . . . – Too much is unhealthy.)

That girl in the shop was downright rude to me. Doesn't let me look at clothes, says every jumper was sold, but has a lot of patience with other people and is nice to them. She definitely detests me. Fancy accusing me of pinching a brown jacket. She said I was the last one to handle it. Anybody might have come in and pinched it. Why me? I shall never go there again, or to the other second hand shop. People in second hand shops are nearly always rude and vulgar. Liebes Gott please help me. Verzeihe mir alle Sunden und Fehler. PS. Jacket had stain on it and too long sleeves.

(*Verzeihe mir* . . . Forgive me all my sins and mistakes.)
I have got enough!

344

Pack it in while the going is good.
Moths!
Enough until death.

CARD FROM GUNTHER
(DEPICTING OLD GABLED COTTAGES BY STONE
BRIDGE)

NO ADDRESS
September 27, 1966:

Dear Gerda:
I hope you had a nice summer with lots of swimming and hiking. Most of my friends have gone to Europe and are still travelling around. I went to Atlantic City, riding the bicycle on the 4 miles long Boardwalk.

I still make great efforts to get established in my own business as piano – technician and instructor and fortunately I am quite successful. The season now starts and I get abundant work from the Board of Public Education and Pittsburgh's greatest Department stores. I cannot get too rich on it, but I am happy doing this kind of work and not to have the slave job in the food factory.

I just got again a "mountain" of documents from the lawyer and I did not get a chance yet to study them. I am disappointed about the results I get out of it and still am left with empty hands. I am getting a little old now and I cannot get around so fast anymore like I used to.
Enclosed please find $10.00
In love
Your brother Gunther

FROM GERDA'S DIARY

17 October, 1966:

Bought 2 lipsticks (reduced). That was quite unnecessary.

No more lipsticks ever now. I have got enough to last me a lifetime.

I do wish people next door would move. They are a blasted nuisance. They make a lot of noise, have smelly fires, and are cruel to cats. Wish they would go!

UNDATED: NOVEMBER? 1966:

What to live for?
My health -
in every way
mental
and physical!

UNDATED: DECEMBER? 1966:

There are 4 suitcases of socks under my bed.
Can't take it with me.
Moths!

FROM LAW FIRM'S LETTER TO GERDA CONCERNING COMPENSATION CLAIM

DUSSELDORF

Den 22.2.1967:

Ich bitte Sie eine eidesstattliche Versicherung mit Aufstellung aller Juwelen und Gold – Schmuck – Silbersachen . . . wann Sie diese Sachen zuletzt im Besitz Ihres vaters gesehen haben (wahrscheinlich vor Ihrer eigenen Auswanderung im Jahre 1939) . . .

(I am requesting an affidavit of all jewels and gold – jewellery – silver items . . . when was the last time you saw these things in your father's possession (probably before your own emigration in 1939) . . .)

LETTERS FROM GUNTHER

Gunther Lynn
5844 Beacon St
Pittsburgh/ PA 15227
U.S.A.

March 27, 1967:

Dear Gerda:
Everything here goes fast and I have to hustle all the time to make a living. Every morning I make 15 minutes exercise to keep me fit. Practically I should use the chest expanders and lift the weights like Peter!
  I heard again from the lawyer who mentioned that she sent

you important documents to fill out, and it was told to me that you must send these forms to me. I did not receive anything from you! I gave her in my last letter some important facts about father's former property and I hope that something will turn out. Don't you have any German speaking friends there who can advise you now and again?

Since my last automobile accident I have a nagging back ache and hope that during summer this will cease. I wished I would be 20 years younger. I always tried to become the "rich uncle from America" but I did not quite succeed in my endeavourments. In the last time I even lost lots of money by my investments in the stock-market, and also from the Department store for what I tuned pianos – it owes me still $127.00! Among my close friends here I am considered a penny - pincher and miser, and you'll imagine how many sleepless nights I had by the loss of money. Nevertheless enclosed find $20.00. Please acknowledge receipt in your next letter.

Generally spoken I must say that right now I have not intention to make any changes. Life here is thrilling and exciting. Though I planned a trip to Europe to see you there, I cannot predict when this I will realize.

Happy Easter greetings and love from your brother Gunther

*5844 Beaconst
Pittsburgh/ PA
U.S.A.*

August 27, 1967

*Dear Gerda:
I never took a chance to answer your 8 pages long letter of March 30, 1967. Oh boy, every line so nice and clean written*

by you and the most part by your children. Even Jacky writes very comfortable too and gives me an advice how to get rid of my backache which I have just at the morning rise. I was afraid it could mean a slipped disk in my back, but the doctor was laughing and he meant I am too heavy and should reduce. I weighed 227 lb, now by diet I am down..

I did not know that there was a dog named Teddy in your house. I would like to know whether you had a nice Summer? Did you go to places? I guess all your children know to swim and like it too. Peter, I think, is swimming every day.

Figure, on June 5 some young kid ran like crazy with his Ford-Mustang in my almost new American Rambler which I had parked in a fine residential section. That guy must have slept for he hit my car so badly in the rear that the muffler and fender were flying around like "flying saucers". My car had been declared a total loss. And I had been congratulated, that I was not inside the car, for I would have been chopped to death. After having gotten quite a lot of money by the insurance I bought a brand new Chevrolet automatic, 120 horsepower. I hate to drive because here the cars go bumper to bumper.

Your children write, "I hope that you will come and stay with us some time since it must be lonely living on your own". They are right! And indeed I am planning a trip to see you there and to give them a chance to see "Uncle Gunther in Person". I would prefer to come by ship to have some fun on my voyage. I would like to know how Gerda thinks about this?? I did not see you about 30 years. Quite some time, isn't it?

Ich habe ganz vergessen, dass Du am 26 Juni Geburtstag hattest, somit hier nachtraglich meine Gratulation.
Dein Bruder Gunther

(I completely forgot it was your birthday on 26 June, so my belated congratulations.)

FROM GERDA'S DIARY

NOVEMBER 1967:

Go on with B.B.B. So be strong! Aller Anfang ist schwer!

Do B.B.B. Again. Every penny helps!

So definitely B.B.B. Again.
   Don't fall by the wayside.

From now on B.B.B. (Only animal charities).

Bought 2 suitcases in Famine Relief for 10/-.
   I think I got enough now.
   So no more Famine Relief either!

DECEMBER 1967:

1.   Never make up to anybody who is rude to you and obviously ignores you. Don't be ingratiating, be aloof.
2.   Don't let people get you down. The more they hurt you, the higher you stretch.
3.   At jumbles speak as little as possible, never haggle or argue too much, just ask the price and keep mum. Don't make up too much or dress too well. They stick the price up too much. Don't be too anxious for anything.
4.   Never be upset if you miss a bargain. What's done is done and du kannst nichts nachholen.
5.   Remember if you look after the pence, the pounds will look after you.
6.   Don't get things you have already got over and over again.

7.   Don't tell Jacky all you buy. It only leads to quarrels and he thinks you are extravagant.

8.   Never let yourself go, force yourself to carry on. It's the only way. Always do your best even if you look and feel hideous.

9.   Don't tell other people (including Jacky) your troubles. It only embarrasses them or burdens them and makes yourself feel uncomfortable afterwards. Fight it out with yourself. Keep away as much as possible from people who upset you.

10.   Keep it all to yourself.

(*Du kannst nichts nachholen* translates as – You can't catch up. But I think what Gerda means is that you can't repeat the moment or opportunity. If you miss something good, then you've missed it; there is no going back.)

LETTERS FROM GUNTHER

5844 Beacon St
Pittsburgh/ PA
U.S.A.

January 28, 1968

Dear sister Gerda:

Almost half a year you did not receive a line from me! The trouble is: I am always on the go and have to hustle more than ever to make a living. Also I must confess the ticklish political situation, inflation, the war in Vietnam distracted youngsters from taking music-lessons.

But I am very fortunate that my health is pretty good in spite *always being outside exposed to winter storms. I travel a lot by my new Chevie. Recently somebody ran in the rear and around $100 was paid to me.*

My birthday of 12 January passed quietly. Nobody was thinking of me.

During the X-mas holidays I had a nice job, I was playing the accordion in Kaufmann's Department store together with Santa Claus. I wore a Bavarian outfit with real short Lederhosen.

Momentarily I am engaged in a High-Class restaurant where I play Honky-Tonk Piano. I look like Uncle Sam. Straw hat with blue-white-red ribbon and a red-white striped vest.

The lawyer sent me last week many letters and documents, but there are not any results. I am pretty disgusted that all my efforts seem in vain.

Right now I have a nice correspondence with Mr. Levy, Baltimore, to whom I owe my entrance to this wonderful country – the U.S.A!

Today I am early to bed because last night I was playing to a bar Mitzvah.

I am with love Your brother,
Gunther

5844 Beacon St
Pittsburgh/ PA
U.S.A.

February 27, 1968

Dear Sister Gerda:
Today I must drop you some lines, otherwise you'll think that already I have died. Practically I have nothing to write of importance. Days pass by smoothly. Generally the inflation and war in Vietnam are unpleasant facts. There is much

discussion about those things, however I don't put my nose in. I am not a political "Heisskopf" like Curt used to be. I keep myself busy with musical matters.

Meanwhile the lawyer informed me that my claim to be compensated for the loss of the family jewelry had been resultless.

Do you still remember Peter Stertz, a Gentile friend of mine in Germany who always came to the house Lewinsohn and played the violin? I tried to find him. His brother sent me a letter and photo snap and told me that Peter at the battle of Stalingrad in World War 2 had died.

I am very sorry to hear that Jacky's sister is suffering of cancer and is down to the bone already. I can imagine that he is very worried. I never knew that you were plagued by arthritis. I still remember that you were allergic to strawberries. Are you still?

I hope that your girls don't look too much anymore in the mirror. Teenagers sometimes have silly habits. It grows out.

In Jemima's Restaurant ("High Class") where I am momentarily engaged, I look always like Uncle Sam, still in straw hat with blue-white-red ribbon and a red-white striped vest.

Enclosed please find another $10 I promised to send you, also not too good pictures somebody took incidentally last night in Jemima's Restaurant, where actually I now play 4 nights a week Honky – Tonky – Gay 90s – style music with a Banjo player.

With love Your brother

Gunther

FROM GERDA'S DIARY

29 April, 1968:

Peter said, "Don't take any notice of her, dad, she is in one of her silly moods". Don't like him at all. Wish he would bugger off to Australia.

Later he said he doesn't want to talk to me. That suits me fine. All I ever get out of him is rudeness and shouting and insults (like: you look like a witch etc. etc.) He is getting more like Gunther every minute, and I can honestly say I do not like him at all. He is a big disappointment as a son. But then – I haven't been a good daughter to my father, so what can I expect. But I still feel very sad and alone. I expect I only get what I deserve. But I shan't talk to Peter again. When I get my big win he won't get any of it. Hope he does go to Australia. Good riddance to bad rubbish.

Gerda was slipping into German – and maybe it was a sign of deep malaise surfacing. In June 1966 she bought herself that grey cardigan for £3. 12/ 6d, **sehr teuer** – but it *was* her birthday. Around that time she writes of her **grosse Angst**. Frightened of what exactly she doesn't say, but it was likely linked to another favourite phrase of hers: **Allzu viel ist ungesund**. *Too much is bad for your health*. As with **grosse Angst**, there is no contextual explication, but by now it is clear what Gerda means by *too much*: spending *too much*, going out *too much* to the charity shops, accumulating *too much*, having *too much* fun, hoarding *too much*, for soon she is asking God to forgive all her sins and mistakes.

There is no reference in her diary to the Aberfan disaster of Friday 21st October 1966, when seven spoil tips on the hills above slipped onto the village and junior school, burying 109 children and five teachers in glistening black sludge. I mention this not because I expect to find Aberfan there – few external events ever made it into her diaries – but because (and I know this for a fact) Aberfan affected her so deeply that it might have just slipped into one of the entries around that time. What I find (on checking again) is this: **Friday 21st Oct = Hairnet (for bath) 1/3**. The following day, **Saturday 22nd Oct**, it is recorded that she **went to Thalidomide shop and spent 3/9, also blue Anorak for £2 5/-**. She then reminds herself: **Do NE from now on. Make do and mend.**

This tells me something about Gerda. It was not that she didn't notice great events in the world beyond charity shops and suitcases. They did get her attention. For days and even weeks, as I recall, the Aberfan slippage was on her lips. But she could not allow it into the private safe place of her diary. There, and only there, could she attend solely to her internal struggles, and limit the impact of the external world to lists of things bought, and divide them into good and bad – **bargains** or **blow-flies**. And her own daily difficulties were quite enough without letting in the world's disasters. There were enough holes for her to worry about from moths, without holes left in the fabric of the world.

The surviving diaries are all I have to go by, and there are extensive gaps in them – days, weeks, months when nothing is recorded – as if even interminable lists of things could not hold her interest for long. And so with my seven-league boots I stride to that entry for December 1967: **What's done is done and du kannst nichts nachholen.** *There is no going back.* She is bemoaning a missed bargain, but as is so often the case Gerda seems also to be thinking of something else. **Analyse** was one of her repeated words. *So, Gerda, that is what I will go on doing with your diaries - analyse them.*

The first difficulty is decoding the acronyms, or perhaps they should be referred to as initialisms: abbreviations formed from initial letters. **NE** = *Nothing Else.* **NE** was the first code I cracked, though as with all codes there are other possibilities. Now that I think about it, **NE** could have meant many things in her world: *No Excitement, Never Ending, No Escape* . . . More possibilities open up in German: *NE = Noch Einmal (once again)* or *Nie erneut (never again)*. Whatever, I am sure of one thing: the *N* of *NE* stands (in either language) for a negative: *No, Nein, Never, Nie.*

Which leaves me with **B.B.B.** As in: **Go on with B.B.B.** And: **definitely B.B.B again.** It is likely that I am the first person to notice the first appearance of **B.B.B.** in her diaries in November 1967. From then on, those combined initials are repeated for the rest of 1967 and through 1968. It remains unclear from the context what they meant to her, because there is no context, or none that helps me, despite repeating all her favourite words beginning with *B*: *best buys, bargains, blow-flies, bazaars, blankets. Books*? No, nothing to do with books. Then flicking through the diaries for 1966–68, I find the answer, hidden in plain sight: **B.B.B. It is the only way to get out of the rut.** A final clue clinches it: **Go on with B.B.B. BUY BONDS!** That accounts for two Bs. Translation: must stop spending and start saving by *buying bonds*. Perhaps Gerda also had in mind slogans like *Back Britain* and *Buy British*. **BBB** could stand for *Buy British Bonds*. I think I'm on the right track here, though unsure about the word *British*. It was not part of her vocabulary.

Recently I came across a photo of wartime women bent over paper-strewn desks at Bletchley Park, and I could swear Gerda was among them: similar profile, similar hair, similar way of not looking at the camera, similar introspection as though preoccupied with more cerebral things. But unlike the code-breaking Bletchley girls, Gerda was not cracking but creating codes, and I wonder if she had foreseen this present moment when someone else would analyse her diaries – translating, decoding her. She could not have guessed it would be me, but she knew it would be somebody some day. Somewhere in her mid '60s diaries, she makes a note to herself to write all future diary entries in German **just in case**... Just in case of what? Gerda doesn't say, but her meaning is clear enough: *just in case* her diaries should fall into the wrong hands! By the wrong hands she meant any hands but her own. As far as the earliest diaries are concerned, she needn't have worried, because the handwriting is pretty indecipherable to anybody but herself. The German is not the problem. It's that barbed-wire script of hers. Even

Gunther comments somewhere (in a pre-war letter) on her handwriting, and if he couldn't read it, what chance have I got?

That's possibly why Gerda, in her later diaries, slips so often into German – as her preferred mode of concealment. It wasn't, as I had always supposed until now, that her own language had become foreign to her. For all her apparent fluency, English remained the foreign language. German was never far underground, like a black sewer. As far as the diaries go, further concealment was needed beyond the German words and phrases. Code. She was developing a form of communication peculiar – unique – to herself. All those **NE**s and **BBB**s. Those itemised lists of everything she bought, with the pennies and shillings and pounds paid, set against the days of the month, running on for page after page. Nothing wrong with that. She is simply accounting for and keeping stock of expenses as a sensible way of managing and controlling them, so that every so often (having compiled another incriminating list) she can write (with blue/black biro CAPITALS and Exclamation Marks !!!, and thick <u>underlining</u>): **I have got enough! Buying same stuff over and over again! REALLY do a complete NE from NOW ON!! No more now! Spent a fortune today! Gone completely mad! Never again! Do NE again and don't forget! NENENEBBB!!! If I am bored, take dogs for a walk or read or knit etc. Willpower for your sanity's sake. Got too much rubbish. No more! VERSTAND! Start anew. Aller Anfang ist schwer.**

That last sentence translates as: Every beginning is difficult. And there it is again – the deeper meaning. In these last diaries, she had to bring things to an end (spending, jumble sales, charity shops) so as to make a new start – *difficult* though it would be. Always the same repeated Sisyphean task. So what struck me initially as *ein bisschen verruckt* about these diary entries of hers, is not crazy at all – not in Gerda's world. They are not signs of a mind unravelling, though they look very like it, with her idiosyncratic way of spelling and writing words like **UTELIZE** and **ERGANIZE** (her capitals) and the frequent ellipses, the absence of words, that leave the reader more intrigued by what has been left out than by what is there. For example, in her blue diary for 1967 and 1968 (by this point she moves backwards and forwards between the years seamlessly, as if they were all one to her), she has written the following, under the title, **People I hope never to see again ignore them all!:**

Woman from Holloway on black bike - Woman with "hairdo" - Woman with "How low can you get at Finefare?" - That fat woman in Thalidomide shop - Woman with blue glasses - Other woman tall and too bony -

Then on 14th April (1968) this:

No more now! Socks or no socks!!

Gerda was thinking about socks on 14th April 1968, nothing wrong with that. It might be simply that she had enough socks, far too many, she despaired of them. It's the way she puts it, as if there comes to every rational person a moment in life when they are faced with an elemental choice. In her case, and at that precise moment, it was **socks or no socks**. But it was so much more than socks.

This could all be making something of nothing. It is easy to find nothing of any interest in these diaries. They are full of nothing in that sense. Much was going on in the outside world just then, and it is as easy to list world-changing events as it was for Gerda to list clothes and household items found in her charity shops. 1967: the summer of love, half a million American troops in Vietnam, napalm burning people like charcoal. January 1968: Vietcong Tet Offensive. March 1968: the massacre of over 500 people in My Lai. April 1968: Martin Luther King assassinated in Memphis, riots and cities burning throughout the USA. May 1968: over a million people march through Paris. 28th August 1968: people demonstrate in Wenceslas Square following the USSR invasion... None of the above global events left the faintest shadow in her diaries. For Gerda, late January 1968 was marked by a visit to the RSPCA jumble, where she **spent 5/- on rather a lot of rubbish, but after all it will benefit the animals so I don't mind.** Her entry for Saturday 16th March (the day of *My Lai*) was just **NE** and therefore (I suppose) a successful day, as it meant she acquired **Nothing Else** for at least a day. 4th April 1968 (when Martin Luther King was shot dead on a motel balcony) was another good day for Gerda as it was not just another **NE** day, but singled out as a new beginning in brackets: **(Do always NE now)**. While **NE** lasted through May and June 1968, there were also warning signs that things were starting to get out of hand again: **No more now!** and (darkly underscored in black biro): **I really must do complete and absolute NE now.** On Wednesday 28th August, while young people were massing in Wenceslas Square in Prague, Gerda **sold wool and bought orange wool cardigan (German woman) and blue petticoat,** but also reminded herself to **Do NE again**.

Nothing unusual about keeping a diary as a purely personal record of everyday events and experiences. These were the things that mattered to *her*. It is quite possible (although I don't recall it) that – as people protested in Prague against Soviet occupation – Gerda was only too aware of it, perhaps remembering her own year in that city in 1937–38, her **beautiful Prague Time**. I know for a fact that she was aware of that other world-turning event of 1968: the release on 26th August of *Hey Jude*. I know this because (and I realise I am repeating myself) Gerda (to my amusement) thought *Jude* could only mean one thing: *Jew*.

There are photos of Gerda and Berliner Joe in London streets in 1939. I assume it is Joe and that it is 1939, though there are no names or dates on the back, only two numbers: on one set of photos this scribbled number looks like L. 32530. On the other, the number L.350099 is clear. The odd thing is, I have studied these photographs many times and only just noticed the numbers on the back. Who now knows what they signify. Photographic print numbers?

In the first set of prints, Gerda and Joe walk arm in arm past the black doorway of a bank or insurance office or government building. In fact, they only appear to be walking past it and have actually paused for the photograph. Joe, stiff and looking a little like Jeremy Thorpe, dapper in hat, collar and tie, dark double-breasted suit, furled brolly, still appears in motion, one knee bent as if eager to resume motion, and he has something in his left hand, possibly a handkerchief. His face, like hers, is out of focus, as seems appropriate for something so unlikely as my mother aged eighteen, with her German boyfriend, in London. Gerda, with dark shoulder-length hair and white blouse, appears well dressed in a matching jacket and knee-length skirt, the jacket buttoned and pulled in at the waist, and there is a dark suggestion of a handbag held at her side. A little distance behind them, indistinct people have paused for the photograph.

In the second set of prints, still with her arm tucked in his, she is looking down at a pavement apparently white with snow, though neither is dressed for the cold. Now that I look at the whiteness again, it is actually over-exposure to light. This time they haven't stopped walking and appear not to see the photographer. But these photos could have been taken on the same day and almost at the same moment, for their outfits haven't changed from the first set. Gerda wears matching jacket and skirt, Joe is dapper as above in suit and hat. Possibly both sets of photos pause them for a moment on the same London street, while 1939 goes on without them. Joe, I see, is looking down at his watch in the second set, pulling back his cuff to see the time.

What prompted me to look at them again was Gerda's diary entry for 4th August 1968. It is easily overlooked, half hidden inside her lists, and it took a minute for the shock to register. **Went to London with Peter.** Her diaries – tedious, repetitive, sad – still had the power to surprise, to shock me. For I had quite forgotten our day alone in London, and suddenly it was all coming back, and here was the evidence.

Because that was *the* day we went to London, and if I needed further proof of it, there is a letter from Miss Stainton, still of S.E.15, who had befriended her in 1939 and stayed in touch ever since. Thanking Gerda for her nice visit in August, and expressing pleasure at seeing her again after all these years, and observing how very relaxed and talkative Gerda had been, just like she used to be. Miss Stainton, while regretting that the visit to Peckham Rye was so short, had found it *most tantalising.*

Here was a further surprise. Was Gerda unusually animated that day – chatty, excited, sociable? That didn't sound like my mother. Miss Stainton was evidently remembering a different woman entirely. If that had registered at the time, it hadn't stayed with me. It had taken a stray letter from a grey-haired woman I saw once and can't recall in any other detail to retrieve a lost moment and restore my mother to me – or rather, not my mother, but the young woman she used to be, someone I never knew.

Berliner Joe wasn't in my thoughts at the time (August 1968), but now – knowing what I know – I can't remember that day out in London without thinking of Joe, as he is inevitably associated with her first few months there, just before and after the commencement of war. Of Joe I knew nothing, other than that she once had romantic feelings for him, pre-dating her life as a wife. Eventually, I would get to know Joe better, read his postcards, see them in bed together. But in August 1968, Joe was nowhere to be seen, and she and I were alone in London. At this distance her reason for going there in the first place is unclear. Probably it was to visit Miss Stainton, the daughter of her long deceased employer, and walk half-remembered wartime streets in the Elephant & Castle and Peckham Rye. As far as I recall, it was her first time back to London. Was she thinking of Joe? If so, it is nowhere recorded. Was she remembering Peckham's deadliest night when a V1 missile hit Savage's old corset factory, killing twenty-four young women sheltering beneath it? No, I don't think so, as by June 1944, when the Doodlebug struck, Gerda was in an ATS camp cookhouse.

Not much has remained of that day in London. Miss Stainton? Faceless and disembodied, though delighted (as I know from her letter) to see her young German friend. The Victorian house in Peckham Rye – with stained glass in the door, Minton tiles in a hallway the length of a railway carriage, plaster ceiling roses and old glass light shades, disused gas fittings, two tall vases with painted birds and blossoms – materialises for a moment. What we did that day after leaving Miss Stainton and her old velvets and mahogany behind, I can't recall – except for one thing. Quite by chance, so it seemed, we came to a lido, which (I have since discovered) was the old Peckham Rye lido long disappeared under ground. In August 1968, it was above ground, and lido-blue.

Gerda often hated me (it came as no surprise to uncover evidence of it in the later diaries) and wished me in Australia. But one thing connected us. Water. The element of intimacy. We both loved to swim. Only in that element might we stay friends. In the river pools of Oxford, like Tumbling Bay and Wolvercote, and in Hinksey lido which, unlike other lidos of England, has never closed. As a girl, Gerda had seen the 1930s black and white Tarzan films – with Johnny Weissmuller and Maureen O' Sullivan. Johnny Weissmuller was once an Olympic swimmer, as could be seen from watching him power through the river after diving from snaking jungle vines, pulling after him a Jane who had left her dress behind. Gerda admired him for that.

In London in August 1968, when I was still sixteen, this shared pleasure was briefly restored to us. Gerda was unsentimental about such things and would be surprised to learn what it meant and means to me. **Went to London with Peter, bought pink towel 10/-. Peter now owes me £5. 16/-** is what she wrote in her diary the next day, but her words hardly convey what actually happened. The pink of the towel is another lost and found detail. The money I owed her must have included the cost of a swimming costume, as I had not thought to bring one with me (not expecting to swim in Peckham Rye) but there is no mention of it. Her 4th August 1968 and mine have only the date in common, and her Peckham Rye and mine are different places; but even at a distance of over half a century, I can just about make her out in the raised seating area for onlookers, looking for me, identifying her son among all the anonymous splashing bodies. The wooden changing huts remain (in my memory) but the big blue fountain, a notable feature of the lido, is gone. In fact, as I have only just found out, the blue fountain is actually all that now remains of the lido. After closing in 1987, it "fell derelict" and remains buried beneath the grass in an unused corner of Peckham Rye, where only ghosts can swim. But I have also read that the lost lido of Peckham Rye is intact under the soil and might be uncovered one day.

Turning back to Miss Stainton's letter, I check if I've missed anything. There is her regret that we could not stay longer, followed by: *I don't know how you managed to get home. I hope they were kind at the Coach Station and that they let you on the next coach, but you must have been pretty dead by the time you got back I'm afraid.*

23

LETTER FROM GUNTHER

5844 Beacon St
Pittsburgh/ PA
U.S.A.

August 25, 1968

Dear Gerda:
Because of the actual hot and humid weather I took my paper and pen to the neighbouring park to answer your kind postal-cards from the Poole and Studland Beach and Bay, Dorset. Did you go by car and did you take your family too?

I spent 12 days in Atlantic City N.J. I had splendid weather and good company.. Originally I had in mind to visit England. However I still hold on to my musical-job I have here only five minutes distance from my home. Also it happened on account of these many riots here, that a series of fire bombs had been thrown in the neighbourhood. The destruction was horrible and even in my apartment windows was broken out. The police and fire wagons were constantly around and I was always watching the touchy situation. By the way, I sent you a card from Atlantic City and I am wondering that you don't acknowledge the receipt.

I came home late last night, we had a pretty good crowd. I play the piano to sing-along with fancy colour-slides. People sit around the piano, I make announcements through microphone and sing a lot. Not quite as good as father Elkan used to sing. To-day is Sunday, in the late afternoon I have to play with my 4 piece-orchestra at a Jewish wedding in White Oaks.

People all around are wondering that an "attractive man" like me is not married yet! They are teasing me! Maybe I am a little too particular. If I meet the right person I still pretend to get married.

Also some day I'll have to move from 5844 Beacon st where I live already 15 years. My landlords are old and shaky and they are not able anymore to clean my apartment and to keep everything in good shape. The landlord is suffering of heart disease and the landlady has cancer. They are very attached to me. I am here in the park with their dog "Buddy". Buddy follows me everywhere I go. Do you still keep your dachshunds?

All around here in the park people are preparing charcoal-broiled steaks. Yum, Yum, I get appetite!! I will get myself a good "Wiener Schnitzel".

Best wishes and greeting your brother
Gunther

FROM GERDA'S DIARY

Saturday 31st August, 1968:

Met that horrible woman in Spastic shop again. She was ever so nasty, started to pick a fight with me, saying how low can you get and I know you from old. Hope I don't have any more trouble from her. I am definitely giving up everything. "Complete NE" unless absolute notig.

(*Notig* = necessary).

368

Wednesday 2 October, 1968:

Bought brown coat. £1. 2/6. Hope it is a success.
   Part exchanged white duffle jacket (originally cost 11/-with cleaning) for yellow quilted dressing-gown (had to pay 10/-).
   Auntie Ivy died.
   2 dessert spoons from Famine Relief.

Monday 7 October, 1968:

Sold yellow dressing-gown and 2 others I didn't like much, got only 7/6 for them. Was rather upset about that and wanted to get my money back, so broke the rule and went to Thalidomide shop and bought blue foam jacket for 10/-. Hope it's a success. Then sold 3 cardis I didn't like for 10/- and got 4/6 off ragman.

Wednesday 9 October, 1968:

Gone mad and bought Peter a Transistor radio 6 EC. When I got back it crackles. Must atone for it.

Saturday 19 October, 1968:

Part exchanged Peter's transistor for a Russian one. Exchanged old small boots for red wool jumper for unpicking. Otherwise NE.

Thursday 7 November, 1968:

Tried to sell brown coat. Am going to keep it now as I would hardly get anything for it. It's OK when fashions get a bit longer and if I wear collarless cardi under it and scarf. I shall not try to sell any more coats, not worth the effort. If I don't like them I shall discard for rags.

Sunday 17 November, 1968:

Went to pictures, spent 11/6 (Gone With The Wind). Shan't go any more pictures. Too nervy!

Wednesday 4 December, 1968:

Wasted 2/-. Bought 2 glasses (one was chipped) and carving knife that isn't sharp. Must make amends for that. Complete NE.

Friday 3 January, 1969:

Spent 25/6 in Thalidomide and famine Relief because it is Sale time and I like a little spend then. No more now. Complete NE BBB!!!

Peter Thornthwaite

LETTER FROM GUNTHER

5844 Beacon St
Pittsburgh/ PA
U.S.A.

January 8, 1969

Dear Gerda:
After all that hustle and bustle of the past holidays to-day I
would like to answer your nice letter of 15th Oct. 68. I am glad
to read that things are all right over there, though you're
complaining of arthritis.

Peter eats lots of food, he is very husky and healthy looking
on the pictures you sent me the other day, not like the "hippy"
boys here with their sexy look. I see them here all around. Many
youngsters grow big beards and I cannot get used to see them.

Things here have not changed a bit. The same old story:
inflation, money-tightness, the war in Vietnam, riots and
endless strikes. As I told you before, my income here has
decreased tremendously.

Right now it is bitter cold with snow and ice, and I am
suffering of back aches. Maybe I strained myself too much or it
might be arthritis too.

Quite often I receive letters from the lawyer who tries to get
more results by initiating a "law-suit" against the competent
German offices. She sent me a form to sign, which would entitle
her to sue the German Government for further pay. I did not
sign that form yet, because she could claim a huge salary for
handling the case. I wrote her that just a percentage would be
acceptable. Also I don't have any further documents and
witnesses available and it seems very doubtful that a law-suit
will be successful.

Did you ever receive any news from our sister in law in B'

371

Aires? I never heard from her since.

I have here a very nice circle of friends and also many friends in L. Angeles are very attached to me, and I have a correspondence with a lovely "Senorita" in Bogota – Colombia.

I hope that very soon I will be able to send you a little "money-gift" but I have to do some "belt-tightening".

My best regards
your brother
Gunther

FROM GERDA'S DIARY

Thursday 16th January, 1969:

Siphon of Soda water 9/6.

Do complete NE again.
No more Spastic shop.
No more Biafra shop.
No more Thalidomide.
No more Famine Relief.
No more jumbles, bazaars etc.

Sacrifice!

1st April, 1969:

Must really pack Thalidomide and Spastic shop in. I get so upset when I miss a bargain. Like today I missed anorak and nightie. I worry too much about it. It's not worth it for my health's sake. The same goes for jumbles. Remember – NE and BBB!!! Sacrifice!

Wednesday 2nd April, 1969:

Spent a lot of money today. Feel very guilty and nervy. I really must do complete and absolute NE!

Wednesday 9th April, 1969:

Went to Market with Jack. Do not enjoy shopping with him, I rather go on my own. He doesn't like it and I can feel his resentment, also he was rude to me. If I have a big win I shall not tell him. I did not enjoy going out with him at all, in fact I got a filthy headache. So take a lesson from that. Do not go shopping with him any more!!

LETTER FROM GUNTHER

5844 Beacon St
Pittsburgh/ PA
U.S.A.

May 25, 1969

Dear Gerda:

Thanks for having sent me your nice letter of April 15. I am very sorry to read that during Winter you were suffering by Colitis and having been steadily under the doctors care you probably felt miserable. And Jacky had much extra work to do.

Maybe you eat too much of fattening stuff which puts much strain on the liver and intestines. Too much candy is not too good either. I lost about 28 pounds by cutting out cake, soups and sugar-sweet food.

I am very fond of Peter because he drinks lots of milk and is a weight lifter. He should keep it up!

I did not know that you own two dogs, Teddy and Dinky. Are they dachshunds?

I came home late last night. I was playing the accordion in my Bavarian Lederhosen and green Hat with feather in Delany's Hotel. I had a swell time there. Good food. Shrimp cocktail and charcoal-broiled rib-steak. Yum, Yum, were they good!

In my spare time still I do as a hobby song-writing with Irene, a lovely, intelligent person. Also I have a correspondence with a Senorita Rojas, who lives in Bogota-Colombia. She always sends me her photos to show how attractive she looks, but unfortunately I am not 29 years of age like her.

My friends in L.A, California stopped writing because they are mad I did not come to the funeral of Mr. Ernst Bruch (formerly of Breslau). Figure, still new immigrants come from Breslau and they tell very interesting stories from there.

Did you hear yet from our sister in law in Buenos Aires? Maybe we should write her once?

The lawyer did not write for a long time. Did you get any news?

Enclosed find $10.00 as I promised to you.

My best regards,

your brother Gunther

FROM GERDA'S DIARY

30th September, 1969:

Pills Doctor gave me made me feel sicker than ever. I am sure that man is trying to poison me!

374

30th September 1969: the last of Gerda's diary entries, not just for 1969 but for the rest of her life. So it is notable for that, but notable too for the coincidence. 30th September happens to be my birthday, and that year, that day, as she felt **sicker than ever**, I turned eighteen. Coincidences like that have dogged my life, and I have just noticed another one. It happened that just yesterday, 16th January 2022, I was yet again going through her diary for 1969 – it being her last and therefore interesting for that reason if for no other. Something I found there prompted another internet search re the August 1968 Russian invasion of Czechoslovakia, and Jan Pallach's subsequent self-immolation in St Wenceslas Square on *16th January* 1969, setting fire to himself as a beacon of political protest. This in turn prompted me to check again what was happening in Gerda's world that same day, and this is what I found:

16 January 1969:

Siphon of Soda water 9/6.

Do complete NE again.
No more Spastic shop.
No more Biafra shop.
No more Thalidomide.
No more Famine Relief.
No more jumbles, bazaars etc.

Sacrifice!

So when Gerda was buying a soda siphon for nine shillings and sixpence, Jan Pallach – a student in Prague – was setting himself alight and burning to death. I bring this up not as a sly dig at her for being so absorbed in the cheap daily trivia of her life as to miss what was happening in the world around her, but because of that word of hers: **Sacrifice**. There is no comparison, of course, between Jan Pallach's sacrifice and hers, yet to write such a word on such a day! And for all I know, his self-immolation reached and touched her, far away though she was in Cowley, Oxford. The distance was not so great after all. Gerda had once studied in Prague (1937-38), leaving just months before Germany annexed the Sudentenland prior to its occupation of Czechoslovakia in 1939. She must have often met her college friends in Wenceslas Square, and Gunther – who knew Prague well from previous visits - enjoyed visiting his sister there, showing her his city, while she showed him hers.

Looking again at Gerda's list of renunciations as recorded on 16th January 1969, I am struck by the melancholy cadence of **No more**, which inevitably reminds me of Edgar Allan Poe: *Quoth the raven Nevermore*. It was only charity shops she was giving up, true, and she was not giving them up for very long, probably no more than a day or two, but even so...

No more. Again Gerda seems to touch, with such doleful words, something darker and deeper than charity shops and jumble sales. Then there is her odd choice of words (9th October 1968) concerning the transistor radio she had kindly bought for me: **Must atone for it.** *Atone*? *Atonement* – making amends or reparation for some great wrong or sin – is that really what she had in mind at the time? The word is more often associated with the crucifixion than with a crackling 1960s transistor radio. Then those glasses (one chipped) and blunt carving knife of her 4th December entry – **Must make amends for that.** *Amends*?

Really? To make amends is to compensate or make up for a wrongdoing. Does making amends apply to wasting two shillings in a charity shop on two glasses, one of them chipped, and a blunt carving knife?

As for that **Transistor radio 6 EC,** I have no recollection whatsoever of it. **6 EC** ? Have I translated her scrawl correctly? An internet trawl nets a surprising shoal of transistor radios from the 1960s, and almost instantly I see **EC** in an Ebay advert for a Vintage Transistor Radio EC 1969 for £270: a "collector's dream radio", a "rare find" of "museum quality" – it "was listened to by my grandfather". Briefly, irrelevantly, I wonder what **EC** stands for – Electronic Communication or Circuits or Capacitors? Should I put in a bid for it? That must be the Gerda in me.

There was something else I meant to research on the internet. I scroll back to Gunther's letter of 25th May 1969: *I am very sorry . . . that during Winter you were suffering by Colitis and having been steadily under the doctors care you probably felt miserable.* Colitis? That *is* news to me. With this I net even more useful information than with transistor radios: "Ulcerative colitis causes stomach cramps and stabbing pain similar to wanting an explosive bowel movement without being able to do it." It reminds me of Elkan, and his intestinal cancer in 1942 – twenty-seven years earlier. As for Gerda, there was to be no cancer, only "inflammatory bowel disease, incurable unfortunately, though not typically fatal." Did she think she had cancer? Her very last diary entry of 30th September 1969: **Pills Doctor gave me made me feel sicker than ever.** After thirty-odd years as an inveterate diarist, those were her last words: . . . **sicker than ever . . .**

Sickness. That's it, the clue, the key, the link. It was

what kept that dispersed family together, and reunited them at the end. Elkan, the father, restored to his one faithful son in January 1942 before dying of intestinal cancer. Kurt, reappearing after his long absence, returning to family – for forgiveness? – before his extreme ageing and death within a year. Gunther – big, bald, bouncing Gunther – twice Gerda's weight at his fattest and her slimmest – 227 lbs of German-American Bavarian Uncle Sam Honky Tonk Piano playing *reiche Onkel von Amerika* – Gunther, if you read between the lines, touches repeatedly on the family propensity for sickness of body and mind. There is no more intimate line in his correspondence with his sister than when he expresses sorrow that, *steadily under the doctors care* she *probably felt miserable*. Sickness brought them together as nothing else could. Though Gunther could never keep up with her hypochondria – what were his occasional back aches to her colitis? – still, you sense that he is trying to keep her company, as in his letter of 8th January 1969, when having acknowledged her winter complaints of arthritis, he wonders if he has the same thing: *Maybe I strained myself too much or it might be arthritis too.* That is so like Gunther. The illness of one Lewinsohn is an illness for them all, to be shared.

In *Tarzan And His Mate* (1934), the white hunters, ivory seekers, with their pith helmets and baggy shorts, observe the fear of their native bearers concerning the planned fourteen-day trek to the elephants graveyard, and comment: "Juju, that's why they're frightened!" To the ivory-bearing "natives", the fabled graveyard is *taboo, sacred ground.* Beyond the high escarpment and through the waterfall, the white waters parting as it passes through the concealed portal, the dying elephant (shot by the hunters) leads them to the hidden valley of death, a forest floor strewn with giant skulls and bones and tusks. This is where elephants go when they feel death coming on. Later we hear once more the "Juju drums".

So what has all this to do with the Lewinsohns? Only this: that they too were drawn back, as they *felt death coming on*, to family. By some intuition or instinct, each sought out the others near the end. Perhaps it was some heightened sensitivity, or what Gunther identified as "nervous" or "mental" stress. This wasn't some kind of dry rot in *the house Lewinsohn*, but an unbreakable bond between them. Even that other bond, the claim for compensation from Germany, the *Wiedergutmachung*, wasn't just to do with money. Naturally, they all wanted the *law-suit against the competent German offices* to succeed - for the money and whatever else it meant to them. From the correspondence it is clear that Gunther initiated it in 1958. Within a year of doing so (8th February 1959) he was feeling bitter about it:

Die Wiedergutmachungangelegenheit" has not shown any results yet. In my last letter to Mr. Levy I pointed out that I am "bitterly disappointed" about this matter.

More agitation arose with Kurt's emergence. Although the *Wiedergutmachung* seemed important to him too, Gunther feared the risks arising from his lost brother's reappearance. That *communistic fighter and agitator* (as Gunther wrote in March 1964) whose *activities* must have been tracked by the West German Government, was jeopardising everything. All this is worth repeating because (as I now realise) it goes to the heart of the matter.

Die Wiedergutmachungangelegenheit, or *reparation matter.* The question of reparation, restitution. Compensation for their father's financial losses, the family's losses, losses enough to bring down the house Lewinsohn. A shared expectation and a shared frustration. Gerda waiting each morning for the post, for news from Germany. Gunther complaining of *the mountain of documents* from the lawyer, the witnesses dying before they could give witness. For Gerda it was the long awaited **Big Win**. The cloud on which, playing her piano, she rose high above **the poor and the proletariat**. In time, the cloud had not a silver but a black lining to it, a dark edge of threat: **When I get my Big Win you won't get any of it!** But it was an anxious and unsatisfying business. This from Gunther on 31st December 1965: *According to newspapers, Chancellor Erhard in Germany wants to postpone restitution-payments for two years. Let's wait and see because the "nazi-victims" are protesting vigorously against the German decision.* It looked like he was never going to get *that restitution pay to have life a little more comfortable.*

Only now does it occur to me to search the internet for information on the reparation program known as *the Wiedergutmachung* (making good again). "Making good again" involved Germany paying $100 million for individual reparations, although by the end of the 1960s that $100 million did not include any payments to Gunther or Gerda apart from the £390 she received early on, *a sizable amount of money,* Gunther wrote in congratulation, while observing less cheerfully that he *did not receive a penny myself for all the tremendous efforts I made.* Gunther had done all the work, finding out about the reparation programme: post-war US, British and French governments requiring Germany to make amends by returning property "or otherwise compensating those wrongfully deprived of such property during the Nazi era." Gunther would have agreed there could be no "atonement" for Nazi crimes, and that the programme's "material approach" in no way meant "reconciliation with those who murdered the six million". But for the Lewinsohns to get something back at last, some recompense for the loss of the family fortune – perhaps even enough for a more comfortable future – that was as much as could be expected.

As for Gerda, how could she have known that her Big Win had been there all the time, in her dark past – in the German Reich, of all places? Nazi Germany, the Holocaust – that was where her future lay. There was no *making good again*. But it meant money, and that could only be good.

ENDINGS

24

LETTERS FROM GUNTHER

5552 Beacon St
Pittsburgh/ PA
U.S.A.

September 27, 1970

Dear Sister Gerda:
I am very sorry that your last letter of June 18th had not been answered yet. Indeed in the last months I went through all kind of troubles! In first place during the months June and July I was ill in the hospital and I underwent surgery by a prominent surgeon. I lost lots of blood and energy but right now I am coming along fairly well. As I mentioned in my last letter, I bought a little cottage not far from the place I used to live 17 years. It is gorgeous! You should see it! I was tired living in furnished rooms. And also the rent went up all the time because of the inflationary trend. I had no furnitures and also to the same time there was "mover-strike". So I bought also the furnitures with which the cottage was provided. Also I have an air-conditioner, kitchen stove, drapes, awnings and a cute little garden. Now I do my own cooking and I am not forced anymore to get my meals in these expensive restaurants. I have my own

phone and phone answering service and a workshop down in the cellar. My former landlord moved about 8 miles from here, out in the country, what I would not like. Though I live in a nice green suburban area, still there are supermarkets and drugstores all around.

I am sorry to read that you still are suffering of arthritis at the shoulders, neck and fingers. You stopped eating candy. I cannot imagine that candy has any influence on arthritis. Did you consult a physician?

After these awful "Indian Summer" with heatwaves now here it gets pretty nippy. I turned on the furnace.

Why didn't you drop me a line. I get so many get-well wishes to the sick-room, except yours!

Now, as the Summer is over I got busy tuning pianos and now and then I am playing with my combo to dances, also I am still in McSorley's restaurant every Tuesday doing the "Schnitzelbank". They always serve me a delicious steak supper after.

Please write immediately. I am very curious to know what is cooking over there?

So far for today
Your brother Gunther

5552 Beacon St
Pittsburgh / PA
U.S.A.

(UNDATED: FEBRUARY 1971?)

Dear sister Gerda:
These stormy winter days, the hustle and bustle of dayly life and the "new worries" to take care of my cottage make me forget to settle down and to answer letters I receive from you

and from all over. I did not even answer your letter of 2nd Oct, 1970. Shame on me! Also I must confess that on account of my severe operation in July I still have not regained fully my strength and after the daily work I am pretty exhausted and even cannot sit up much to watch television.

Though it is not easy to take care of the house, I am really happy to have my independent living quarter. I do my own cooking. I have a wonderful kitchen with refrigerator etc. I bought it completely furnished and still I hope that Jack and you and perhaps your children will be my guest here. There is lots of room for all of you! Also I have a little garden and a porch with awnings, out of this world!

Right now I am totally snowed in. From time to time I have to shovel snow. As you know, I am very handy and I do all the house repairs myself. Unfortunately inflation is increasing every day and these many strikes paralyse the whole business-world, but thanks God, I have not to complain, I am doing fine. I am doing quite well in the line of piano-tuning and repair and do mainly work for schools, stores, churches and very refined private families. Having a perfect pitch ear, I do an excellent job. Besides of this, there are very few piano-tuners in this area.

If I would not have been ill last summer I would have paid you a visit there. After all, I did not see you for almost 33 years!

Your house must be rather deserted since your children more or less stand on their own feet. You're going to be 50 years old and I am on my way to be 60. Oh boy, Oh boy, the years passed by quickly. Is not your birthday on June 16?

I am shocked to read that arthritis still bothers you. Why not consult a physician constantly? They always find new ways for treatment. I hope that Jacky got rid of these symptoms of lumbago. Here in Pgh is the air polluted with smoke and dust from the nearby steel-mills. I wished I would be in Florida! Some day, when being retired, I will do so.

Last night I was engaged to play to a Valentine-dance. But after a short while they sent the musicians home because 8 inches of snow made it impossible to come to the dance-hall.

Some times I go to the Spanish-Club, to brush up my Spanish language. Cant you find a nice girl for me to get married. The American ladies here are very particular and not my taste.

Enclosed please find $10.00. As soon as I receive your answer letter I'll send another $10.00.

Did you ever hear from our sister in law in Buenos Aires? Maybe you should write her once. Meanwhile my best wishes and regards to you, family and dachshunds.

Please write me about everything!

Tausand susse Kussen

Von Deiner Bruder Gunther

TELEGRAM FROM BENJAMIN SWEAR ATTORNEY
LINCOLN BUILDING PITTSBURGH

16 APR. 71
REGRET TO INFORM YOU THAT GUNTHER LYNN EXPIRED APRIL 15TH STOP YOU ARE ONLY KNOWN SURVIVOR AND BURIAL WILL BE DELAYED PENDING WORD FROM YOU STOP CALL IMMEDIATELY AND CHARGE TO MY NUMBER STOP

LETTER - NO ADDRESS (PITTSBURGH)
(LAST PAGE MISSING)

April 22, 1971

Dear Gerda

Please accept my sincere sympathy on the death of your dear brother Gunther.

It came as quite a shock to me as he was a close friend. My husband passed away very suddenly of a heart attack last November. He, too, was a fine musician and worked with Gunther for many years. He lived very close to us and would pick up my husband in his car when they had musical engagements together. Another musician friend, who booked engagements for them, was called to identify the body, and he then called me to ask about the religion. I told him all I could, and then arrangements were made. I want you to know that if he had been a king, the funeral could not have been finer. Rabbi Goldblum delivered a most beautiful Eulogy, and the Cantor's singing was divine. All of Gunther's friends from the Friendship Club, of which he was a member, came to the funeral, and after the graveside ceremony all joined in Kaddish. These shocks are very hard to bear, but we who are left behind must carry on. This is Life, and we must accept it . . .

Though I knew almost nothing about Gunther until I started to read the letters that were never sent to me and never meant for me to read, when I go back over them now, the last ones especially, they remain terribly poignant:

I bought a little cottage not far from the place I used to live 17 years. It is gorgeous!

I get so many get-well wishes to the sick-room, except yours!

After all, I did not see you for about 33 years!

Oh boy, oh boy, the years passed by quickly.

Cant you find a nice girl for me to get married.

That missing apostrophe in *Cant*: that alone is enough to bring me to tears. Even now I can't quite believe that Gunther is dead, having so recently resurrected him. It may not be the deep, irrecoverable loss that Gerda expressed (to herself) when her beloved Sandy died. More a shadow passing through me, a ghost. It is hard to find the words for it, but that shadow passing through is not the first and won't be the last. I again mark the moment of his passing by scanning the internet for other dead Lewinsohns.

Search *Lewinsohn – Breslau*, and they multiply! So many Lewinsohns I never knew existed, at my fingertip, from Breslau Synagogue records of 1930:
  Elkan Lewinsohn, b. 1877, Kaufmann.
  Kurt Lewinsohn, b. 8 May, 1909, Cand.Jur (Master of Law/Lawyer?)

Dr. Klara Lewinsohn of Victoriastrasse 18 and 120, b. 21 September 1869.

There are women who become Lewinsohns by marrying into the family, and others who marry out of it... Emma, Anna, two Fredas, Henrietta, Johanna...

And Bertha, of 12 Hofchenstrasse. Tante Bertha! The birth date confirms it: 8th December 1888. *The* Aunt Bertha who made coffee for Elkan, added her words to his letters to Gerda, and wrote her own letter to her. The Aunt Bertha who (unknowingly?) *so very often provocated strife*, as Gunter wrote, provoking him to remember her with such venom. The same Tante Bertha who wrote to Gerda about the possibility of her own *Auswanderung* to England, but who lacked the *Gelegenheit* – the opportunity – to leave. And who looked after her older brother, before being deported on 25th November 1941 to Kowno, Fort X1, where she was murdered four days later. Aunt Bertha, once reviled, later mourned, by Gunther...

Other Lewinsohns listed... Hedwig, Joseph, Theodor. The first two, doctors, the third a *Reisender,* a travelling salesman. Lewinsohns new to me, with Breslau addresses, all listed in in the Breslau Synagogue Community Archive of 1930. Gone now; Breslau, too... Then I notice something. Kurt is there, but no Gunther or Gerda. Gunther was eighteen in 1930, Gerda, nine. Kurt was twenty-one. For that reason maybe (his age), Kurt is on the list, being the eldest. In the end it is only a list. There is no indication of what became of those listed. What became of Kurt, I know (or know as much as I'll ever know) – Kurt, the good-looking one, with his Rhett Butler moustache, his double-breasted white linen suit, and his sudden premature ageing at the end so that he was mistaken in hospital as his wife's *sick FATHER*.

I know what became of Kurt and Gunther. Probably, even if what happened to them as a family had never happened, theirs would have been very different lives. In 1963, when he arose from the dead, Kurt wrote of his *raging life*. For Gunther what really mattered was feeling *gemutlich*, comfortable. Always thanking his sister for her comfortable letters. Feeling comfortable was what he seemed always to miss – until just before he died. It was the one thing lacking in his new life, the thing he could not recover or do without, for all his American get up and go. A line from one of Gunther's letters comes back to me, without my having to look for it: *You almost will believe that I am dead because your comfortable letter has not been answered yet.* So thrilling was his life in the US, all hustle and bustle, that he had no time to settle. Always on the go. If you have to keep straining for the high grapes Uncle Sam dangles above your head, there's no time to settle. What he most wanted was just to feel comfortable – and he found it at last, in his little cottage with its drapes and awnings and cute little garden. He had arrived at last at a more restful place. Re-examining his letter of 27th September 1970, I conclude that he must have bought his gorgeous cottage late summer. He refers to having informed Gerda in his last letter of the move, but that last letter is missing so I can't be sure of the date. At any rate, if he moved there, say mid-August – not long after his *severe operation* and copious loss of blood and energy – then at least Gunther enjoyed some comfort for eight or nine months before being found dead.

To state that Gunther, throughout his years of exile, found comfort in writing to his little sister, whom he chided (as older brothers sometimes do) but clung to as his only link, is to state the obvious. *The Elephant never forgets*, he once wrote to her re the lost diamonds, but there were other things he could never forget – her childhood, that holiday *in the "Lotte - car" to the Zoblen-Mountain*, his visits to her in 1937/38 during **the beautiful Prague time**, as Gerda came to refer to it (after it ended). There is something prelapsarian about his recollections of their time together in Germany. Whether Gerda ever shared his nostalgia is doubtful, but it is hard to believe it made no impression, even on her. For all that she blanched at the prospect of a visit from Gunther, what bound brother and sister together was greater than what pulled them apart. It is no coincidence that, within eight to nine months of Gunther's death, something equally dramatic and life-changing would happen to her.

There is no evidence that she mourned him. She was capable of mourning the passing and loss of certain loved ones, like her **one true friend**, Sandy the dachshund, who at the end was slithering on his belly with a slipped disc, like a great sandy slug. A late diary entry refers to **Gunther the bully! I never want to see him! I hope he won't come to England!** Another entry advises Gerda to **Keep away from relations – and that goes for my brother too!** This was the same brother who ended his letters with *in love* and *ein Tausand susse Kussen*. The only family left to remind her of times when she was still happy in Germany. Whether she mourned him or not, Gerda was certainly grieved to find out, soon after his death, that she was not the only beneficiary – as she had always assumed – and that half of Gunther's estate would be going to the widow in Buenos Aires: Elena Italia America Scarfi Messima de Lewinsohn.

That was a shock, though typical of the shocks she had come to expect. Half Gunther's money going to a widow and her family in Argentina. What I am now about to suggest may not be true, may be grossly unfair (in which case she is entitled to a posthumous apology), but it does appear that Gerda kept on replying to Gunther's letters, and maintaining what was for her consistent close family contact, so that *der reiche Onkel von Amerika* would one day leave all his money to *her*. It was doubtless a difficult time for her, too painful to talk about, as were all the other painful things in her life. Maybe she mourned him in her own way. *After all, I did not see you for about 33 years!* Who could not feel touched, recalling such words. It would not even surprise me if she re-read his last letters, scanning the tissue-thin airmail paper, picking out the poignant phrases, and recalling other letters and lines from other times: *My goodness, already you're 33 and I myself 42. Do you remember when you was "sweet sixteen" and we went with Tatzel, Tante Bertha, and Pussy in the "Lotte-car" to the Zoblen-Mountain? . . . Do you still remember the days we spent in Prague – Victoria College? . . .*

But even with half of it going to the widow, it still counted as *the Big Win*.

Although he had left behind a Gunther-shaped hole in her life, a little part of Gerda was surely encouraged by this turn of events. By April 1971 she was not yet fifty, though she thought of herself as old. She had thought of herself as old since 1951, when her hair and teeth started going and starvation diets were needed. But by 1971 there was no mistaking it, no reversing it, no going back. Though always of a nervous disposition, or *nervy*, as she said, it had become more noticeable. His money, even half of it, was at least some compensation for all her losses.

I have just fished out (again) the letter in which Gunther wondered if there was a *nervous condition* in the family affecting (infecting?) them all. Interestingly dated 25th December 1964 (such thoughts occur on Christmas Day?) the festive greetings to Gerda include this: *Some friends of mine found strange definitions for my nervous condition. Some say it could be change of life. You think it must be in the family because you too pretend to be nervous once in a while. Curt in his last letter confessed that he was rather nervous too and he blamed it on our ancestors.*

That *pretend* makes me smile. Gerda never had to pretend to be nervous. But that's Gunther for you – still a foreigner in his use of American English. Unless, and this has not occurred to me till now, he meant that she was making it up, putting it on. There is something in this – but no, she really was nervous – whatever *nervous* meant when applied to women like her, I mean women in her kind of situation. That year I was away much of the time and so didn't see much of her, but when I did it seemed that her usual hysteria and histrionics were more exaggerated and that they were surfacing more after her brother's death – that her nervous condition was coming out with a vengeance.

Gerda recorded in her last diary that she was saving up for a portable TV, so as to watch it in private, without interruptions. Nothing wrong with that. I expect we were most annoying when we interrupted what she was watching. But it wasn't just the TV. Here is a diary entry (yes, I know, but it is worth repeating) from around that time: **No more shopping with Jack. He is always grizzling and ticking at me and standing behind me worrying. I just had enough of the constant ticking and telling off. Gunther all over again!** There are similar diary entries for all the family. We all got on her nerves. It was the one thing we had in common: *we got on her nerves.*

Gerda was *all nerves,* as if the usual layers of skin had been scraped off and the nerve-endings exposed, red-raw to the careless touch. This was more than "just a touch over-sensitive". On the whole "over-sensitive" seemed to me a good thing, a sort of refinement. Gerda had always wanted to be left alone. Fine. So had Garbo. Pre Gunther's death she could be found most of the time in her armchair, swaddled in layers, a half-knitted patchwork quilt on her lap, watching *Peyton Place.* Of course I exaggerate – it could not have been "most of the time" – yet it is not too great an exaggeration, for the internet informs me there were 514 episodes of *Peyton Place* from 1964 to 1969. Gerda, I know, watched all of them. That was her way of being alone, since we were not allowed to interrupt and usually left her to it, undisturbed, to travel to New England twice a week and live through the characters and crises, their loves and lives and lies. In her own way, if left alone, Gerda was happy, and none of us begrudged her that.

After Gunther's death it was different. Though no one knew it at the time, the diaries had ended, and with them

whatever outlet they represented. When I wander
through them now, the last diaries, and read lines such
as, **Moths! - Enough until death!,** or **I might get into serious
trouble one way or another**, I understand that even her
most alarmist utterances were actually therapeutic – or
maybe I mean cathartic. They were her *Peyton Place*, her
dramas – and not little trivial dramas either, but of a
depth and intensity requiring all the CAPITAL letters,
the exclamation marks !!!, the blue/black biro
underlinings at her disposal. Before Gunther's death, life
was still a dark and dangerous undertaking, with pits
opening at her feet. **BEWARE PITFALLS! NOT GOOD FOR
MENTAL HEALTH! STOP NOW BEFORE IT'S TOO LATE!** How
scary that was for her, how exciting! Really, she was more
like Kurt and his *raging life* than Gunther seeking
comfort. It was not comfort that Gerda was after, but
excitement. Hence the savage dialectic of her diaries.

25

"When she gets better, I'll buy her a new TV." Jack's faith in the power of television to rouse her from such sleep was as touching as it was pathetic, but maybe he was not so far wrong. If anything could wake her from a coma and restore her to her old self, it would be a new TV. We had nothing better to offer. Gerda was leaving us. She had done it before – leaving everyone and everything behind – and she was doing it again, though I don't suppose I saw it like that at the time, knowing then almost nothing about her first *Auswanderung* in that mythical time before I was born. Alone in her bed and dreaming whatever visions come to those on life support machines, she was too distant to be recalled. Still, if anything could bring her back, it would be a new TV.

Jack waited in the waiting room, unwilling or unable to venture further into colder clinical regions, and asked when we returned from them, "How is she?" It was an uncomfortable question. To accurately report her comatose and bloated appearance was not likely to reassure. There was nothing to be said. In late December 1971 I knew nothing of his love letters to her at the end of the war, and if asked I would not have thought him capable of writing them. Perhaps, as he looked up at us fearfully, expectantly, he was still re-living the moment he had found her in her bedroom on his return from another night at the Pressed Steel. Thinking about it now, I imagine some spool in his head going round and round, like a film only he could see. In 1971 there were no televisions on hospital walls to take your mind off such things. In truth, I can't really see Jack at all in that waiting room, or just the faintest edge of him, and the thinning grey hair. I can see that. But I'm sure that, during every visit, there was the same expectation in him as he looked up on our return. He was waiting for us to say: "OK, Dad, now you can go out and get her that new TV."

There were things Jack could not be told, things we had witnessed on the ward. As I recall, Gerda had her own private room, which she would have liked if she had known it. The things Jack could not be told included any description of her physical appearance, such as the size of her. It was as if someone had taken a bicycle pump to her body and vigorously inflated it. By late December I still knew nothing of her diaries – except that they existed, and she had recorded unflattering things about us in them – so I could not have known that in January 1967 she had written this: **She said it's impossible to get as fat as me. I don't think I am all that fat. I am one stone overweight, and I shall try my best to get that down and be slimmer. Willpower!** Who "she" might be, I don't know, but it was a female who clearly knew how to upset her, though that hardly narrows down the likely suspects. Summoning back the body on display during our repeated hospital visits, its eyes squeezed shut between folds of bruised flesh, its blown-up body with that drowned appearance beneath the tubes and bottles keeping it alive – I can easily imagine her own revulsion at waking to find herself looking like that, irredeemably unattractive in ways even she had not believed possible, fat beyond the help of the most skeletal of starvation diets. So it was perhaps as well that Gerda kept her eyes closed throughout and did not open them, or wink conspiratorially at me when that nurse said: "Speak to her, she might be able to hear you."

The nurse clearly did not know her very well, but how could she in the absence of any conversation? She did not understand that the very last thing Gerda would have wanted was to be aroused. Probably I did say something – if only because it was expected and seemed impolite not to – such as "Hello Mum, how are you doing?" – in what I hoped was an encouraging tone of voice. Thankfully, that bit of our interaction is a blank, for even fifty years later it is mortifying to recall. And it seemed foolish to begin a conversation (about what?) with a woman in a coma. She would have been cross to find herself still here and wouldn't have thanked me for the discovery. Looking back, I think she had already arrived in a heaven of her own choosing – where she would never have to watch her weight, where jumble sales and charity shops open up seven days a week just for her, where *Peyton Place* is on more than twice a week and without end, and where Sandy is always there to greet and lick her and never scrapes his slumping belly on the floor.

Reflecting again on her suicide, I am reminded of something Gunther wrote to her in January 1949: *You always make your own decisions in life.* I find something disapproving in his tone, yet suicide turned out to be one of her better decisions. She'd have hated to grow old, and at fifty the horror of it had already arrived. Reading the Obituaries section in the Saturday Guardian, as I regularly do, I sometimes amuse myself by writing hers. It goes something like this: *My mother, who has died aged fifty from a massive overdose, was an unknown housewife who did not have a crowded career, or any kind of career for that matter – unless one considers frequenting jumble sales and charity shops a career. Gerda Thornthwaite, nee Lewinsohn, was born in Breslau (now Wroclaw) in 1921. Her father was a successful and well-established businessman until things changed after 1933. As a Jew Gerda was lucky to leave Germany in May 1939 and work as a domestic servant in London until joining the ATS in 1943. It was there, in the cookhouse, that she met Jack, who was to become her devoted husband – though a disappointment to her in later life when she realised that he'd never be anything more than a factory worker. Ironically, the financial compensation she had sought for so many years from Germany - the "Wiedergutmachung" as it was termed - benefited Jack by default following her untimely death, enabling him to leave work. Gerda is survived by her husband, her three children, her two beloved doggies, and well over a hundred suitcases . . .*

Her fake obituary leaves me wondering what Gerda achieved in her life, if anything. She achieved a family of course, and a family is not nothing. Considered alongside other post-war women in Britain, she managed no better and no worse, given the shrinking of their world after the war. Gerda enjoyed the war – especially the air raids, the bombings, the disruption of ordinary life. They were **thrilling**, she wrote in her diary. Then there is that folder marked *Privat*, containing the love letters. They were thrilling too. After 1945 she found herself shrinking into a wife and then mother, and all she had then to look forward to were the jumble sales and charity shops of the 1950s and '60s. The stuff she was after half her life – the stuff packed into over a hundred suitcases – is not the stuff of your average obituary. So I'm sorry, Gerda, but there's not much more I can say about you other than: *You mattered to* *us only because we were your family.* She mattered to Gunther because they too were family and they had corresponded for over thirty years. After Kurt's death, they were the last of the Lewinsohns, and after Gunther died – well, then there was one.

And she mattered to Jack. Whenever I think of the ending she chose, I still think she was cruel to him – inadvertently so, perhaps, but that almost makes it worse. I am thinking here not so much of her suicide as her suicide note. **Look after the dogs. I've had my chips.** Not a word to him, or about him, the man who never stopped loving her. Before Virginia Woolf filled her coat pockets with rocks and walked into the River Ouse, she wrote to her husband that she owed him all the happiness of her life. Gerda was thinking only of the dogs. At the time – when I first read her suicide note – I thought: *That really sums you up.* As for the suicide itself, well – as Gunther once wrote – *You always made your own decision.* She decided, and I admire her for that – for deciding exactly when and how and where to die. And I have a different view now of the suicide note – its scrawled words, as I recall, almost falling off the page as the pills took effect. At the time, though, I was thinking more of their impact on Jack. When I again see him, in that hospital waiting room, grey head bowed, thinking perhaps that if anything could pull her through it would be the promise of a new TV, not knowing that while he was looking away his wife had become an alien – I wonder if he had ever seen her as she really was. Now, with the benefit of distance, and having read his wartime love letters, I can appreciate just how much she meant to him. The Gerda-shaped hole she had left. They are still there, the letters, in a khaki-coloured folder marked PRIVATE, all undated yet evidently from 1944-45, when they were courting.

My dear Gerda

You are such an Angel to write me such a charming letter, at first I could hardly believe it was from you, and I kept putting off the pleasure of reading it until I was quite alone, and then I made myself comfortable in a nice big chair by the fire, lit up a cigarette, and . . .
We have lots in common and ought to have a perfectly wonderful life in front of us . . .

You are my Dream Girl. I know I am very lucky and certainly dont think I deserve such happiness. Cant you feel my love for you even though we are so far apart . . .

You are my whole life, without you I dont live just exist, nothing matters nothing is of any interest without you . . .

What a terrible place this is. We are herded together on little wooden beds . . . Am dreading my wash in the morning amid the tombstones. Lights out now. Goodnight, Darling . . .

Such unlikely words of love from the man from Sunderland to the girl from Breslau. The unlikeliness of it all – the meeting, the emotion, the marriage – strikes me anew as I randomly select lines again from the pile of letters before me on the desk, and as I am about to return them to their wartime folder, I find this: *You are so very different from other girls. You have ways all your own.* That was it – her great appeal. She was foreign. German. It inspired unsuspected eloquence, even moving him at the close of one letter to write: *Ich liebe Dich.* The uneducated Geordie from Tyne and Wear was speaking German to a Jew.

The other day I read (Saturday Guardian) about a mother appearing and making a speech at her own funeral. She was in fact a hologram, created by her loving son using the latest A1 technology. If Gerda's ashes had come back together after the cremation, and she had stood before us – looking a little odd, but still recognisably her three-dimensional self – she might have parted her lips but then said nothing. No last words. Just an uncomfortable silence. The first time we sat there looking out, from a house still eerily empty of *her*, must have been just weeks after her death, for it was around the time of the first miners' strike in January 1972. Whether it occurred to me then that they were turning out all the lights in England to mark the occasion of her death, I don't know, but I doubt it as we were still too close to the event for such whimsical fancies. The newspapers, as I recall, were hailing the return of the Blitz spirit in the strangely lightless streets of London and reporting that people were friendly again in the new blackouts. However, as it happens that wasn't the occasion I am especially remembering – the time when he opened up about his life with Gerda. She was not yet a wholly taboo subject. We had been sitting there a while in a not uncomfortable silence, waiting for darkness, and I suppose I must have asked him if he thought about her a lot, and though it was fifty years ago I recall his exact words: *There were times when I thought of leaving her.*

BEGINNINGS

26

Gerda spent most of her life in search of an ending. Each new beginning – marriage, family, Nissen hut, council house, compensation from Germany, a house of her own, Gunther's estate – soon became another ending, and usually a bitter disappointment, a failure, for all the initial promise. But for me her own ending was just the beginning. It was probably the hundred or so suitcases she left behind – her legacy to us, her own *Wiedergutmachung* compensating for all the losses. At some point, most of them were moved into the attic which, in his readiness to do anything to make her happy, Jack had boarded and lined and lit, and transformed into a vast and usable space quickly accessed by a loft ladder. There she was stowed and stored, in old brown cases and trunks and tea chests, in perpetuity – no one (least of all Jack) having the heart to return all the lovingly folded, categorised and labelled second hand clothes (her life's work) to the charity shops from whence they came. As for the cases of diaries and correspondence and photograph albums – all the written and pictorial evidence of her extraordinary ordinary life – these had to be kept for posterity, though nobody really expected to go through any of it. And, as much of it was private and marked as such, it was evidently not for the eyes of strangers.

If I added together all the minutes and months I spent in that attic, it would amount to the best part of my life. Whenever I visited Jack, who lived alone in the house in the decades following her death, it was always the attic that drew me. Gerda exerted a more irresistible attraction after her suicide than before. I was well aware of this from the start, and regretted it, because she wasn't very likeable at the best of times, but she had two distinct advantages over Jack as a person likely to be remembered in the years to come: she was foreign, and she was dead.

Now (January 2022), having partially translated the German diaries (some entries are beyond me) and the German letters, and having read and re-read the English ones, and having searched all the photographs for further evidence – I find myself closer to the beginning than the end. When seventeen-year-old Gerda, writing in her diary almost exactly thirty-three years before ending her life – when, in December 1938, she wondered what the future would bring, she was closer to me than she ever was in later years. Because even now, after all the translating and reading and looking, her life is still a mystery to me. Those Saturday Guardian obituaries – those remembered lives are distinguished by shape and purpose. They achieved things. There is a beginning, an end, a discernible trajectory. Gerda did not shape her life; her life was shaped by externals. Extraordinary though they were – the Third Reich, Holocaust, World War – they were the panzer tracks that left on her their indelible deep imprint. Then came marriage, family, the end. So I summarised her life. Yet once it had ended, and only then, did the fascination really begin. A time would come when I couldn't get enough of her – when I wondered what surprising revelation awaited me in a suitcase or trunk or tea chest. I have been obsessed with Gerda for the past fifty years, and I am still just starting out on my long search – and yet, viewed dispassionately, her life didn't amount to much. For all the Jewish background, the Holocaust, the war, it was after all an ordinary enough life, ending prematurely and rather pathetically. It was a promising enough beginning – I mean in the sense of promising an interesting life – but really her life never lived up to its initial promise. In fact, it fell well short of it. That at least was my callow assessment at the time of her death. How little I knew her – and myself.

As for Gunther, with his tendency from the start to inflate and boast of his many accomplishments, he did not have to wait for me to write his obituary; he was writing it himself from his arrival in Ecuador in autumn 1939. Admittedly it has taken me years of sporadic attic research to grasp the full measure of him. From early on – within a year or two of the suicide – I was finding all there was to uncover of the big balding German-Jewish-American brother, and there was a lot of him to find. Though I had known of him since the 1950s, from the blue airmail envelopes and occasional $10 bills enclosed, it was only after he died that he spoke to me for the first time from the old brown suitcases in which he had been laid to rest; and it was then that I got to know him in all his expansive dimensions. Where epistolary Gerda was silent (she left few letters, as one might expect of *sent* letters) Gunther opened up and couldn't stop talking, mostly about himself, from the start of the war until the moment *Rabbi Goldblum delivered a most beautiful Eulogy and friends all joined in Kaddish.*

With Gunther, as I was to find, there are earlier beginnings than 1939 in New York, but that was where he began in the first trunk of letters to be opened in the attic. A little later, after only two months in Ecuador, Gunther wrote: *Since I come here I have become member of the greatest Ecuadorian Jazz Orchestra, "Blacio", playing in the smartest night-club restaurant.* Within less than a year after leaving Germany, Gunther could be found in *the smartest Bar of this country, leading there the Band* and quickly finding *the way to glory.* By August 1944 he was back at the *Boris-Palace* in Quito, leading the orchestra and *playing Boleros, Rumbas, Tangos, and swings and hot music in the new bounced Boogie-Wooggy style.* In a more or less random selection of his self-descriptions over subsequent years, Gunther appeared variously as the *famous Accordion-player, as der reiche Onkel von Amerika* champing on *a big cigar,* as front man in a *Bavarian outfit with real short Lederhosen,* and as *Uncle Sam in straw hat with blue-white-red ribbon and a red-white striped vest.*

These Gunther-incarnations were (I soon realised) impersonations. Even as I pick out these particular descriptions from the piles of paper, I know they falsify him. There were other Gunthers. I remember reading somewhere, in some Holocaust memoir, that *you don't separate the family, the family stays together.* That's what Gunther was always doing. A line from an early letter comes back: *Consider, we all belonging to one family have brought us in security.* He maintained a lasting correspondence with his sister; he helped his father leave Germany in late 1941 when Jews were being deported and murdered en masse; he looked after his father at the end. He sought his absent brother, though Kurt was a *filthy fellow* who seemed to want nothing more to do with them after 1939. For all that he advised and chided her, Gunther praised and was proud of Gerda, reminding her of happier times even inside the Third Reich – as when they walked in the *Sud-Park in Breslau*, and when she was once *sweet sixteen*. He liked to boast (though not without self-irony) of his abilities and achievements, but it was as a survival strategy, and he could also see himself for what he was: a factory slave, a man destined never to marry, for all his talk of it; a big brother destined never to visit his sister, or get what was due to him – his *Wiedergutmachung*. And at some point in our acquaintance, I must have wondered what he really thought as he squeezed his 227 lbs into that *Bavarian outfit with real short Lederhosen*. Did he ever see it as the degradation it was? And for what? For an audience's amused applause for the comic German-American accordion-player, in little leather shorts and flowery suspenders, from a make-believe Bavaria – the land of Wagner and mountains, of Berchtesgaden and the Berghof.

So I began to see Gunther differently, unfiltered by his sister's caustic fears. Behind the aspiring, the successful Gunther, the man who, in the absence of applause, applauded himself – *Is that not really something?* he liked to say when displaying yet another accomplishment – there was an anxious and fearful man. Though he made much of his citizenship of the USA, *the greatest country in the world,* it was there – in the *filthy city* of Pittsburgh – where he froze in the sub-zero temperatures needling his arthritis, and extolled his thick *woollen underwear*. There was an underside to Gunther. In fact – as I now realise – there was nothing but *underside*. Once this occurred to me, I wondered how I had not noticed it from the start, and when I recently returned to his letters, another Gunther emerged; an anxious, anguished man. Even when jesting – which was the front he presented to the world and his sister – he was afraid. Gripped by *the grippe* in New York in May 1939 and *forced down to bed,* he pinned a notice on his door: *Mr. Lewinsohn is out of order.*

Gunther was *out of order* more than he cared to admit, but once you notice it you notice nothing else. Occasionally he saw it too. In one letter from America, referring to himself as a *displaced person*, he admitted he still has *in mind those days of fear, days of concentration camps and persecution, and now and again the outlook for the next future makes me fear.* He was more afraid in the US, but could seldom admit or even recognise it, because what he wanted, what he longed for, would always elude him. That was the fear. That was why – as a German, as a Jew, as a displaced person – Gunther gazed longingly at American women, with all their *vices and frivolity*, their powdered faces and rouged cheeks, their cigarettes stained red from their lips, as they roller-skated in front of him *in sports-hats with feathers of an altitude of about one foot.* It is obvious to me now. Gunther was afraid, and at last I think I understand why, I am beginning to grasp his situation. When he warned his sister that she was *gliding poco a poco to misery* – really he was thinking about himself. That was his fear, more than hers – that the *distinguished Professor Gunther Heinz*, the *rich uncle of America*, the band-fronting *Booggie-Wooggy* man, might one day also find himself *in the neighbourhood of filthy people*. Probably he was thinking of *sliding* rather than *gliding* to misery – and as I wonder again what lay behind his idiosyncratic summary of his sister's degradation, I find myself remembering Sandy the dachshund, Gerda's **one true friend**, Sandy with his slipped disc, no longer able to support his own weight, scraping his belly on the floor, much to the children's amusement, until they were told he had to be put down.

Among her surviving early photographs, first found all those years ago in a trunk in the attic, and now in front of me (stored on my phone for ease of access and scrutiny) one in particular holds my attention. It differs from the others because of the dachshund at the centre, held up by a woman I take to be Aunt Bertha, who by then (the photograph is dated 1936) was presumably a fixture of the place in the absence of the deceased mother. Gerda, at the back with her father and lightly touching Aunt Bertha's shoulder, looks down at the dog. Meanwhile a white-shirted, grinning Gunther assumes an almost horizontal pose at the front of the photo – presumably because if he sat upright he would block out Aunt Bertha, dachshund and half the family. Next to the date is the apparent location, *Balken*, which is puzzling as it translates as Bar or Beam – unless it is *Balkon* = balcony. This is the only photograph I have found in which Gunther and a dachshund seem to vie for attention and a place in family history, though he often acknowledges the lasting importance of dachshunds to her in subsequent letters. In one from 1947 he remembered her as *the 12 years old school-girl when we walked with a bag of "Borxel" and "Pussy" through the Breslau Sud-Park.* When I

first happened upon this reference to my mother as a girl in Germany in 1933 – the year Hitler became Chancellor – I was puzzled by *"Borxel"* and *"Pussy"*, but assumed that the first, being in *a bag*, was some kind of sweet or titbit. *"Pussy"* reappeared seven years later, in a letter dated 26th August 1954, when this time he remembered his now thirty-three-year-old sister as *sweet sixteen* and on holiday with him when they *went with Tatzel, Tante Bertha, and Pussy in the "Lotte-car" to the Zoblen-Mountain. Tatzel* I understood as a pet name for their father, *Tatta*, but *Pussy* was never again referred to or explained. Only now do I begin to understand that *Pussy* was – must have been – the name of the dachshund, the same *Pussy* held by Aunt Bertha in the 1936 photograph. Why does any of this matter? It matters not just because this is about family – families long since vanished but surviving in photographs and letters and diaries – but because, however closely and over how many years you scrutinise the evidence, the truth remains hidden until suddenly, in a blinding moment, you see it. And what I didn't get until this moment was the nature of Gunther's love. That he loved her throughout their long correspondence is evident from the *thousand kisses* ending so many of his letters, but the meaning of that love somehow eluded me through half a century of sporadic research into family history. It walled him from the fear. Gerda, whether she knew it or not, was Gunther's abiding security, safety, refuge. Hence the panic of one of his letters, as he complains that he has received no reply from her for months: *You are absolutely silent.* It is the same panic evident in his wartime letter (October 1940) to her employer, pleading for information about Gerda who had been *absolutely silent for a couple of months: Has she come in a concentration-camp or has she had an accident?* Gunther could not bear to lose her along with everything else. If Gerda returned his love, she kept it to herself, though as far back as 1951 she confided to her diary: **Gunther still writes to me but he is a dreadful old miser. Wish he'd leave me some money some day though.** She had to wait a further twenty years for that wish to be granted.

When it was her time to die, there was no evidence that she was thinking of anything but the dogs. But having now read and re-read all the available, decipherable written evidence, and having pored over every photograph as if they were paintings in a gallery, I have come to a different view. That Gunther was behind her decision is now obvious to me, given the timing of events. But some other realisation has also started to emerge: she was thinking of family. Not of *us* of course. The thought that she wasn't thinking of us misled me for many years because it led me to conclude, wrongly, that she was therefore thinking of no one – at least nobody human. That seemed entirely plausible as she was always alone in her world. But now I understand that she must have been thinking of her origins – her first family, the Lewinsohns, the family she left behind in May 1939 and never saw again. We – her subsequent family, who visited her body in hospital and attended its cremation – how could we ever weigh on her like the family she had left and lost? Leaving: it was the one thing she could still do. She had done it before. Seventeen-year-old Gerda was so excited then, leaving her father in Hamburg, boarding the President Harding, delighted to be getting away at last. So this second *Auswanderung* – thirty-three years after she began planning the first – must have seemed exciting too; a decisive break with her life, a seminal moment. This second time around Gerda was – I am sure of it – thinking of *them*. Was *Tatta* on her lips as she kissed those pills? Yes, yes. Gunther too, and Aunt Bertha, and Pussy in the Lotte-car – up, up to *the Zoblen-Mountain*. And as she swallowed her own life, she was sweet sixteen again, then twelve in 1933, then a child in the 1920s and on the beach between her father's legs; then she was nobody and nowhere and nothing.

THE BEAUTIFUL PRAGUE
TIME

27

One of the things I learned about Gerda was that in 1937, almost two years before leaving Germany for good, she went to Victoria College in Prague, or, to give its full address, as written in thick black ink on the envelope (stamped BRESLAU) at the side of my laptop:

Victoria College Prag 8 (Liben) Kosinka 502 C.S.R.

The envelope is addressed to Frl. Gerda Lewinsohn (the Frl standing for Fraulein), and the G and L of her name and the P of Prague are embellished as if done on stained glass rather than paper. The Deutsches Reich stamp appears to have Hindenburg's head as the Reich President, though he died in 1934, when Hitler merged the Chancellorship with the Presidency and became the Fuhrer. The date stamp is 14.5.38. The name and address on the back of the envelope are: Abs. Gunter Lewinsohn, Breslau 18, Deutschland, Scharnhorststrasse.31 (the Abs. Standing for *Absender, Sender.*) The letter is missing. It was missing when the envelope first appeared. For once, I can remember the precise moment that empty envelope surfaced. It was autumn 1972, about nine months after Gerda's suicide.

I was in the attic, conscientiously going through her things – a decent period having elapsed since her death – and, opening one of the photograph albums at random, I found the envelope apparently marking the place where her **beautiful Prague time** at Victoria College began. In 1972 I didn't know that it had been a beautiful time for her, but I sensed its significance. She'd actually spoken of it once or twice when we were young, so it was too special even for

silence – one of the few memories escaping that unreal time before the war. It was always my understanding that Gerda went to Victoria College after being removed from her Breslau school for being a Jew. Maybe Tatta thought it would be good for her to get away from Germany for a year, and in the meantime things might settle.

Evidently, he still had enough money to pay for a year's private education at a "college for young ladies".

What Elkan Lewinsohn paid for Gerda's year at Victoria College is nowhere recorded, but (as I later discovered) it cost him more than money to send her away. At age sixteen, she was happy to leave. And something happened that year in Prague, which even her subsequent layers of silence couldn't smother. She did not speak of it much, but when she did, it was more as the end of an era than the start of an exciting new life: her last year as a girl. When she turned seventeen in 1938, the year of *Kristallnacht*, she missed that **beautiful time** almost more than she missed her family after 1939. In time Gerda came to hate even her beloved Tatta, if only for a while, and her feelings about him afterwards were complicated by shame.

Nothing ever shadowed that year in Prague – other than it coming to an end. Looking back, it was perhaps the most significant year of her life. Of course I did not know this until quite recently.

Victoria College was a boarding school for girls. With its Prague address in a Czechoslovakia not yet occupied by Nazi Germany (though soon to be), it welcomed Jewish girls like Gerda, whose father – an established *Kaufmann* in Breslau – still had some assets, status, standing.

A photograph from that seminal period of her life, presumably with Victoria College in the background (no location is indicated) shows Gerda and three friends standing by a dark doorway. It must be late or early in the year because the branches of the tree in the photograph are leafless. The girls are smiling, the white wall behind them reflecting brilliant sunlight, and the tree's shadow branching above. On the back of the photograph are these names: *Ada L, Gerda L, Steffi,* and the word, *Rausgeschnitten,* which means *cut out.* Three names, four girls; it is unclear what has been cut out, or why the fourth girl is not named. As far as I know, this is all that remains of them, but recently information previously unknown to me came to light concerning Victoria College, formerly known as Grab's Villa.

Grab's Villa once belonged to Hermann Grab, a Jewish "tycoon". It was originally a farm with a vineyard called **Kosinka** (the name in the address on the envelope of the missing letter to Gerda). In 1879-80 Hermann and his brother, Josef, established an oilcloth factory on the site of the farm and vineyard, but it was not until 1928-9 that the family villa was extensively renovated and its terraces and sculptures added. Notably, above the north entrance is a large terrace with decorative railing, balustrade, and two statues of angels holding lanterns. It's possible; probable, even, that Gerda and friends walked along that very terrace and saw stone angels, as the search now brings me to Victoria College. In 1936 Grab's Villa was rented to a teacher, Josefina Victoriusova-Mockerova, who established a girls' school on the site, principally for "well-to-do" boarders. Gerda Lewinsohn was one of them a year later. Victoria College lasted under three years. It was all over by 1939. Under the German occupation, the entire estate was confiscated as Jewish property by the Gestapo. By 1941 it was used by "the Prague branch of the Hitler Youth".

The internet images of Grab's Villa on my phone show a classical style of architecture, set amid lawns, gardens and trees. In Gerda's old album there are no interior photographs of Victoria College, and it is difficult to imagine her in those rooms with their high windows and ornate marble fireplaces, but there she must once have sat and walked and chatted with her friends. In her photographs they are outside the college, in gardens, on lawns, on benches by sunny walls, near trees. They are all group photographs and the girls are always smiling. In the one I am studying now, she is standing at the back with five of her friends, while the three in front sit on the grass, and here in her bright patterned dress she is actually grinning. It comes as rather a shock. Another photograph has *1938 Victoria* on the back. A young woman sits by a pool, which has been mysteriously drained and a wine bottle placed in the centre of it. She wears a long dark dress and a white hairband, but her face is turned away from the camera. Could that really be *her*? In another (also *1938 Victoria*), the friends perch on the back of a bench against a wall, and the weather, though sunny, must be colder because of her long dark coat with Astrakhan collar, and as usual she is smiling as she playfully leans nearly out of the picture.

Other than *1938 Victoria,* there is nothing to locate these pictures in a more specific time and place, and (as it now occurs to me) there was no need for her to do so. Gerda *knew* the times and places, the gardens, the grounds, even the trees. She required no other words to find her way back to them again. There is something about them which still eludes me, more than the surprise of seeing her with friends, smiling. *With friends. Smiling.* That's it. That is all it is. It's so easy to overlook the obvious. Once she became a mother (the only Gerda known to me), she had no friends, and that did not seem unusual; it was the way things were. And as for smiling, she must have smiled sometimes, but never again so naturally. It was different in *1938 Victoria*. As I study them again, these surviving images of a time and place that did not survive, these smiling faces, Gerda's among them, checking if I have missed something else, it suddenly comes to me, and again it is the obvious that I missed in my countless previous viewings. In all the family photos – the family of which I was a part; her second family, not her first – Gerda looks somehow out of place. That is missing from these pre-war photographs, especially from those recording her **beautiful Prague time.** She belongs there, as they all do, Gerda and her college friends, relaxed and smiling, in that time, that place.

One of the many internet images of Grab's Villa is of a classical octagonal wooden gazebo in the grounds; a good place to sit and chat with friends, but it is in none of her photographs. And it could not have been, I discover, as it is a new construction built "during recent reconstruction of the park surrounding the Villa". The Villa itself is now used by the City District of Prague 8 and "houses the housing, property and construction departments". Had I thought to research the history of Victoria College when I visited Prague ten years ago, I could have visited Grab's Villa, entered its rooms; but at that time I wasn't thinking much about Gerda and the Lewinsohns.

It lay at the bottom of one of the old brown suitcases, her year (1937-38) in Prague, underneath piles of legal papers from Dusseldorf dealing with the *Wiedergutmachung*. Such papers accumulate over decades (they did not stop with Gerda's death), which probably explains how I came to overlook the black Prague diary. Unaccountably apart from all the other diaries, it drew attention to that year as separate and apart from all the others. Having reached January 2022, the fiftieth anniversary of her death, and (as it seemed to me) the end of my search, I was loath to go on digging, and that mess of legal correspondence in German actually nauseated me. *Genug ist genug, Gerda*, I could hear myself reproaching her, not for the first or last time. Inevitably, I found myself sifting through it, selecting sheets at random and reluctantly translating the odd phrase or sentence:

. . . Schonfeld & Co (Name der Firma) and sole proprietor (Einzelinhaber) Elkan Lewinsohn . . . Business (Betrieb) Gentlemen's clothing, hats, caps Herrenartikel, Herrenhutte, Mutze . . .

. . . (Draft letter to lawyer as requested): Im Jahre 1939 gelang es mir durch einen speziellen Kindertransport nach England zu entfliehen. Ich war bei meiner Auswanderung 17 Jahre alt . . . (In 1939 I managed to escape to England by special Kindertransport. I was 17 when I emigrated . . .)

. . . Ich bitte Sie eine eidesstattliche Versicherung mit Aufstellung aller Juwelen und Gold – Schmuck – Silbersachen – wann Sie diese Sachen zuletzt im Besitz Ihres Vaters gesehen haben (wahrscheinlich vor Ihrer eigenen Auswanderung im Jahre 1939) . . . (I am requesting an affidavit of all jewels and gold – jewellery – silver items – when was the last time you

saw these things in your father's possession (probably before your own emigration in 1939) . . .

. . . saddened to hear of the death of your wife . . .

And then I found it, the black book underneath the paper piles, a German diary from one of the lost years. This discovery, at the very end of the year I had allowed her, and already well past the date (2nd January 2022) marking the 50th anniversary of her death, was a frustration. But it could not be ignored. The dates in it were from 1937 and '38, significantly pre-dating my original and preferred start date for her story of December 1938 in the red *Tagebuch*. Loose inside the front cover of the black book was a *Semestralzeugnis* (Semester Certificate) dated 29th January 1938, with the list of subjects. So – I had found it at last. Victoria College. Her mythical year in Prague. The year she would afterwards refer to as **the beautiful Prague time.**

The list of subjects include Deutsche, Englische, Franzosische, cultural history, geography, practical philosophy, accounting, correspondence, commerce cooking, serving, sewing, and shorthand. Her grades at this "Halbjahre" (half year) point are "vorzuglich" or "lobenswert"(excellent or commendable) and "mit Auszeichnung" (with distinction) for her overall progress. This is her year out, her year away, at Victoria College in the Cechoslovakische Republik. Kristallnacht is far off in the unseen future. Her address, on all the letters to her, , is Kosinka House, Prag V111, with the college described as an "English Boarding School For Girls" or "Ladies College". 29th January 1938 is the half-year point, so the term must have commenced September 1937, three months after her 16th birthday, with the magical year in Prague ending in June 1938. By Gerda's 17th birthday, she is back in Breslau, with Prague behind her.

26th June: Gerda's birthday. Unlike Gunther, I have not forgotten. *Es ist ein ganz besonderer Tag, den man nicht vergisst (It is a very special day not to be forgotten).* But it was not a birthday Gerda was particularly looking forward to in 1938.

The black diary makes no mention of Victoria College before 23rd July 1937: **Hoffentlich komm ich bald nach Prag.** *Hopefully I will soon be in Prague.* I have gone backwards and forwards searching for Prague references in her almost illegible script. Considering her beautiful time there, I was hoping for more, but there are other things of interest to compensate for the absence of Prague. On 6th May 1937 she writes: **I want so much to be beautiful and to have a beautiful figure.** There are many references throughout 1937 to a boy she likes, who is identified only as **33. 33** makes his first appearance on 1st February 1937, when Gerda **war vereisst** (was travelling) in Spindlermuhle. I see that she was there for fourteen days, and that Spindlermuhle (now called Spindleruv Mlyn in the Czech Republic) was and still is a ski resort. Franz Kafka was there fifteen years earlier, in January/February 1922, writing *The Castle*. It is there that Gerda keeps thinking about **33**, who turns out not to be ein Junge at all, but a man of about twenty-five or twenty-six - **10 Jahre alter wie ich, wer hat eine gute Figur.** So an older man then, ten years older, but with a good figure. He wears glasses, has lost some hair **(hat vorne die Haare etwas verloren)** but is on the whole a well-groomed, good-looking youngish man from whom Gerda receives a marriage proposal **(ich habe einen Heirartsantrag bekommen).** Even then she declines to name him **(ich soll seinen Namen nicht niederschreiben)** beyond referring to him as **33.** At the end of May 1937 she writes: **In one month I'll be 16. Hopefully it will get better with me because, if I think of someone kissing me or anything like that, I won't know if I really love him.** Then this: **Now it's Spring, the sun shines all day (except today) and I am mostly happy. The thoughts I live by are different: Be good to everyone, and they will be good to you. Have no**

enemies. Be neat and tidy. Early to bed. Work (but not too much). Get lots of fresh air for your health. Be always in a good mood.

33 surfaces again on 12. Juli, but is now eclipsed by Prague which makes its first appearance on 23 Juli 1937 as an imminent journey, and it appears that 33 gives his blessing to it, telling Gerda to: **Go ahead**. That same day the weather is bad, and she sits alone in a **cloudy** mood, a hopeful but doubtful state of mind: **I don't know exactly what I'm hoping for, and I don't care how it happens.**

Prague then disappears from view until 18th January 1938, and unfortunately the entry is barely legible, although 33 can still be made out midway through. By 31st January the script is legible again, briefly, when it is recorded that yesterday at the cinema she heard a beautiful song which she now sings all the time: **Sweetheart, Sweetheart, will you love me always/ Will you remember the day when we were happy in May/ Sweetheart, Sweetheart.** For her this is the sound of love and happiness and sunshine, and she has such nostalgia afterwards. There is then a half-legible entry for 1st February 1938 Prag: **I walked 10 times round the garden and when I got fed up with that, I lay in bed. I experienced something very romantic there. You are not allowed to go to bed on the spot, and suddenly Miss W – came into the room, and I had to leave lightning fast – usw.**

USW means *und so weiter* (and so on), but it is unclear to me what it signified for Gerda just at that moment as she lay in bed. She **experienced something very romantic there**. I still wonder about that.

LETTERS FROM GUNTER

(TRANSLATED):

Scharnhorststrasse 31
Breslau
den 13. September 1937

Liebe Gerda!

Now, after Tatta's return yesterday from his travels to Bad Reinerz after 3 weeks away, I take the opportunity to write you some lines. Although I planned to write to you in English, I refrain from doing so since I need the help of the English dictionary. I have tried to translate some of my explanations below, but I am missing the following vocabulary. You can tell me the translation of these words:

Abenteuer = ? (Adventure) Hindernis = ? (Obstacle) Spion = ? (Spy) Katastrophe = ? (Disaster) Zukunftig = ? (Future)

I have already been some weeks in Breslau and I am sorry to have returned so early without having had the opportunity with you to visit the old churches, temples and museums in which you were so interested at the time. I hope you have already made up for what we missed and at least you have seen the old Synagogue in the old town. I have told Tatta about the beautiful film we went to see during my visit. There are only 2 things I cannot understand: firstly why, as a "resident" of Prague, it was so difficult for me to find the passage where the cinema is, and secondly, how the woman in front of us could sleep through such an exciting film! We would have had to put something very cold, eine Portion Eskimo, on her head to make her wake up! Tatta was very amused to hear about our adventures.

What is Fraulein Slink or Fraulein Link doing? - I no longer know the correct name for her. How is the nice little Italian lady? Does she still have something left for me? Please give her my regards. My future wife, Fraulein Kate wanted to write to me, but I wait in vain for her letter before the love sickness and nostalgia are wasted.

I couldn't get used to the inn food after my taste was spoiled by your delicious titbits such as potato pancakes and roast veal, where you don't need cutlery but just a hammer and chisel. What has been said so far should suffice for today and I await your reply! Above all else, don't forget to choose a really good bride for me – you know my taste!

Gruss and Kusst (Ha, ha, ha, ha)

Gunter-Heinz

PARTIAL LETTER
PRESUMABLY WRITTEN FROM SCHARNHORSTSTRASSE 31, BRESLAU
DATE (MISSING) BUT LIKELY OCTOBER 1937 AS GUNTER REFERS TO HIS LARGE PAINTING OF TATTA (WHICH IS FURTHER REFERENCED IN HIS SUBSEQUENT LETTER DATED 28TH OCTOBER 1937.)

. . . Tatta is, as you perhaps know in Baden-Baden. Father ist voyaged with Mr. Siedner, and I fear that frequently he will drink much liquor and pay a visit to the gambling hell, which in Baden-Baden is famous! Today I have been in the temple, because we have Zimches taure and the temple was totally fulled up till the last place. This evening is the Zimches taure feast, where I will also go. It is to be hoped that Edith Bohm will be present to this arrangement, for you knows I love she with all my heart. In the passed week I have painted Tatta and this

large picture tomorrow will be exposed in the window of the shop on Schweidnitzerstrasse. That will cause a great sensation! My dear Gerdala, have you already chosen a nice fiancee for me? I've written to Kate Hesse in Prag, but my writing is come back with the postal remark Inkonnu (Unknown). I have great fun in my life. Please send by return to the father in Baden – Baden, Hotel Regina, a writing.

Scharnhorststrasse 31
Beslau

28th October 1937

Dear Gerda!

Many thanks for your kind letter, which has just been already read by the Tatta, who this week just come back from Baden-Baden. We have taken note with the greatest pleasure, that you shows yourself as a very good pupil. And Tatta is agreeable surprised that you has got a price for your conduct. Tatta shows your letters in the Cafe Fahrig etc because he is proud to possess such a famous daughter. Nevertheless you has made a severely mistake in writing the German word "sturzten" with two "t"s as sturtzten. Here in Breslau there are in the moment no noveltys. Frequently Tatta remains at home. To day I play with the EJO Orchestra in the Toymee-Hall, and I trust to meet a great approval.

I proceed in my Spanish lessons and will in the next time make a try in writing anything on Kurt. Before some days the little Miss Hofter has told to me that Steffi Apt has been one of the nicest girls and she is living now in Helvetia (Schweiz). How please you the life in the college? In the next time will Mr. Born pay again a visit to Prag, perhaps I will voyage together with him, and if I enter Prag and surprise you there – it will give one catastrophe! The Picture of Tatta, announced here in the shop window, had been a sensation. All people passing there sayed: Oh that is Mr. Lewinsohn.

Instantly I'm in the shop at Schmiedebrucke with Tante Bertha, and the little Pussy lies down at my feet. Now I shut my letter and await from you a very large writing in communicating us what has happened there in the last time.

Your accordially

Gunter-Heinz

(A handwritten addition to this letter, from Tatta, begins in English as follows):

My darling!

You shall be astonished because I begin in English, for observe in the meantime I have learned English fluently. However, as I fear that you cannot English enough in order to translate all, I prefer to write in German . . .

(Unfortunately he then does precisely that, and apart from the odd word the thick black script is indecipherable.)

Scharnhorststrasse 31
Breslau
den 1. Dezember 1937

Liebe Gerda,

A miracle happened and you actually wrote a 20 line letter to Tatta! When I read it, I first noticed the metamorphosis your handwriting has recently undergone. The letters all slant to the right, whereas before it was still a vertical script. That says a lot about your character, which doesn't seem to be balanced, as is the case with Kurt.

But quite apart from that, nothing stands in the way of your taking part in the dance evening in 8 days, for which you happily intend to practise. That you have chosen Fraulein Kate Hesse to be your companion is "a very agreeable circumstance". When Frau Hiller took note of this, she laughed mischievously as always and said, "Gerda definitely wants to get you married off" ("unter die Haube bringen"). Although I really want to be there at this dance evening, nothing will come of it because the foreign currency applied for at the bank has not yet been cleared, and without money to get there it would be a disaster.

On Saturday evening the Reich association of Polish Jews organises its foundation festival, with the EJO Orchestra playing.

Meanwhile Gerda Flur has had endless telephone calls with me because she wants me, on this evening, to sit next to her at the table. By the way, she sings a Polish song, to which I am supposed to accompany her.

Bubi Brand and Lilo Benger send greetings to you. They have already steamed off to Rio de Janeiro.

By the way, how are you getting on with Fraulein Kate Hesse? I liked her a lot this time, but I can't say more because I only saw and spoke to her for a very short time . . .

Peter Thornthwaite

Scharnhorststrasse 31
Breslau

7th March 1938

My dear Gerda!

In receipt of your letter, I beg to-day to answer him immediately. Naturally father is most enjoyed of your excellent English correspondence, and he cannot but showing him all his acquaintances and the father has even his joke to translate your writing. Father says that the hand-writing this time is most ugly. Also I find that your English style is still so simple and filial – where shows the education? Such a English as you write you has already learned in the first class of the Augusta-school. Furthermore, the father cannot understand why you not get butter to the meals. For the much money what we pay monthly for your state, you get all what you want. In the meantime I have written a letter to Miss Hesse, however she does not answer. Perhaps you have said her that to Christmas day I have burnt your letters.

I have to let you know that Mr. Hartmann, who has marriaged this month, goes in the shortest time with his woman to Buenos Aires. Also Mr. D - intends to go to North America on beginning of May. By this facts the existence of chapel EJO is most threatened. Also myself have solicit for one position in Middle-America, in the branch of importation and exportation.

Now it may be possible to pay you a visit in your boarding-house. Is the nice Lotte again well healthy, for I take care of her. The father has remained this evening to home because he has sinned severely in the last time.

Yesterday I have payed a visit to the monumental and splendid cinema named Roxy-Palace. There are a nice film for only 70 Pfennig.

Separately you find the permission here of the father, necessary for the visit of the ball, but the father and generally myself wish to hear what happened there. Because Tatta will spend to you a greeting I shut the letter.

Your affectionate brother Gunter-Heinz

(Tatta's "greeting" is illegible.)

Scharnhorststrasse 31
Breslau

20th April 1938

My dear Gerda!
Herewith I acknowledge receipt of your letter by which we have taken note that momentary you don't intend to come here to Breslau. By this fact we have spent alone the holidays of Easter. Frau Hiller has gone away from us for some time. In the meantime we have got a new cook, named Clara. While the Easter holidays there are meals most amazing, for instance broth with the finest dumpling. Furthermore, roasted hens, sweetnesses etc, in short, there are all we got on our arrival in the college where justly the ball took place. I remember sitting on my place, no more capable to eat tart and cake. I remember of this fact to have made the acquaintance of the nice Lotte, of the moment where she danced untroubled with this ridiculous fellow.

And now, nearly one month has passed since that handsome time in Prag. It was a pitty not to have had more occasion for a expensive loitering with you. At your dismissal about Whitsuntide I will come once more there showing to you all the curiositys of Prag. Perhaps I loose my pass-port at that time so that would not be possible my visit.

As soon as in Prag will be again a darkness I will arrive in your boarding house and sit silent by the piano, and all the girls shall participate as sincerely in their dressing-gowns.

Momentary I learn besides Spanish now English. Look at my perfect English of this letter!! Without mistakes!! Bravo, bravo!!

Yours sincerely, brother Gunter Many greetings at the very kind Lotte (master in swing-dancing)

FROM GERDA'S DIARY:

1 May 1938:

I received a letter from A – . He seems to be a very famous man. He has written many famous books. I'm absolutely not in love with him, so I won't reply. I want to fall in love with a boy here, but I think it's hopeless. I still think about 33 a lot. He is always there. I would so like to see him again before I go to Palestine. Yes, yes, Palestine, it is time. But I have absolutely no desire to travel. I so much want to stay here another year and learn Spanish and then go with Gunter to Argentina. Life is difficult. I'm not in a particularly good mood. I haven't received any post for a long time, which I'm angry about. Gunter must go to Argentina with me. Hopefully tomorrow evening I'll write about something lovely.

(UNDATED) 1938:

PRAG Zu Ende
Breslau beginnt.

8 August 1938:

For nearly 2 months I have written nothing. The beautiful Prague Time is over. As expected I have only good memories. Everything was wonderful. All the bad hours I experienced forgotten. So that's life. Perhaps it gets better.

31 August 1938:

Yes, dear diary, I have to cut my heart out again. Life is not easy. So what is actually the reason for my anxiety? There is actually no reason. I have everything my heart desires – except for one thing: love is missing.

Love was not all that was missing, for there is a gap in the diary until this undated entry (under Freitag) concerning **33: I have today read about his engagement. He is living in Berlin. But I can laugh and sing because he wasn't the great love. 33** ends there, and I am wondering why that particular number? Could it have had significance for her because 33 signified 1933: the year Hitler was appointed Chancellor. The first year of the German Reich. The year of public burning of books?

In the black diary there are no further entries for September, October, November, and most of December 1938, only blank pages, with no explanation other than **siehe rotes Buch** (see the red diary for 1938/1939), and there was either no correspondence, or there is no surviving correspondence from that period. Considering what was happening in Nazi Germany at the time, the absence of any written record is puzzling. There is nothing concerning Gerda in that four-month gap.

Nothing about going to Palestine in October, or about *not* going. Nothing about *Kristallnacht,* the night of broken glass, and whether it could be heard in her father's stores. And so it is back to the red Tagebuch, and the entry for 27th December 1938:

Soon another year will come. Soon we'll write 1939. What will the new year bring? The future looks quite black. We Jews . . .

EPILOGUE

I wonder why Gerda identified him only as a number. Some things you never find out. I can see why that number resonates. **33.** 1933: the beginning of the end. In 1938, after Gerda had left Prague and returned to Breslau, and it was the last month of the year – the month after Kristallnacht – Gerda had thirty-three years of life left. In April 1945 Eva Braun, having married Hitler in the Fuherbunker, then bit and swallowed a capsule of cyanide; she was also thirty-three. Funny how certain numbers keep cropping up. *My goodness, you're 33,* Gunther wrote to Gerda on 26th August 1954. *Do you remember when you was sweet sixteen and we went with Tatzel, Tante Bertha, and Pussy in the "Lotte – car" to the Zoblen Mountain?* There is no connection between these things, of course, no hidden linkage to be found. Yet the strange correspondence – the symmetry of certain numbers – almost makes me believe otherwise. There is another number also worth mentioning: 50. Gerda died aged fifty in January 1972, and it took me another fifty years to write her story. That it has taken me half a century to complete this memoir (by January 2022 she could have lived her life twice over) is surely more than coincidence. It was evidently predetermined. Her date of death had set off some kind of timer in me, triggering me fifty years later to complete (more or less) what I had set out to do. I was simply on a timer. Did that also apply to her? She cut out the past, yet carried it with her, never let it go, and it never let go of her. *I'm split in two*, Anne Frank confided in her final diary entry. *On one side: joy, flippancy, the lighter side of things. On the other . . .* Gerda was also split in two, but there was no clean split of light and dark; each was veined with the other.

She let go of her life. Now I can do the same. Looking back at her diary entry for 27th December 1938, it occurs to me that I would not have wished on her the life she had, the woman she turned into. *Don't go there*, I can hear myself saying. *Take a different direction. Don't mind me.*

When I started (2nd January 2021) delving more deeply into her past and Lewinsohn family history, I also started watching BBC's *The Repair Shop*. Filmed at the Weald and Downland Living Museum in West Sussex – a restored barn in a bucolic English setting – it seemed a sentimental and comforting corrective to what I was doing, and I was moved, almost to tears, by the extended family stories. In episode after episode, supplicants bring to the old barn some treasured family heirloom, long broken and neglected and in terminal need of restoration. The experts awaiting them offer not only a wide range of specialisms and skills but also, in congruent looks and words, acknowledgement of what these broken, neglected, unforgotten things really mean. Families return to find the personal past and loved lost ones restored. "Are you ready?" the repairers ask, before lifting a cloth to reveal – a miracle. An old shop sign; running shoes running out of time; a worn leather suitcase; a dilapidated diary; a stopped clock – whatever the particular heirloom, it is always the same thing that is repaired. Family. Family history. Family past and future form again an unbroken chain. They got what they asked for, often more than they asked for, those fortunate families, and I wonder if I did too. In last night's episode, the first object to be restored was a writing case; a badly worn red leather "code-breaker's writing case" belonging once to a woman doing secret work at Bletchley Park. The woman bringing it in to be repaired was her daughter. Restored and returned to her, complete with writing paper and envelopes, it could be used again to write the letters almost nobody now writes or receives. The next story concerned a "spinning clown" called Jimmy, who had stopped spinning and had a hole in his head. He could only grip his trapeze, arms rigid above his head, locked. Little Jimmy with his red and blue acrobat costume, dark hooped eyebrows, black eyelashes, red nose, rouged cheeks, yellow hat, and red lips parting in a grin. The red gash of his lips reminded me of Gerda, and momentarily I saw not Jimmy, but Gerda the Clown, grinning, gripping the swinging trapeze between its yellow and white candy cane supports. Restored to how it used to be, its blue and red costume clean and new, wood-filler plugging the hole in its head, at the touch of a lever round and round it spins again.

There is no *Repair Shop* for Gerda and the Lewinsohns. Bringing her back to life through her diaries, Gunther and the others through their correspondence – well, it was worth a try. Maybe something has come of it – not a miracle – but something worth finding out. She was often afraid. **Liebe Gott, ich habe mich sehr grosse Angst.** But brave, too. The seventeen-year-old who found a way out of Germany on her own. The refugee. The domestic servant of S.E. 15. The young woman who could see Joe both as **the big love** and the **asshole who stank lately so much that I felt nauseous.** The ATS recruit who had **to stick it out and cook for a thousand men.** The struggling wife and mother. The woman who amassed and hoarded suitcases of clothes for the family's future.

Gerda's story does not particularly stand out among all the memoirs of Jewish victims and survivors. She was one of the lucky ones; she got out in time and, other than suicide, nothing much happened to distinguish her. In her case there would be no extraordinary account of survival in the heart of Nazi Germany; no "going to ground" in wartime Berlin; no walking about without her yellow star, evading the Gestapo, while other Jews drew up lists of their possessions before being deported. For Gerda, there was to be no unforgettable and extraordinary journey of discovery – no surprise packages in the post – no black-lettered **JUDE** on yellow cloth – no false identity card – no Holocaust expert to decipher her handwriting. Unlike Hans Neumann, the subject of the recent memoir to which I am alluding (*When Time Stopped* by Ariana Neumann), Gerda Resi Lewinsohn did not want her story told, certainly not by the likes of me.

As survivor memoirs go, nothing much happened to her. I have read enough accounts of life in the death camps to draw up a list of the horrors she missed – the ghettoes, deportations, herding in cattle wagons, selections, bodies bulldozed into mass graves, dead women clutching the red lipstick donated by the British Red Cross when the camp was liberated. References to such things are noticeable by their absence in Lewinsohn family records. From Gunther I'd have expected more than his passing reference to Aunt Bertha's likely end: *Though no information and no lists with regard to survivors of Jews in Germany I have in hands, it can be said that Aunt Bertha and the rest of the family who lived in Brandenburg have perished . . .* Even their father's situation, abandoned in Breslau, gets the briefest of mentions – from Gunther of course, nothing from Gerda – when he describes him (July 1939) as *desperated and of broken heart* and subject to *daily persecutions* from the Gestapo. There is a telling phrase in Gunther's letter of 8th May 1945: *Just to-day I got a nice letter from an American friend. He advised me not to leave this continent and to try to forget Europe forever!* Maybe that was what they were trying to do in 1945 – forget the Europe of the war, the camps, the mass killings, and cut the past out of their lives. Afterwards came news reports, documentaries, Nuremberg, but they left no shadow in Gerda's diaries or Gunther's letters, and probably in the long aftermath of the war few people wanted to know. Following the liberation of Belsen in April 1945, a ten minute BBC radio report was broadcast concerning the thousands dying there; the smell of death; the fleshless faces at the windows of wooden huts; living skeletons; bodies strewn, stacked. A British Ministry of Information official documentary, ordered in April 1945 and compiled with footage shot as the camps were liberated, was shelved, unfinished. It took a further fifteen years or so for my mother to fill suitcases with newspaper cuttings of these past events, and for the Eichmann trial in 1961 to arouse interest in them.

None of the Lewinsohns did anything remarkable or memorable, as far as I know – unless it was to leave, survive. There is no Parisian haute couture, or art collection, or friendship with Picasso to be found in their history, as there is in a recently published account of a Jewish family in France during the war and post-war years. The closest Gunther got to haute couture was wearing *Lederhosen* or dressing up as *Uncle Sam.* If anything distinguished Gerda, set her apart, it was her obsession with the old clothes she stashed away in suitcases. As for Kurt, who wrote of his *adventurous and raging life,* most of it remains hidden and unlikely ever to be found. There are millions more forgotten than remembered people. So why recall them at all – the Lewinsohns? The answer, I suppose, is they are family, and family matters. It mattered to them. They got out, they dispersed, they lived their divergent lives, they looked for and sometimes looked out for one another. So, while Gerda may not approve of my partial and personal account of her life and the fragmentary lives of the other Lewinsohns – may not even recognise herself in it – it is in remembrance of their *extraordinary ordinary* lives that I have done what I have done.

The closest Gerda came to fame (Gunther mentioned it) was when she was interviewed on TV for a polo mint advert, though I don't recall ever seeing it. She may have had plans, but in the end it came down to a **plan of suitcases**. Suitcases were her most remarkable achievement. Still, I was proud of her – proud even of her overdose, which set her apart – though it was not an unusual way to go, I realised, after reading of the death of the American poet, Anne Sexton, who put on her mother's old fur coat, poured herself a vodka, and locked herself in the garage with the engine running. Nevertheless, Gerda's suicide turned her into a person of interest. Being interesting and being my mother had seemed two separate things.

There is one last thing I can do for her. Gerda was always more at home in Hollywood – more at home, that is, than in the places she found herself: a post-war camp of Nissen huts; a raw new council estate, Cowley. The other day, having concluded this memoir, and having no desire to go back to or add to it, I selected from the shelf of classic Hollywood films on DVD a particular favourite, *Now Voyager*. As it turned out it was exactly the right choice. A superficial viewing reveals little if any connection between Charlotte Vale, a Boston heiress in search of independence and self-respect, and Gerda Resi Lewinsohn, formerly of Cowley, deceased. There was no Paul Henreid in Gerda's life lighting a cigarette for her, and she didn't smoke anyway. There was no great love in her life, unless it was Sandy the sagging dachshund, and it is difficult to imagine him in a white dinner jacket, standing up on his stubby hind legs, lighting two cigarettes, and handing one to her. There was no kindly father figure, no psychiatrist to advise her, as she was about to leave, to "be interested in everything and everybody." That was never going to happen to Gerda, though she could not have known it when she set out on her first voyage. Nor was there anybody to ask her at the end: "Will you be happy?"

And yet, watching it again, it was impossible not to see connections. There is the "dark secret" of Charlotte's identity; the past "looks dark to her"; she tries to escape it by going on a voyage. Aboard the ship she meets Jerry (as Gerda met Joe) and they end up alone together after leaving the ship. Admittedly, their stories soon diverge. There was probably no "butterfly design" on Gerda's evening wrap, if she was wearing one, and it is unlikely that Joe would have spoken of her "wings" as Jerry does. Unlike the Bette Davis character, Gerda (though glad enough to get away) was not turning into a butterfly, leaving behind forever the bushy-browed bespectacled caterpillar. This was not her butterfly moment. She was already beautiful long before leaving, as she and others couldn't help but acknowledge. This was her break with the past, though, and with herself, and Whitman's lines – *Now Voyager, sail thou/ Forth, to seek and find* – could have been written for her. 1939 was the year of Gerda's first *Auswanderung*. Thirty-three years later, she left another family behind. On both occasions things had turned ugly for her, and she had to get away.

Now Voyager came out in 1942, when she was twenty-one. Gerda's story, it occurs to me, is of its time, not just because of the cataclysms of the 1930s and '40s, but because it could only emerge through diaries and letters. If such written evidence had not survived, then she and the Lewinsohns would be lost beyond retrieval. As it is, they are paper people, yet endure for that reason. Those more or less obsolete means of communication are integral to their story. Would Gunther have panicked, as he did in October 1940, if the gap in their correspondence had not led him to imagine the worst? The sometimes lengthening gaps between them – as when it took Gerda several years to acknowledge in writing the death of their father – can be more revealing than the letters themselves. They could not tap into a mobile phone or ping off an email. Just as well. For Gerda, the worst imaginable thing was to be easily reached.

January 2022.

*

It is now April. The war in Ukraine is far from over. Refugees are always in the news. There is a plan to send asylum seekers, who cross the Channel in small boats, to Rwanda, and I read that Alf Dubs, Member of the House of Lords and himself once a refugee on a Kindertransport, condemned it as an "awful, shocking decision". The story of Gerda and her first family is the story of refugees. That was something she could never leave behind – being a foreigner, not belonging.

Theirs is one refugee story that is over. It ended as planned on 2nd January 2022, which was good timing on my part. Or so I thought. Then, a few months later, I received two emails with substantial attachments from a descendant of Kurt, that *absent-minded Wine-drinker and bad boy* – as his widow, Elena Italia America Scarfi Messima de Lewinsohn, described him at his death. We had recently found and kept in touch with Silvina, Kurt's granddaughter, who lives in Canada having emigrated there from Argentina some years ago. Silvina was intrigued and saddened by what could be revealed of the Lewinsohn story, and I must here acknowledge her own significant contribution to it by arranging the translation of the more indecipherable letters from the 1930s.

Silvina's last emails (April) imparted new information. "Here are my discoveries": 1). *Hedwig Lewinsohn, geboren Schonfeld...* This was the name of the absent mother: the mother missing from all but possibly one or two of Gerda's old photos; the mother she never mentioned, and who died young, before she could be remembered. None of the children seemed to remember the cause of death – or if they did, they never mentioned it. Even Gunther, who forgot nothing (*the Elephant never forgets!*) forgot his mother's date of death, and asked Gerda if she remembered it, and her reply is missing. There was something of particular note in the information from Silvina: *Die tote Mutter wurde Schonfeld geboren* - ie the dead mother's maiden name was Schonfeld. *Schonfeld!* That's the name on all the headed letters from their father:

Elkan Lewinsohn.
Inhaber der Firma Schonfeld & Co.,

Breslau, Scharnhorststrasse 31.

So Elkan, the *Inhaber der Firma*, the owner of the company, had taken its name from his wife. Had he then married into the business? How little I know about the Lewinsohns... But to continue with Silvina's "discoveries": 2). *Manifest of Passengers, Nov 3rd 1938, SS New York.* Among them is *Guenter Heinz Lewinsohn: Hatmaker. Last Permanent Address: Breslau. Nationality: German. Race or People: Hebrew.* Guenter (spelled with a *ue* instead of an umlaut) aboard a ship bound for New York, 3rd November 1938, and here is the written evidence, to be found if you know where to look. It comes as a surprise to see him designated as a *Hatmaker,* though I don't see why, since his father was a *Hatmaker* before him. And as for *Race or People: Hebrew* – to see it recorded simply as a factual descriptor/designation, as Gunther leaves Germany for the US just a week before *Kristallnacht* – adds to the strangeness of finding him there at all, one of a long list of passengers on the *SS New York,* all his complexity and contradiction reduced to *German, from Breslau, Hatmaker, Hebrew...* But already I am reading on, finding Silvina's next "discovery": 3). Kurt's Birth Certificate, dated *8 Mai 1909.* Enlarging the attachment, it is just possible to make out the date, but nothing else, apart from his father's signature at the bottom: *Elkan Lewinsohn.* Kurt's date of birth I knew already, and fragments of what happened to him afterwards. The wonder is that someone else – his granddaughter – is also looking for him, entering the story. For her, this is just the beginning. It looks like the Lewinsohns have life in them yet.

Yet another email from Silvina today (27th April), disclosing the date of death of the mother, Hedwig

Lewinsohn, 15th April 1927, and place of burial: Lotnicza Street Jewish Cemetery, Wroclaw. This information she got from a *jewish.gen.org* database. Silvina found other web pages, about the cemetery, revealing that the "necropolis" was discovered, some years ago, in a "neglected and demolished state", half hidden in a "huge jungle" of "luxuriant greenery", with many of its gravestones defaced and "anonymous". Website visitors to this gallery of graves are asked for any information they are able to provide to help return the identity of the lost inscriptions.

As well as unearthing new information about the mother – the mother conspicuous by her absence in the family records – Silvina did something else of far-reaching consequence. In a further email, she confided she had not previously heard of Gerda, knowing only that her own mother once had "some uncle in the US". Kurt had "another sibling somewhere in the world", but where exactly, and whether "a man or a woman", remained a mystery. After now discovering from newly translated letters that in 1939 Gerda – having recently reached safety in England, could do nothing to help Tatta and Aunt Bertha escape from Germany – Silvina commented: "It seems that your mother had a lot of pressure from her father. I feel bad for her . . . she was very young."

That opened up for me a new view of Gerda...

Subsequent emails and attachments disclosed several other Breslau addresses for Elkan and Hedwig following their marriage on 26th August 1907. Silvina had discovered that Elkan was not German in origin but was born (6th June 1877) in Girtakol, Kovno (Kaunas), Lithuania, then part of the Russian Empire. It was my turn to reveal something to her: Elkan's younger sister, the "Aunt Bertha" who wrote to eighteen-year-old Gerda in London, was deported in November 1941 from Breslau to Kaunas and died there four days later. "It appears that Aunt Bertha was sent back to the city of her birth to be killed."

BIBLIOGRAPHY

Books:

Ascher, A (2007) *A Community Under Siege: The Jews of Breslau Under Nazism* (Stanford, California: Stanford University Press).

Atkinson, H (2012) *The Festival of Britain: The Land and its People* (London, Taurus, L.B).

Barthes, R (2000) Camera Lucida (Vintage, London), translated by Howard, R. First published 1980.

Berger, J (2009) *About Looking* (London, Bloomsbury).

Bronte, C (1847) *Jane Eyre* (no specific edition referenced).

Cawthorne, N (2004) *Turning The Tide*, Index Books, Kettering, Northants.

Davies, N and Moorhouse, R (2002) *Microcosm: Portrait of a Central European City* (London, Jonathan Cape).

Delbo, C (1995) *Auschwitz And After*. Yale University Press, New Haven and London. Translated by Lamont, R.C.

Fallada, H (2009) *Little Man – What Now?* (Melville House Publishing, Brooklyn), translation by Susan Bennett, 1996. First published 1932 (Rowohlt, Berlin).

Frank, A (1988, c 1949 by Otto Frank) *Das Tagebuch der Anne Frank* (Fischer Taschenbuch, Frankfurt am Main, Germany).

Freeman, H (2021) *House of Glass* (London, 4th Estate, Harper Collins), first published 2020.

Gilbert, M (1999) *A History of the 20th Century* (London, Harper Collins).

Gill, A (1988) *The Journey Back From Hell* (Grafton Books, Collins, New York).

Ginsberg, A (1984) *Kaddish* (written 1957–59) published in *Kaddish and other Poems* (1961) and included in subsequent Collected Poems.

Grimm, J. and W (2007), first published 1812, *Vintage Grimm: The Complete Fair Tales* (London, Vintage Books). Reference in text to *The Old Man And His Grandson, p. 353.*

Hastings, M (2011) *All Hell Let Loose: The World At War 1939–1945* (Harper Press, London).

Hoffmann, H (1845 original publication, Germany) *Struwwelpeter (Shock-Headed Peter)*. No specific edition cited.

Jalowicz Simon, M (2016) *Gone To Ground* (Profile Books, London), translated by Antghea Bell, first published in Germany in 2014.

Kafka, F (1999 in this edition, first published in Great Britain by Martin Secker & Warburg 1974) *Letters To Felice* (Vintage, London).

Kafka, F (2000, first published in Great Britain by Martin Secker & Warburg 1930) *The Castle* (Penguin Classics, England).

Kafka, F (1983) *The Complete Stories* (London, Vintage/Penguin), including *The Metamorphosis* (first published 1915).

Lambert, A (2006) *The Lost Life of Eva Braun* (Century, Random House, London).

Larkin, P (1990) *Collected Poems* (London, Faber and Faber/Marvell Press, London).

Louis, E (English translation 2022) *A Woman's Battles and Transformations* (Harvill Secker, London). Translation from the French by Tash Aw.

Lucas, J (1986) *Last Days Of The Reich* (London, Cassell).

Nabokov, V (1951) *Speak Memory* (London, Victor Gollancz).

Neumann, A (2020) *When Time Stopped: A Memoir of My Father's War and What Remains* (Scribner, London).

Overy, R (2001) *Interrogations: The Nazi Elite In Allied Hands 1945* (London, Allen Lane, The Penguin Press).

Plath, S (1999) *Ariel* (London, Faber and Faber). First published 1965.

Plath, S (1966) *The Bell Jar* (London, Faber and Faber). First published 1963.

Primo Levi (1989) *The Drowned and the Saved* (London, Abacus), first published in Britain 1988.

Rees, L (2005) *Auschwitz: The Nazis and the "Final Solution"* (London, BBC Books/Ebury Publishers).

Saunders, F.S (2022) *The Suitcase: Six Attempts to Cross a Border* (UK, Vintage), first published 2021 by Jonathan Cape.

Sebald, W.G (2002 in this edition, first published in German 2001) *Austerlitz* (Penguin, London).

Sebald, W. G (2002 in this edition, first published in German in 1993) *The Emigrants* (Vintage, London).

Shirer, W.L (1998) *The Third Reich* (London, Arrow Books). First published 1960.

Smith, L (2006) *Forgotten Voices of the Holocaust.* Ebury Press, Great Britain.

Films and Television:

Casablanca (1942) directed by M. Curtiz (Warner Bros, USA).

Cat People (1942) directed by J. Tourneur (RKO, USA).

Gone With The Wind (April 1940) directed by V. Fleming (Metro-Goldwyn-Mayer).

Groundhog Day (May 1993) directed by Harold Ramis (Columbia Pictures).

House Of Strangers (July 1949) directed by Joseph L. Mankiewicz (20th Century Fox).

Marathon Man (December 1976) directed by John Schlesinger (Paramount Pictures).

Now Voyager (October 1942) directed by Irving Rapper (Warner Bros).

Peyton Place (1964–1969) American Broadcasting Company, USA.

Tarzan And His Mate (1934) directed by C. Gibbons (MGM, USA).

The Man Who Knew Too Much (May 1956) directed by A. Hitchcock (Paramount, USA).

The Phil Silvers Show (1955 – 1959) directed by N. Hilsen (CBS television Network, USA).

The Repair Shop (Current) BBC iPlayer.

The Snake Pit (November 1948) directed by A. Litvak (20th Century Fox).

Websites:

research@holocaust.org.uk

Second Generation Voices:
www.secondgeneration.org.uk

Wikipedia: https://en.m.wikipedia.org

www.friedhofcosel.info/fields.php.
and
www.friedhofcosel.info/kwatery/urnanonim.php:
Information re Lotnicza Street Jewish Cemetery, Wroclaw.

ACKNOWLEDGEMENTS

I am especially grateful to those who encouraged me to write and complete this book and who must therefore bear some responsibility for it. In particular, I wish to thank my partner, Sue Challis, for her support and resilience, and her sensitive and careful criticism. I know that, during the researching, writing and endless revisions of *Remember Who You Used To Be* in the Covid years, she must have wondered when she was likely to see me again.

I wish to thank friends – Guy Holmes, Biza Kroese, Martin Costello, Rob Warin – for also agreeing to be readers of a book which underwent so many changes before arriving at its present form, and which would not have arrived where it did without them.

Special thanks to Silvina, Kurt's granddaughter, who left Argentina for Canada some years ago. When I started researching and writing this book, she was unknown to me. Indeed, I knew almost nothing about Kurt, my mother's eldest brother, his place in our family history being marked mainly by absences. Silvina would still be unknown to me but for Sue, who followed lost Lewinsohn connections in Argentina through Facebook. I acknowledge in the Epilogue the significance of Silvina's contribution in getting key letters translated, unearthing information about the old family, and helping me look at things anew.

Silvina was not the only unknown family found through researching and writing this book. The looking glass of Facebook also led us to Brazil, and so to Soledad and Mariano, Kurt's other grandchildren. Thanks to them for becoming family and a continuing part of this story.

Katharine Smith, novelist, has reviewed this emerging book and prepared it for publication. Without her enthusiastic engagement with it, and kind, incisive input, it would not be the book it has become.

Thanks also to the Senior Researcher we met during our first visit to the National Holocaust Centre, and to whom an apology is due. Dr Claudia Reese subsequently emailed us in May 2021, apologising that we had lost touch, and acknowledging the scanned German diaries as "an outstanding source", though beyond her capacity (as she acknowledged) to translate the script. She had arranged for two German exchange students to work on it in the summer of 2018 and they also struggled with the translation. Diary excerpts translated by one of the students were attached, and Dr Reese subsequently gave me permission to use these. She followed this up with several further helpful emails, one of which informed me of an event in which "second generation" speakers share experiences of "Writing the Holocaust". She also referred to our discussion at the time about applying for German citizenship, feeling it "very unjust" that I couldn't get a German passport. I had quite forgotten our post-Brexit conversation at the Holocaust Centre, when my undiminished dismay at the Referendum result was such that I had considered becoming German, only to find that a German mother (and a Jewish one at that) is not enough in itself, in the absence of a German father, to meet the requirements of the Vaterland. Those at least were the regulations then, though I understand (from Silvina) that they have since changed and that a Jewish mother will do. My thanks, anyway, to Dr Claudia Reese for her part in the evolution of this book.

Thanks to Gerda for her diaries, and to the Lewinsohns – Gunther especially, as her lasting correspondent – for their letters. Without these paper records, they (I include my mother) would be almost entirely unknown to me. Regarding parents, we only really begin to get to know them when we cease thinking of them as such and start uncovering their other lives. The diaries and correspondence have made this possible. At last I am getting to know her, half a century after her death. Of course I must also thank my mother not only for keeping a diary – however sporadically and with more absences than entries – but for keeping all the written records, packing them away in old brown suitcases. Why she did remains an unanswered question. That was her habit – to store and hoard. It was surely not that they might prove useful one day (though they have to me). Maybe it was the sense of security they gave her; with all its gaps the written record of a life perhaps made it seem more real. Anyway, it is important to acknowledge Gerda's vital contribution to the book I wrote about her and her family, though she was unaware at the time that one day I would be there, looking over her shoulder. Such lines of communication with dead family are not always available, I know, so I consider myself fortunate that the diaries and letters have found their way to me, and that I have not finished with them yet.

Finally, thanks to my twin sister, who accompanied me to Wroclaw to look for Gerda.